Abel Brown, Abolitionist

ALSO BY TOM CALARCO

The Underground Railroad in the
Adirondack Region (McFarland, 2004)

Abel Brown, Abolitionist

CATHARINE S. BROWN

Edited by Tom Calarco

McFarland & Company, Inc., Publishers
Jefferson, North Carolina, and London

LIBRARY OF CONGRESS CATALOGUING-IN-PUBLICATION DATA

Brown, C. S. (Catharine S.)
 Abel Brown, abolitionist / Catharine S. Brown ; edited by Tom
Calarco.
  p.   cm.
 Includes bibliographical references and index.

 ISBN 0-7864-2378-1 (softcover : 50# alkaline paper)

 1. Brown, Abel, 1810–1844.   2. Brown, Abel, 1810–1844 —
Correspondence.   3. Brown, Abel, 1810–1844 — Diaries.
 4. Abolitionists — United States — Biography.   5. Antislavery
movements — United States — History —19th century.   I. Calarco,
Tom, 1947–   II. Title.
E449.B8755B76   2006
973.7'114092 — dc22   2006004511

British Library cataloguing data are available

Cover photograph *(detail)* Sand Lake Baptist Church in Sand Lake,
N.Y. (photograph by Tom Calarco)

Manufactured in the United States of America

McFarland & Company, Inc., Publishers
 Box 611, Jefferson, North Carolina 28640
  www.mcfarlandpub.com

This book is dedicated to all those, like Abel Brown,
who devoted and sacrificed their lives
so that all people in America, regardless
of race, color, or creed, could be free.

Contents

PROSPECTUS OF THE LIFE AND WRITINGS OF REV. ABEL BROWN.

C. S. BROWN proposes to publish the life of her late husband, Rev. ABEL BROWN, including many of his private journals and letters, together with an account of his labors in various causes of reform, particularly in connection with the temperance and anti-slavery movements of the age. The opposition and persecution he encountered in the form of mobs, indictments, &c., will be given; also an account of his travels, in connection with his wife and partner in the anti-slavery enterprise. The work will comprise from 250 to 300 pages, good sized duodecimo, and will be illustrated by wood engravings. Price 50 cents, bound in muslin: twelve copies for five dollars.

The authorised Agents to receive subscriptions are as follows: Albany, William L. Chaplin, T. Townsend and Julius R. Ames; Troy, Rev. H. H. Garnet, Rev. Fayette Shipherd; Poughkeepsie, Rev. C. Van Loon; Utica, Alvan Stewart; Canandaigua, J. Mosher.

Advertisement promoting Catharine S. Brown's book about her husband (from *The Albany Patriot*, 2 December 1846).

Preface
by Tom Calarco

Sometimes I think it was fate that led me to the Rev. Abel Brown — a man now largely forgotten but who in his time was both hated and beloved. Hated, because he passionately espoused an unpopular cause. Beloved, not only because his position against slavery was morally upright, but because he was utterly selfless in providing personal aid and comfort to people in desperate need.

I discovered Abel Brown in the course of research I was doing on the Underground Railroad in Washington County, N.Y. (which eventually led to my book *The Underground Railroad in the Adirondack Region*). The year was 1998, and I found a listing at the New York State Library for a weekly abolitionist newspaper, the *Albany Patriot*. Though I had never heard of it, I was intrigued by what might be in it. A preliminary search in the library's warehouse, which housed the inactive collection, turned up empty. But library staff said they would keep trying, and their persistence paid off. A month later, I received a call that they had found it in a mislaid box.

It turned out to be a full two-year run of the tabloid-size newspaper tied up in a heavy green binder. It was laid out on a table for me in the library's manuscripts room, and I would spend weeks perusing its small print with numerous reports of the area's fervent abolitionist activity. But on that first day I made what was perhaps my most important discovery. In the December 2, 1846, issue of the *Patriot*, C.S. Brown, widow of the Rev. Abel Brown, advertised that she was preparing a book about her late husband. It would include "many of his private journals and letters, together with an account of his labors in various causes of reform, particularly in connection with the temperance and anti-slavery movements of the age."

I had never heard of Abel Brown, and he sounded like someone who might be worth learning about. I wondered if the intended book was ever completed, and if it had been, where it might be available.

I decided to try the SUNY Albany library.[1] I searched online and to my surprise found it listed. When I reached its location in the stacks, I found this little book exactly where it was supposed to be. I couldn't believe it. Here it was, printed in 1849 and available for circulation. What luck! Even more important were its contents. This forgotten book was filled with stories about Brown's efforts in the antislavery cause and included a number of anecdotes about his aid to fugitive slaves, as well as their personal stories. The book was a veritable gold mine of information about abolitionists in New York State, especially in the eastern corridor along the Hudson River.

I wondered what authorities on abolitionism might know about Abel Brown. I contacted a member of the then newly formed New York State Freedom Trail Commission, Syracuse University History professor Milton Sernett, a recognized authority on abolitionism in New York State. No, Professor Sernett said, he had never heard of him. But the biography claimed that Brown aided more than 1,000 freedom-seekers during his short life of 34 years! Sernett put me in touch with Stephen Zielinski of the New York State Museum, who was organizing the 1999 Conference on New York State History. Mr. Zielinski arranged for me to be part of the panel discussion on the Underground Railroad, providing me the opportunity to introduce Brown. The forgotten abolitionist no longer was to be forgotten.

Since that time, Brown has become known to serious students of the Underground Railroad, but few have read his biography. Only about 30 copies are alleged to exist in libraries and archives scattered around the country. The book reveals information, hitherto forgotten or discarded, that corroborates much of the legendary Underground Railroad activity in eastern New York State. It also provides an intimate view of the reflections and motivations of an evangelical Christian abolitionist — thoughts usually expresseed only in dense theological treatises — and shows

[1]I later learned that the New York State Library also has two copies.

how these beliefs were translated into action through the life of Brown. Though the narrative may be filtered through the rose-colored memories of Brown's widow, it does give us a record of ceaseless activity and selfless devotion to the cause of human betterment.

This book will keep alive the memory of Brown's suffering for the cause of ending slavery, and it will add insight regarding the forces that drove white abolitionists. Its reprinting will make Brown's story available to a broader audience as well as assist those researching the Underground Railroad.

The book consists, in large part, of Brown's correspondence, journals, and newspaper articles. Catharine Brown's narrative is used mainly to unify the many quoted sources. The first six chapters relate the early years of Brown, though only a brief opening chapter is devoted to his roots and youth. When chapter II begins, Brown is entering manhood, and the next four chapters deal with his schooling and maturation, as well as the motivations that led him to the ministry. Not until the end of chapter VI is there any indication that Brown is considering becoming involved in the antislavery movement. At that time, he was 25 years old and devoted to the causes of temperance and Sabbath schools. His goal in life was to become a missionary and preach Christianity in foreign lands.

But during this period, when his zeal for temperance resulted in him being harassed, hounded, and publicly whipped on a number of occasions, his life turned, and his staunch character was revealed. Before long, he became an antislavery agent and lecturer, and no longer was there any mention of missionary work overseas. He had found his mission in the antislavery cause in America.

Once I learned Abel Brown's story, it seemed I was destined to come into contact with his memory again and again. I had a remarkable experience in Canandaigua, a village north of the Finger Lakes in central New York where I had journeyed to visit the Ontario County Historical Society. According to my research, they had a run of copies of the *Tocsin of Liberty*, the earlier title and more inflammatory incarnation of the *Albany Patriot*, of which Brown was for a time the publisher as well as the general agent. I had seen only one hard copy of the newspaper at Cornell University. The newspaper is referenced numerous times in the Brown biography.

When I entered the society's library, I was told that a search of the archives would be required. While I waited, I talked with one of the research assistants. I told him about Abel Brown, who had died in this very village of Canandaigua. I knew the date of Brown's death, and the research assistant was able to locate the brief obituary published in the local newspaper. He also said that the historical society had records of the village's cemeteries on a computer database. He suggested that perhaps he could locate the gravesite of Brown. I was still waiting for the newspaper, so I thought, Why not? As he was searching, I learned that they were unable to find the *Tocsin*, so I turned my attention to the gravesite search.

I waited only a few minutes more. This time I was in luck. The research assistant had located it in a cemetery only a couple of blocks away. He showed me a map and pointed me to the approximate location.

At the old West Avenue Cemetery, there were many broken and fallen headstones. Many were unreadable or barely readable. I wondered

Gravesite of the Rev. Abel Brown, West Avenue Cemetery, Canandaigua, N.Y. (photograph by Tom Calarco).

if Brown's was one of those broken or worn away by time. After walking through the area pointed out to me and not finding the stone, I began to think that this likely was the case, or perhaps that it was even missing. But I kept walking up and down the rows, crisscrossing back and forth.

Suddenly, I turned and gazed at one stone standing in the middle of some others that had fallen. I thought I was seeing things. It was faint, but readable in the right light. I could just barely decipher the words I saw — Abel Brown. There was a lot of worn, unreadable writing below it, but his name was clear enough. I felt a rush and a chill. It was as if Brown had reached out across the centuries.

The Rev. Abel Brown lived and performed deeds worthy of a saint. His life serves as a noteworthy example of the antebellum Christian evangelical. This reprint brings back to life the full measure of the man. Included with it are all of its original woodcut illustrations, as well as photos, graphics, illustrations, and letters not in the original edition. It is hoped that this book will stimulate further research that will unearth additional documents and information about Abel Brown, and keep the memory of his courageous and selfless deeds alive.

Tom Calarco, 2006

Notes on the Editing

My chief aim was clarity without sacrificing the original document. Spellings and capitalization used by Catharine S. Brown were retained, but some superfluous commas were removed, and erroneous punctuation was corrected, as were errors of spelling and basic grammar. Here and there, I have provided context or clarification, either by inserting phrases in brackets or by furnishing a footnote.

In the original work, very little distinction is made typographically between quoted material and Mrs. Brown's own writing. In this edition, quotes of more than one or two lines are set apart as block quotations in a reduced type size. When quotations are not set apart, quotation marks have been added as necessary to distinguish quotations from Mrs. Brown's words.

Mrs. Brown's book made frequent use of italics for emphasis, probably representing underlined words in handwritten documents. Often the words that nineteenth-century writers chose to stress, and the patterns of stress, differ enough from current usage to be distracting to today's reader. (For example: "I hope to have a message for some of those who *sleep* in Zion.") In the interest of readability, some of these emphases have been removed. Italics in articles from newspapers are retained.

In Mrs. Brown's original publication, the chapter titles did not always precisely match the table of contents. In this new edition, the table of contents matches Mrs. Brown's original, and chapter titles have been edited where necessary to make them match that table of contents.

Except where noted, the illustrations are not original to Mrs. Brown's volume.

Tom Calarco

INTRODUCTION

It seems due to the character of an individual, who has labored long and assiduously to promote the best interests of his fellow-beings, that his life should be portrayed, after he has ceased to act in his corporeal nature, and when his memory or the influence of his life alone remains, endeared to his friends and spectre-like to his foes; for, "though dead, he yet speaketh." Then let him reiterate the truth in his own words, and let his deeds be recorded as the best evidence of a life devoted to the service of his fellow-mortals, and of his God.

Offering no apology for this little volume, I merely would premise, that I have done the best that my precarious health and circumstances would allow, and that I have been obliged to rely essentially on the correspondence and papers of Mr. Brown, in connection with my own personal knowledge. Having little available information from even known resources, many important incidents may have been omitted, but an index, I trust, has been given to his general character as a Christian and an humble reformer of the age in which he lived and wrought.

The character of an individual, whether good, neutral, or evil, is held in various degrees of estimation as it is seen and appreciated only by partial lights, and not by the just blending of all its colors. These produce the harmony of the whole, and the general effect is often different from that of the separate tints and shades. This, which is frequently the case with those engaged in affairs of the state, who are held up to the scrutinizing gaze of the public, is still more so with the reformer, from the peculiarity of his position. Boldly arrayed against popular institutions, he awakens and excites personal feeling and indignation by his appeals to the conscience, as with demonstration and energy he exposes the odious sin or vice to view, causing the evil-doers to behold and comprehend its enormity, and seek for its removal. In such a position, people are influenced by interest or prejudice in deciding on the reformer's character. One doubts his sincerity, another his talent, another perhaps his object — as being unworthy of popular excitement or attention. Thus it is, and however self-denying a reformer may be, his efforts obtain him little credit for disinterestedness of purpose or benevolence of action. So selfish are mankind generally in their aims, that they can hardly conceive how any person can be actuated by different motives from their own, they not having experienced the divine principle of love, which animates his spirit in every obligation, and in every pursuit of life. For these reasons, the writer has dwelt somewhat in detail on minor points of interest, deeming them essential, in no small degree, to the delineation of a true picture. Could these memoirs only stimulate others to a life of greater self-denial and perseverance in the cause of the persecuted, she will have fully attained her object.

C.S.B. [Catharine Swan Brown, 1849]

CHAPTER I

HIS DESCENT — BIRTH — NATURAL ACTIVITY AND LOVE
OF BUSINESS — HIS GUARDIAN SISTER — HIS EXPERIENCE
OF A NEW LIFE — AND CHOICE OF PROFESSION

The subject of this memoir was born at Springfield, Massachusetts, in the year 1810, Nov. 9th. His parents were respectable, inasmuch as they were Christians, and trained their family by precept and example in those virtues that adorn the Christian character. Abel was the third of six children, including an only and dearly beloved sister of whom some account will be given in succeeding pages, — indeed, sufficient to throw light on the subject of this volume. His father, Abel Brown, was a native of Spring-field and son of Collins Brown, "a respectable farmer of retired habits, known but little abroad." His mother was a native of Hadley, Massachusetts, whose name was Joanna, the daughter of Timothy Lyman, who graduated at Yale College in some year between 1775 and '78, and after-wards studied the profession of medicine, in which capacity he settled in the vicinity of Northampton. The ancestors of Abel, on the maternal side, were members of the church in charge of President Edwards,[1] and his mother seems to have imbibed much of the spirit of those times when the Lord moved as upon the face of the waters, [and was one of] the vast multitude who thronged to listen to the eloquent pleadings of the inspired preacher. In those days of earnest devotion, to be a Christian implied something more than "a name to live." Who knows the extent of such an influence even to the present hour. It is for this reason that I notice the membership of those venerable fathers and mothers.

---

[1] *The Rev. Jonathan Edwards (1703–1758), remarkable evangelist and theologian, began a series of revivals after becoming pastor of the Congregational Church in Northampton, Massachusetts. This sparked a period of great religious fervor in the American colonies that was called the First Great Awakening. — Editor.*

Abel spent his earliest childhood at the home of his parents, in the place of his nativity, until his removal with them at the age of eleven years to the state of New York, Madison County.

In size he was of ordinary stature with proportionally large head and chest, affording him much of the sanguine united with a quick nervous temperament. His forehead, finely arched, indicated intellectual powers of no ordinary character; while with a cheerful yet steady and determined eye, he pursued every object of his undertaking with resistless energy. Still, [he was] "easily governed as a child" by persuasion and appeals to his consciousness of filial obligation, yet not a subject for arbitrary discipline.

His swiftness in pedestrian plays with his school fellows was somewhat remarkable — as with the speed of an antelope, "he would often outstrip them in the race." Of dancing too, he was fond. It is needless to say, however, that with him it was mere pastime in an hour of childish glee confined to his younger days — the ebullition of a joyous heart when nature showed naught but a sunny face (the mirror of his own) and the world itself seemed one enticing charm. Such is infancy — and sin alone unfolds a different view to the weeping eyes of manhood, throwing its darkening shadows over all that is beautiful and fair, and filling the cup of life with bitterness and woe.

He was said to be "a natural scholar, and quick to learn," yet when young was sent to school as convenience would permit rather than receiving the benefit of a systematic course of instruction (I should judge).

It is certain that at an early age he manifested a disposition for business. Some kind of employment he ever sought. Inspired by this natural disposition, enhanced by necessity, the child of poverty — at the age of twelve (as he himself informed me) he was extremely solicitous to enter a store — and accordingly did — business of some kind seemed to be his life. Affable in his manner and prompt in his calling, he gained many friends. I have heard him speak also of assisting in the care of children in a family when young, and of visiting with them and sharing equally in all their privileges as social guests. This fondness of children and tender solicitude for their welfare was very noticeable in after life in his intercourse with families as a lecturer abroad, and was a subject of remark. I have heard him speak also of hearing political discussions in stores, which may have contributed to interest his mind in matters of this kind.

He is represented in the following terms, in the numerous credentials he received as clerk, at different periods, as being "faithful, trustworthy, competent, &c.," and as "never having abused the unlimited confidence reposed in him."

CHAPTER II

FAMILY LETTERS—CHRISTIAN EXPERIENCE

The correspondence between himself and his sister evinces a kindred sympathy and interest in the welfare of each other. Indeed his sister seems at an *early* age to have been to him a guardian angel, to keep him from temptation, waywardness, and folly.

Deeply imbued with the love and knowledge of divine truth, she was abundantly qualified to counsel and advise her younger brother, and her little sermons undoubtedly exerted a salutary influence over his heart and life. While at the Academy at Fredonia, Feb. 8th, '29, she writes—

> I feel much interested in your prosperity, and hope you enjoy yourself in G——. Yet remember, Abel, that perfection is not to be found in any person or situation in life. Let me entreat you, dear brother, not to seek happiness from the things of this world exclusively, entwining your affections around them as your only treasure. Consider they are of the earth, earthly, and must soon return to dust. We ourselves also are passing away fast as the wheels of time can carry us. Religion will prepare us better to enjoy the things of this life and fortify our minds to meet all events with calmness and resignation.

In another letter she remarks—"Abel, if we have so far sustained a good character, it is highly important that we strive for it through the remainder of life."

At nearly the same time, he writes to his brother Edwin:

> Since leaving home, the Lord has (I trust) shown me my perilous condition "out of Christ." I have been made to feel that I was a great sinner. I have thought of joining the church in this place, but do not know that I am fit to belong to a people devoted to God as much as that body ought

to be. Such a responsibility is resting on a person of this description that I think and fear I should be a stumbling block to poor sinners.

Brother, do you think of the obligation you are under to live as a christian? Do you think of the Covenant you made with your God when you were buried with Christ in baptism? Oh, if you do, as you value your soul, do not break it. "He that putteth his hand to the plough and looketh back, is not fit for the Kingdom of Heaven."

During this period (at nineteen years of age) he joined the church at Fredonia, and immediately became interested in Sabbath Schools and the cause of God universally — and in whatever he engaged for the cause of Christ, he entered with his whole heart.

Even from his first experience in the divine life, he seems to have been confirmed and established in those high and holy principles of religious obligation, which he ever manifested in after life.

FROM HIS SISTER

... I am exceedingly anxious that you live devoted to God. In all thy ways acknowledge Him and He will direct thy path. Your young companions may forsake you, but let them take knowledge by your life, that you have learned of Christ. After relating her own experience, she further adds: And let us live a self-denying and Cross-bearing life, and that Being who has been the God of our dear parents will be ours also.

While interceding at the throne of grace for ourselves, let us not forget our dear brothers at home.

[TO CYNTHIA]

Dunkirk, Sept. 4th, '30.

Dear Sister, — As I am deprived the privilege of attending Covenant meeting this afternoon, I write you a few lines. I was quite disappointed in not attending Association, yet endured it very patiently, but Mr. informed me that I could no more attend meetings during weekdays, while I live with S. H. & Co. I have heard you had a good meeting at Carroll, and am glad others can have the privileges and enjoy them if I cannot. But Cynthia, I hope I shall not always be obliged to live as I now do, although I think it is all for the best. I have enjoyed myself much this afternoon thinking of my dear brethren and sisters. Oh Cynthia, how pleasant it is to get away from the cares and troubles of this world and sit down with those we expect to meet in heaven!

From a certificate of commendation given him (at twenty years of age) by a mercantile company, it seems that he was eminently qualified for business, and that "his integrity and moral character were irreproach-able."

He was alternately engaged as a student and behind the counter as a means of support in the prosecution of his studies — while his sister was much employed in teaching school. There seems also to have been a reciprocation of favors between them, always so delightful and praise-worthy in families.

At this time his sister writes thus:

I believe our trials have served to increase our union and strengthen those ties of divine love, which should entwine around the hearts of all the children of God. Oh yes, Abel, I begin to think trials are good — they only serve to make the path of the righteous to shine brighter and brighter. We all the time need something to wean our affections from this world and cause us to love and serve God more and better. I do sometimes feel to confide in God, "Lord I believe, help thou mine unbelief."

March 31st, '31. To a friend Abel writes as follows:

I never, until within a few days, felt to give myself up to the service of God in all respects, but I now feel willing to put all on board Zion's ship and give God the helm.[1]

Mr. P. is getting the Presbyterian yoke on so hard, that it will gall his neck (I think).

Remember me to all friends. Tell brother Hale, that God has seen fit to bless me in a straightforward course, &c. What my future destiny is, I know not — my only desire (as respects myself) is, to live so that I shall be approved in that day, when I am called to the judgment seat of Christ.

---

[1]*At this time, Abel was living in the midst of a moral and religious revival led by the mesmerizing evangelist Charles Finney, who was working his magic in upstate New York. It is possible Abel came under his influence through personal observation — Finney in fact had conducted a number of revivals in western New York while Abel was living in Forestville. However, there is no mention of it in the journal entries or letters referenced by C.S. Brown, though it is possible that Mrs. Brown passed over those references or perhaps they were lost. But if Abel did not personally experience Finney's preaching, he certainly was indirectly influenced by this Second Great Awakening of religious fervor whose call to overcome sin "burned over" the fields, hills, and villages of upstate New York as one author has so poetically described it (Cross, Whitney R. The Burned-over District: The Social and Intellectual History of Enthusiastic Religion in Western New York, 1800-1850. New York: Harper & Row, 1950). This moral awakening spawned the great reform movements and revolutionary epistemologies in America of the next 20 years, especially evangelical Christian abolitionism, which was the path that Abel would soon follow. — Editor.*

THIS IMPRESSION OF A REVIVAL CAMP MEETING ILLUSTRATES THE RELIGIOUS FERVOR THAT OVERTOOK MUCH OF AMERICA DURING THE EARLY DECADES OF THE NINETEENTH CENTURY, ESPECIALLY IN THE BURNED-OVER DISTRICT OF CENTRAL AND WESTERN NEW YORK WHERE ABEL BROWN GREW INTO MANHOOD (LIBRARY OF CONGRESS).

FROM CYNTHIA

Sept. 30th, '30.

... I plainly see that I love this world so much, that there is very little of the Father dwelling in my heart. A[bel] undoubtedly, you think, you have many trials and disappointments to encounter — well, these are the common lot of all God's people. "Through much tribulation ye enter the kingdom of Heaven." You and I have but just entered the field of battle — shall we desert at the commencement? No, my brother — the victory is for those who fight. Let us endure as good soldiers of "Jesus Christ, the great Captain of our salvation," who will shortly bear us conquerors, through him who hath loved us, away to His heavenly mansions, where we shall sing "the song of Moses and the Lamb, forever and ever."

Do Abel, trust in God for direction in every affair of life. Let us pray for each other, long as health and life remains.

In a subsequent letter to his sister, he writes — "As for the things of this world, I have come to the conclusion, that it is all vexation of spirit. The more I engage in them the more perplexities I find."

Lockport, May 6th, '31.

Oh, my Dear Sister,

What shall I say — In viewing the situation of my father's family — those near and dear to me by the ties of consanguinity, I am almost resolved to say, I will turn my attention (exclusively) to their temporal welfare and to the affairs of this life. The Lord has (I trust) taken from me the desire of possession in this world, with all its vain pursuits and delusive charms — and I now think myself willing to relinquish all for the service of Christ, could I only see my dear brother (for whose interest I feel deeply) in a way to obtain an education. Yet God is able to banish all my fears and place all my hopes on His blessed cause. Think calmly while you read. If I could see you, I could then unbosom my feelings, but I tell you, and I hope in the fear of God (strange as it may seem) that I feel it my duty after asking of God as I trust — to preach — and my dear sister, if you ever felt to pray for your brother, pray now, that he may be willing to go forth and discharge his duty, relying on God alone to bless and sustain his efforts.

When I look around and see how "white are the fields," — and the laborers so few, I feel anxious for the time to go and thrust in the sickle and share in the bounties of so glorious a harvest. I feel as though I want to wear out this body and these lungs in the service of God.

The path to riches and honor in this world look easy, but not inviting. It is nothing to be rich in this world, but to be rich in grace, is all I wish — or to be more plainly understood, I desire (I think) nothing so much as to be a faithful minister of Jesus. God has seen fit to bless me abundantly since I tried to serve him — and he has said, his grace is all-sufficient.

The church in this place, has precious jewels, although some are dead weights in Zion. Should Providence permit, I shall go out to Chautauque in about two months, when I hope to have a message for some of those who sleep in Zion. Oh remember me at the mercy seat.

P. S. I expect to leave the business I am in, in about six or eight weeks if the door of Providence is opened. (My employer is now in New York.) You may keep this letter within your own breast, until you hear from me again, as I may be deceived on this subject, but talk to God much about it. I hope all will trust in God, not in Abel, — I cannot give the things of this world.

A. B.

Many things of a family nature in their correspondence (not suited to the public eye) tend equally with the preceding to exhibit his character in the kindred relations he sustained — such as proffers of assistance to his brothers in obtaining an education, which were duly appreciated and readily accepted.

Such simple exhibitions of his views and feelings, as these frank and unassuming letters present, carry far more evidence of his true character than the most labored arguments in ethics, or the mere solution of intellectual problems in divinity. In consideration of such valuable testimony, it is hoped the compiler will be excusable for making such copious extracts therefrom.

Lockport, June 17th, '31.

Dear Sister,

Yours I have — Jesus reigns — Let the earth rejoice — all I can say is, what hath the Lord wrought! I have often thought of the youth in fair Chautauque, and when in a measure, I have realized their situation at the bar of God, I think I have felt in heart to say, Lord, save or they perish! Let us for one moment look back, when we were without hope and without Christ in the world, busily engaged in decorating these mortal bodies, which soon must be food for worms, and see if we are not under obligation to serve God while we live for even permitting us to bear some humble part in accomplishing his purposes. Oh, how humble should christians feel when God in his infinite mercy has vouchsafed unto them his Holy Spirit, to guide and direct them into all duty — and to assist them to speak and pray to divine acceptance. christians should ever realize that their strength is perfect weakness, and depend alone on the strength and merits of Christ.

If you who are Baptists, are now, *all* only willing that *God* should reign, and will lay by your party feelings, you will soon be built up a spiritual house, against which the prince of darkness or his followers cannot prevail. I hope you and those dear sisters with you, will do and realize, that the cause of Christ is worth infinitely more than all earth beside — and pray God to keep you humble, that you may never cease your efforts, until you see 'the church coming up out of the wilderness, leaning upon the blessed Jesus.' All that is required of you is, to perform the duties allotted to you as individual christians, in the love and fear of God, and leave the event with Him who knows what is best for his children. Christians are apt to have an unscriptural anxiety about God's affairs, are fearful he will not manage just right — but if you ever feel any thing of *this*, be assured that *you* are not right. Don't trouble yourself about the affairs of God, he will permit *error*, delusion, strife and tumult to reign just as long as he sees fit, and then will bring it to an end. — Would that I were more reconciled to the will of heaven. I wish to make a few plain remarks to you, and others, could I see them, on the example those in your situation should exhibit.

For several years you have professed religion, yet you are still young. Those younger than yourselves will probably make the same profession; to whom will they look for example? To sister Brown, Burgess, Mallery, &c. If then young christians should thus look to you for instruction, what conduct should you bear towards them? In the first place, you should always greet them with that pleasant salutation, *sister.* Oh, how my feelings have been dampened by the title Mr. from one whom I really thought to be my *brother.* This affectionate salutation is often omitted in the presence of strangers — but it is wrong so to do — for see, says the stranger, those christians are ashamed of each other.

2d. We should be careful to enquire after the welfare of their souls, whether they enjoy the presence of Jesus or not — and very soon, it would be our greatest delight to tell each other how much of heaven we have enjoyed since last we met.

3d. Let our conversation be in heaven from whence we look for the Saviour. Finally, we should endeavor so to act that we can look up implicitly toward heaven and ask God for a blessing on our labors. We are apt to forget to pray together. We should make it a practice (on all proper occasions) when we meet and when we part, to begin and end at the mercy seat.

Again he writes —

I am at present busily engaged in the things of this world, but expect ere long to be liberated, and with pleasure I look forward to the heavenly employment, to which I trust, my Saviour has called me. Although, I must say with one of old, "Who is sufficient for these things." "Praise the Lord," for the arm of the Jehovah is *Almighty.* I love you all dearly, but hope I love Jesus and his cause more. I want more humility; I cannot tell you all my wants, but Jesus knows them. The road to heaven lies through this world, and as our Captain went before, let us follow and submit cheerfully to the temptations of Satan and all the enemies of God, recollecting that "they work for us a far more exceeding and eternal weight of glory."

"Then shall I be satisfied when I awake in his likeness."

Let us so live, that when called upon at *death,* we can say, — I have done what I could. That we may be permitted to reign together in heaven, is the earnest prayer of your brother,

ABEL.

CHAPTER III

STUDIES DIVINITY AT HAMILTON— CONTINUATION OF CORRESPONDENCE WITH HIS SISTER— LETTER TO HIS PARENTS AND BROTHER

Although kind offers of commission were presented him (at this age) in mercantile business, he declined on the ground that "the Lord had *other* work for him to do." And being still desirous to continue his studies with reference to the ministry, he entered the Lit. & Theo. Sem. at Hamilton.

Soon after his arrival in H. he thus describes his journey from Forestville,[1] &c. being a review of former scenes and acquaintance, together with his new abode.

Oct. 29th, 1831.

My Dear Sister,

I arrived in Lockport Sunday after I left you about ten o'clock — found all warm friends and well. Started on Monday Morn, "on board boat" with Elder Tucker. Arrived at Elbridge[2] in time to hear the first sermon at the sitting of the Convention. Elder Elliott stood in the pulpit and spoke from Rom. 8th: 3d and 4th verses.[3] I think I never heard a sermon from mortal lips, that exhibited more of the greatness, goodness and love of God. He indeed showed himself to be a man of talents, eloquence and powers of reasoning, yet he appeared desirous to use them all in showing the love-

---

[1] *A hamlet seven miles east of Fredonia, New York.—Editor.*

[2] *Brown evidently took an Erie Canal boat to Elbridge, a hamlet five miles south of the canal, about 15 miles west of Syracuse.—Editor.*

[3] *"What if some did not have faith? Will their lack of faith nullify God's faithfulness? Not at all! Let God be true, and every man a liar. As it is written: 'So that you may be proved right when you speak and prevail when you judge.'" The context of this passage is Paul's treatise on the Jews, who though they followed the law of Moses would not be saved because they lacked the faith to believe in Jesus Christ.—Editor.*

liness of *the Saviour* and not himself. It was a very interesting season and they indeed appeared to sit together "in a heavenly place" in Christ Jesus.

Thursday, proceeded on our way and arrived at Syracuse in the evening — heard the converted Jew preach. Started in the morning and arrived at Morrisville about noon. I now feel quite at home. Called on most of the friends, visited the grave yard, and there saw the little mounds raised over the bodies of many whom I once beheld walking the streets of Morrisville. There is a sweetness in the thought, in viewing these sepulchral homes, that the *mortal* part only rests there. It seemed very pleasant to read the names of those who (as I trusted) died in the triumphs of faith, for while I gazed on the earth that hid their bodies from sight, I looked — and by the eye of faith, saw them rising in the likeness of Christ. I saw the grave of Miss L. (Oh, that fair form is now wasting away.) I felt as though I could weep, but something whispered, she has gone to God who will do no injustice.

All my young acquaintance received me very cordially: those of us who were once boys and girls together, now, apparently took more delight in conversing with each other than ever. But my sister, they don't love Jesus. I endeavored in my feeble manner, to tell them that Jesus had died to save sinners, and that they must believe on Him if they would be saved — yet none but God can turn them. I hope I love to pray for them. I went to Messrs. _____; the young ladies inquired particularly about you and expressed a wish to see you, which I think was real.

I arrived here last Monday evening — called on brother Dean and was welcomed to his abode, and for the first time was permitted with him to address a throne of grace. We rise in the morning at half past four — assemble in the Chapel at five and attend prayer (O Cynthia, it is a pleasant place.) Breakfast at about half past six — have porridge and bread for breakfast — meat, sauce and bread for dinner, or leave the meat and take butter, as we choose. For *tea* we take *cold water*, bread and butter. This is the fare of most of the students or of the abstinence society; but tea, coffee, &c. are furnished for those who wish them. Cynthia, the word self-denial means a great deal. Inform yourself in what duty consists, and "go thou and do likewise." Sister, I would write more on this subject, did room admit. I do not like to write such a letter as this, but knew you would expect it, therefore comply. I had much rather be telling you about the Saviour, for he appears exceedingly precious to me at this time. The closet has been very sweet to me, although I have the same temptations of sin and of Satan to withstand as ever. I hope you grow in grace every day, for this is your privilege. I think I feel more sensibly the presence of God — that He is ever looking into the innermost recesses of the soul. It is a fearful consideration,—but if we can hide under the Saviour's wings we are safe. What unholy creatures we seem, when we realize that the all-piercing eye of Jehovah is upon us!

To all. I hope none of you meet at the mercy seat without remembering Abel, especially in a family capacity. God will hear prayer. Remember me to all the dear brethren and sisters — especially to those who bade me such a hearty farewell.

Yours in a precious Saviour, A. B.

22d Feb. — This morning have been reading the 18th chapter of Matthew. I find that I owe God ten thousand talents,[4] and that when I had nothing to pay, He, as I trust, forgave me all the debt. On examining my heart, I find also that I have been like the wicked servant who took his brother by the throat, when he owed him but one hundred pence. O, shall I ever possess the forgiving spirit which characterized our Saviour. I have often thought if I could go to Fredonia, I would with pleasure confess to those who stood opposed to me in opinion, that I did not feel the forgiving spirit of Jesus. My sister, it is our duty, if we do wrong in the least, even to a person who has all his life-time abused us, to go to that person and confess our fault. We must confess and forsake our sins, if we would find mercy. Have all the dear brethren and sisters in Forestville church, confessed all their wrong feelings toward and expressions about their opposing brethren and sisters? If they have not, they cannot expect to he blessed in soul, and they certainly have not done their duty. We must *do* those things in which we ask God to bless us or we cannot have free access to the mercy seat, and if we are shut from that blessed place, we are surely in a lamentable condition.

Sunday Eve, Feb. 26. — I have just received a letter from brother Thomas. He tells me he hopes he is a christian. I hope you will lead him along. I want to talk with you about self-denial. Bear with me a little longer. I find it is our duty to deny our taste as well as any other, vain desire. I find by experience that I enjoy good health and live without pies or cakes, tea or coffee. A plain, simple diet is for our health; it costs the least, and God approves. A contrary course injures our health, costs more, and God disapproves. I only mention this subject, and leave it with you to pray over. In doing the will of God, there is great reward.

---

[4] *This refers to the Parable of the Talents. Ten thousand talents is an enormous sum, meant to imply an unlimited amount. This parable suggests that we can never repay God the debt we owe him, but that he will settle his accounts with us at the Judgment Day if we obey his commandments. — Editor.*

Hamilton, May 25, '32.

Very Dear Br. Edwin:— I know not how to address you as you may be in eternity before I am ever permitted to see you. I know not why you are afflicted, while I enjoy health. You cannot be a greater sinner than I am, therefore *that* cannot be the reason. I can only say, "Even so, Father, for so it seemeth good in thy sight." I hope, my brother, you will neither mur- mur nor repine at your lot; for the Lord does all things well. He knows when it is best to send affliction upon his children, and when best to take them to himself. Only resign all into his hands and trust in Jesus for salvation, and you can meet death with a smile. Do not think your situation and lot hard; for when compared with others they are not. A short time since, I was at the County Poor-house — went around among the sick and conversed with them about their eternal interest. I found many without hope in Christ; two in particular were miserable, compared with your situation. They sent for me to visit their chamber. I immediately complied with their request. I went to the bedside of the first, a black woman, about middle aged. She was in great distress — told me she had a hope in Jesus and expected soon to be with him. Yet, said she was willing to bear all the pain the Lord saw fit to inflict, as he would not send one too many. The other was an intelligent looking young woman, whose husband had become a drunkard, and left her, with a dear little child after bringing her to this land of strangers, sick and alone, without any friend but the mercies of the public. In this situa- tion she was carried to the poor-house. She was almost overpowered with grief. She said that she had an aged father and mother in Massachusetts; but they were unable to render her any assistance, and she was unwilling to have their hearts broken by the sad intelligence of her situation. After telling her about Jesus and his suffering, she, looking at the little child, said, "Were it not for this, I would willingly die." I looked at her and then at the black woman, who asked me if I was willing to pray with them. I kneeled by her bed-side, and tried to commend them in the name of Jesus to Him who hears prayer. After I arose they thanked me for what they esteemed kind- ness, and I soon retired. I have reflected much upon the scene since that time, and have endeavored to compare their situation with yours and mine. They have no father who prays for them; no mother to soothe their anguish and answer their calls; no affectionate sister to sympathize with them in their affliction, and no friend to call and tell them about Jesus. I hope, my brother, you will be calm and undisturbed when thinking of your situation, and try to realize that you are not at your own disposal; but that God has sent this affliction upon you for some wise purpose, and although you may not think or see why it is so, yet, trust in God, and believe him when he says, "all things shall work together for good to them who love him."

The only desire the christian should have to stay in this world, should be to warn sinners to flee from the wrath to come. The Lord knows when to take them — to accomplish his purposes. You may at last meet around the throne with hundreds of immortal spirits, who were brought to see their situation through the instrumentality of one converted at your death.

Death, to the impenitent sinner is the "king of terrors"; but to the christian, it is the beginning of life. Is it a terror to be free from sin, and to be like Jesus? The thought of being like Jesus has many times filled your soul with joy inexpressible. But, O my brother, what will the reality be! Now we look only by an eye of faith into Heaven, seeing Abraham, Isaac and Moses, with angels and Jesus — and even this infant glance almost overcomes us; but what will be our joy when seated in their midst! I have sometimes been ready to inquire, why am I not one of their number? It is because this clog of clay holds me down to earth. But I trust you will soon have the privilege of leaving this hinderance, and death alone can separate this mortal from immortality. Then do not fear to die, for death is no more than raising the curtain which hides Heaven from our view. We should be willing to stay here just as long as God would have us, and bear with patience all the afflictions he sends upon us; for we never can suffer as much as Jesus did. I want to see you very much, but do not expect it in the flesh. There will be no death around the throne of God. There, we can praise that Jesus who died to redeem us without interruption. Oh how sweet his name will sound when sung by an immortal tongue! Were there not a world of sinners who never heard the sweet name of Jesus, I would gladly go with you to His Father's mansions. I must bid you adieu. I shall, in my feeble manner, try to pray that God may give you a calm and unmoved spirit; and that, whether He permits you to live or die, you may be His. Oh, my brother, *trust* in God and *fear not.*

Farewell.

In the prosecution of his studies he was obliged, as he had hitherto been, like many other students, to rely entirely on his own exertions for support, accepting occasional favors from his family, always given with a good will and a hearty "God speed," which to him was more than an encouragement to effort.

In his sister he never failed to find a sympathizing friend to cheer him onward in his course, as from her lips and pen she dropped the words of consolation and of love. Hear her say in that angel voice, "Go on, my brother; my soul says, go — Yonder is the prize laid up in heaven above." Then pointing the way she proceeds —

but ever be mindful that through much tribulation we enter the kingdom of heaven. There are many enemies to encounter; but they shall be destroyed, and we come off more than conquerors through Him who hath loved us. Oh that I could do something for God during the little time I may be permitted to live. I feel that my life is almost spent. Had it been spent in usefulness, then I could meet death with a smile — but Jesus lives; therefore have I hope. I have enjoyed many pleasant seasons in my little retired chamber since you left. Sweet have been my meditations on heavenly things, and you, my dear brother, have not been forgotten. May the Lord ever be your guide is the prayer of your unworthy sister. I now retire —

and there, in the sanctuary of a sister's heart, was he again and again remembered.

In a letter dated, Hamilton, Dec. 5, '31, he thus writes:

Dear Parents: — I trust, I have felt and do still feel grateful for your unceasing kindness to me. I am led to thank God for permitting you to live, and be a guide to me in youth. But the privilege of receiving religious instruction in childhood is one that I never have realized as I ought. Where should I have been or what my fate, had I not have had religious parents to instruct me — God only knows. I think I have (of late) had a small view of the blessings resulting from praying parents.

You appear precious to me when I think of the circle around a father's fireside, or when I think of you as earthly friends, who will always sympathize with me in affliction, but when I think of you at the mercy seat, pleading in my behalf, then it is, the cord is fastened in my inmost soul. Then we are cemented together with a Saviour's blood.

We ought to be very humble before God for permitting us to labor in his cause. We should not think we are making sacrifices when we are called to give up Father, Mother, Brother or Sister, or even our children for Christ's sake. I hoped to have been permitted to have supplied your temporal wants when old age deprived you of strength — but I trust Jesus will then lend you his sustaining arm on which to lean, and will not only go down with you to the borders of the grave — but will lead you through the valley of death — and present you spotless before the throne of his Father, while he exhibits his wounded side and points to Calvary, saying, there I purchased these with my blood!

N. B. I hope you will not trouble yourselves about my temporal welfare.   A. B.

Writing his sister, Dec. 25th, '31,

In view of the heathen world, he was led to exclaim — Where is the christian, who thinks enough of the Saviour and the souls of men to leave the parental roof and all civilized society, to go and teach them, how to escape the wrath of God. I have asked myself, are you willing to make these sacrifices, leave home, Father, Mother, Brothers and Sisters and America with all its enticing charms, for the privilege of teaching poor benighted heathen that Jesus Christ was crucified that sinners might live? I do not know what to answer, but sometimes trust I can freely say — here Lord, am I — if thou canst accept of so sinful a creature. I know not *where*, it will be my duty to labor, I must leave it until future years to determine; hoping, I shall be willing to go wherever the Lord would have me. You are bound to me, my sister, by endearing ties, and I vainly hoped to have strewed your path with temporal blessings, but the Lord in mercy has shown me (in a degree) that *this* world is neither an abode of pleasure or of rest, and that we ought not to think of resting here below, but rather be anxious to wear out these mortal frames in the service of our Divine Master. With these feelings I ask you solemnly — are you willing to become a Missionary? Are you willing to live, labor and die, pointing sinners to the Lamb of God? I do not ask you to go to Burma, there are heathen *this* side of that benighted region — I only ask, are you willing to give yourself up to the cause of Christ, and pray God to open the door and make you willing to enter in. The poor Indians call — The distant vallies of the west cry, "come over and help us"; and on all sides the voice is heard, "tell us how to escape an eternal hell — and who Jesus Christ is." I feel as though I could with pleasure give you the parting hand and say, go, labor for Jesus. I know we are not fit or worthy to be Missionaries; but Jesus is worthy. These feelings are not of the moment, and the more I inform myself upon the subject, the more I long to have my desires granted. It is not impossible for God to open a door that you may go out and labor for Him. I trust we feel that we are the Lord's and not our own. We ought not to have any interest of our own separate from Christ; and christians must devote their time, talents and influence to the cause of Christ before the isles of the sea shall rejoice, or Ethiopia stretch forth her hands unto God.

To his youngest brother he writes:

Dear Brother Lyman: — I love you dearly and want to see you very much. Yet I am not sure that I ever shall see you again in this world. I wish you to remember that you are not too young to die; and if you die a wicked boy you can never go where Jesus is. Jesus loves to hear little boys pray, and delights to see them good boys. I hope you go to the Sabbath School and to meeting every Sabbath. I send you this little map in order that you may find the place where Jesus was born, and where he was crucified. And when you find these places, think that this Jesus died and was crucified because we were sinners, and that he might save us from going down to hell. — Please to keep this map very nice, and learn to answer all the questions in the table. Go to school and learn all you can now, while young, so that you may know something when you come to be a man. I want you to write me the first opportunity you have of sending a letter, and tell me whether you go to Sabbath school or not, and what you study at the day school, and all about what you are doing, and what is done in Forestville.[5] Tell brother Edwin, I want to see him very much. From your brother, Abel.

[5]*Apparently, Abel's family had moved to Forestville when he was working there as a clerk. — Editor.*

CHAPTER IV

SECOND YEAR AT HAMILTON—HIS PRACTICAL
EFFORTS IN THE CAUSE OF SABBATH SCHOOLS—
MISSIONARY LETTERS—JOURNAL

He seems to have considered a theoretical course of studying Divinity, as it is termed, best promoted by a divine course of action. He therefore was not satisfied with being cloistered within the walls of an institution without doing something toward the great object for which he was preparing himself. He accordingly was much engaged in exhortation and prayer with his fellow students, and in study of the scriptures with stated seasons for meditation and devotion.

In writing to his sister, he casually remarks:— I have charge of two Sabbath Schools and two Bible classes, one in each.

Severe in self discipline, he practiced every self denial requisite with his limited means in the prosecution of his studies, which also served fully to develop his principles and mould his character to the requirements of the gospel. He also improved whatever time he could command in publicly teaching the gospel of Christ, as indicated in his journals and letters.

Hamilton, Feb. 6, 1832.

My Dear Sister:— I know not as this will ever get to you, but will pen down a few thoughts.

I have just returned from Morrisville, where I have spent three weeks, it being vacation. Have attended meeting almost every day in the village and vicinity. I have visited most of the people in M. with whom I was acquainted, and tried in my cold hearted and feeble manner to tell them about Jesus; but I know so little about Him myself that I could neither do or say but little. Oh that I was more like my blessed Master. While I live, let me labor for Jesus. This world, my sister, how vain it is! What will the heathen do — no Saviour to shelter them from that Almighty storm that is fast approaching. Can we meet them at the judgment seat of Christ, and stand ourselves acquitted, unless we do all we can to deliver them from this awful state. The youth of our land must come up to their rescue. I hope you will train the dear children under your care, with the blessing of God, in such a manner that they will not live for themselves.

TO THE SAME

14 Feb. '32.

I have thought, and am daily thinking, concerning the subject I have before written you; but no favorable opportunity has yet presented itself for consideration. I trust that you are laboring for the Lord where you are. We should make it our object to glorify God in every position of life. Self must altogether be laid aside, if we would labor acceptably in his cause.

15th Feb — I was unexpectedly called to lay aside my pen last evening, therefore resume it tonight. I have been thinking what I have done for Jesus in my life, and my feelings and thoughts I cannot describe. I received your letter to day, and this evening I have been thinking about you, and have thought God would humble you at the feet of Jesus, if he never did me — That he would permit you to labor for him successfully, if I am not. I think if I could see you I should talk as follows: —

Dear sister, we profess to love Jesus, and say that we wish to labor for him; therefore it becometh us to lay aside every thing that keeps us from the Mercy seat and hinders us from serving Him. Now are we willing to show by our actions what our words say we desire; are we willing to put off the fashions of the world — our fine clothes — and are we willing to sacrifice our good names — willing to be called singular, enthusiastic, self righteous, fools, and all other slanderous names which a wicked world can heap upon us. Are we willing to deny self entirely and take up our cross and follow Jesus, if he heads us into the burning furnace? The blessed Jesus had no where to lay his head. Methinks I hear you say, gladly would I make any sacrifice; or, I would not think any thing I could do for Jesus a sacrifice.

I have not mentioned the subject to any one, and shall not until I hear from you; and if you answer me as I trust you will, I shall use my influence to obtain for you a situation, that you may go and labor until you hear the voice, "Child, your Father calls, come home." I take great pleasure in meeting you at the mercy seat.

Adieu, my sister.

ABEL.

In his Journal he thus describes his labors on a preaching tour.

Springfield, Sept. 8, 1832. I have only a moment to write. I have been in town two weeks, and the Lord I trust has been with me. Have preached nine times.— The Lord appears to be hovering over this place (Chicopee Factories).[1] I have not as yet had time to visit any of my relatives; but am under the delightful necessity of meeting an audience every evening. There are about eight hundred inhabitants in this place. My heart entwines around this people; but duty will soon call me to leave them. I have had some views of eternity, and of the awful condition of the sinner in the world of spirits. Oh, when will men learn to be wise and consider their latter end! Have seen Eld. Ezra Going today, and heard him *preach*. He is a *going* man, and may the Lord bless his labors.

I take satisfaction in praying the Lord to forgive and "wake up" those drowsy professors who clog the wheels of Zion. The time has already come when christians must show, by their acts of benevolence, that they are such, or be accounted drones in the hive of Christ. I feel to bless the Lord that the *youth* in the church of God begin to live and act some as Jesus did. Our *Saviour* became poor, that we might be rich. And dare we refuse to follow his example? May heaven forbid.

VIEW OF CHICOPEE, CIRCA 1839 (COURTESY CHICOPEE [MA] HISTORICAL SOCIETY).

[1]*Because of the abundant water power, mills and factories sprang up during the first half of the nineteenth century in Chicopee Falls, near the Chicopee River's intersection with the Connecticut River not far from the Massachusetts border with Connecticut. The first business at the falls was an iron works, which was followed by large cotton mills, metal works, and gun factories.— Editor.*

Avon, Hartford Co. Conn. Sept. 13.
I am attending a protracted meeting in this place. God has seen fit to bless
me since I came here — but I stand almost alone. Ministers do not preach
here as in N.Y.; and Christians are not awake to their eternal interests. I
do not know why I have been brought to this place, or what the Lord is
about to do with me. I hope I am willing that God should do with me as
seemeth good in his sight. When I look back, and see where most who
have lived upon this earth have gone, and reflect that most, *now* on the
stage of action, are hastening to the same dark abode, *what can I do,* but
throw myself in the way, and try, with all the powers which God has given
me, to stop men from plunging into the abyss of woe. A soul in hell eternally! how *awful* the thought! who can endure it?

I came through Hartford on my way to this place, but had not time to
go about the city much — took a view of the place from the top of the Baptist Church. It is pleasantly situated, and contains about ten thousand
immortal souls. There appears to be much wealth and talent in the city.
Oh, that it was all devoted to the cause of Jesus! But let others do as they
may, here Lord, accept of my unworthy self— time, talents and all — and
for Jesus' sake use them to promote Thy glory, or take me from the world —
"Thy will, Oh God, be done."

Springfield, Sep. 15.— Arrived here this morning from Avon. Have had
a precious time during my absence from this place. It appeared to me that
God was willing to save sinners; but his professed ministers and people
stood in the way. In view of this, I felt to pray "in groans that cannot be
uttered," before the Throne, that God would break the hearts of His servants.

On Friday morning, the man who preached on Thursday P.M., with
a heart apparently almost insensible, this morning got down upon his
knees, being the first who had kneeled, and offered a petition, with all
that childlike simplicity with which the ministers of Jesus should pray. It
was pleasant to see the tears roll down his stately cheeks. The church
began to weep, and sinners began to cry, "Pray for me." In this situation
I left them.

South Hadley Canal, Sept. 18, 1832.— On Saturday evening last found
myself very much fatigued, but attended meeting. Tried to preach two sermons on the Sabbath at the Factories, and one at Willimansett in the evening. The great God, I trust, helped me. On Monday came to this place —
shall continue about two hours.

During his visit in this region, he notices the attention and kindness of various relatives, also the respective character and condition of

their families, in all of which he manifests the most lively interest for their spiritual welfare. Some are represented as being without hope in Christ, others as devotedly pious.

> J_____ is like the man in the gospel, "I have married a wife and cannot come." R_____ has built him a house and is soon to be married. His heart is all full of farms, houses, cattle and sheep, and everything else, except Jesus, and his religion. Grandmother Pendleton is still living, although 94 years old. She is a poor, helpless, insensible old lady. I have visited the house and farm where I was born; but it does not appear as it did in childhood. The beautiful bed of lilies is gone. The stately oak has been removed — the shed has fallen and decayed — the fine peach trees are not seen, and even the house itself is decaying, and fast falling to pieces.

On this scene he makes no comment, for he never allowed himself in vain regrets and sad reflections. This was a peculiar trait in his mental disposition. He was too much engaged in the duties of the "ever varying present," to indulge in the dreamy shadows of the past.

> South Hadley, Sept. 26.
> Last evening, tried to preach in this place, and realized in some degree the presence of the Saviour. I know not why I am thus favored, for I am fully sensible, that I am one of the most sinful beings on earth — having sinned against great light, and crucified the Saviour afresh, again and again. Still, God, in His unbounding mercy, has seen fit to bless me abundantly. When I realize how this sinful world has used the lovely Jesus, I am constrained to wonder and am astonished that He has not left it to its own choice. I am aware of my indifference to the great concerns of eternity, compared with what I shall feel in the light of another world. Yet still, I am under the painful necessity of seeing those who are even more indifferent than myself — but they must soon awake or be called unprepared, to give an account of their stewardship.

TO CYNTHIA.

With reference to a prospective field of usefulness in some Missionary Station.

> South Hadley, Sept. 26th, '32.
> ... Ever be found using all proper means to facilitate the object you so much desire to accomplish. I love you as I do myself, but I love the cause

of Jesus more than I love your society. I hope we shall get where Jesus is in a few short years: until that time, let us be willing to be separated, if the bleeding cause of a suffering Saviour thus demands. The poor perishing heathen call up all the energies of my soul at times. Were I prepared, I would gladly leave my native shores for those where darkness reigns. I have enjoyed myself very well since I have been in this section of country. I have spent most of my time at S. where the Lord is moving upon the hearts of the dear youth. I have preached every Sabbath but one since coming here. Six have been baptized, others are waiting and some are saying, "What shall I do to be saved?" The people in W. are in a cold dead state. Dea. P. is the most engaged of any among them, and he is not more than half awake. I have tried to talk to them, but there appears a mountain of ice hanging over them. Many of the old professors and even ministers seem to press me down into the dust. "Awake, thou that sleepest and Christ shall give thee life." The more I think, do and see relative to these things, the more I realize the importance of Christians acting according to their profession. But sister, there is a generation of youth coming into the churches, who will unshackle themselves from past errors in the church, and give their all to Christ and his cause. Be faithful to young Christians, talk to them, pray with them and impress on their minds the importance of giving all to Christ. Not only do your duty to the world, but arouse others that they may help you in doing this great work.

We can do but little, yet if the multitude of youthful friends take hold with us, great things will be accomplished. When you see a young Christian in an error, tell them frankly in Christian meekness of it, and God will bless you and them also. I have of late, talked to some of our sisters about their curls, ribbons and rings — and to brethren about their watch trimmings, and nearly all of them have said, I am wrong. Some have even taken them off in my presence and said, I will no longer wear these unnecessary ornaments. The only way is, to be faithful, or these errors will not cease to exist. The friends, one and all, speak of you in the warmest terms, and seem to desire your welfare.   Yours, ABEL.

CONTINUATION OF JOURNAL.

On way to New York, Steam Boat McDonough Oct. 2d, '32.— I have just left the dear young friends at C. Factories. I have in that place, I trust, enjoyed the presence of the Saviour. Never have I found a company of young friends, who one and all, gave so many tokens of their love and untiring zeal in the cause of Christ. The spirit of Missions is fast rising in their minds. Last evening at a Monthly Concert of prayer, while relating to them the circumstances of Boardman's death,[2] they seemed in heart to say, let me like him labor and die in heathen lands.

In conclusion of a scene — he adds:

I often had the pleasure of hearing A. talk about Jesus, with a heart broken by his grace, and I saw her weeping when speaking of her sinfulness, and at last had the satisfaction of seeing her come rejoicing from the watery grave.

Hamilton, Oct. 8, 1832.

Arrived home on Saturday last, having been absent seven weeks. I have found the only way to do any good in the world, is to live in the closet. It is the only place in which I can at present take solid satisfaction. There I find Jesus, and He is always ready to hear. There I see my own sinfulness and exalt the blessed Saviour. There I feel for sinners and try to pray for them. There I get my spiritual strength renewed, and I catch some of the flame of Heaven. Yes, 'tis a blessed place, for Jesus shows his smiling face. I prize it above all other places below the sun, for there I get my daily food, and there I drink my daily draughts to slake my thirsty soul; and the water is ever pure, for Jesus has cleansed it with his blood.

He seems not to have been satisfied with entreaties to his sister to become a missionary, but actually made enquiries of the Baptist Board of Foreign Missions in relation to the subject. On finding that "single females were not permitted to go out under their protection," he advised her to labor for the Indians at the West, and to this end an early opportunity presented itself, as the following communication will show.

Hamilton, July 7, 1832.

Dear Sister Cynthia, — Sister Bingham, a Missionary at Sault De St. Marie, three hundred miles from Detroit on the straits of St. Mary's, is here, and informs me that she wishes a young lady to return with her or to go up this fall and join the Mission. She says that Indians have been down to the stations from many hundred miles west, who were desirous to have the Missionaries go and settle among them. The station is in a very prosperous condition, yet they want more help, and my sister, will you go and help them, if the door is opened? Think, dear sister and try to do as Jesus would have you. I shall wait all farther proceedings until I hear from you.

Yours in haste, ABEL BROWN.

[2]*George Dana Boardman, Baptist missionary from New England, who went to India and Burma (now Myanmar) and died at the age of 30 in 1831.— Editor.*

The invitation found a welcome response in the heart of her who had long waited the mandate of her Saviour to some field of Missionary labor,—and now how could she refuse. Accordingly, the ensuing autumn she started for the expedition.

With reference to the departure of his sister, under date of Oct. 14, he writes:

> I am unable to express the gratitude I feel to God for permitting me to be born of parents who are willing to give up their children to the cause of Christ. My father and mother never appeared so precious to me as within a week past. I am almost led to think that I never loved them before. Yes, my mother, it is better to wear out this mortal part in teaching Indians about Jesus, than to lay it in the tomb before the vigor of life is spent. Let her live among the heathen—labor and die among them. Then when Gabriel shall blow the trumpet of God, let Cynthia rise with the dear red sons of the forest, and go up and reign with Christ.

> Nov. 9, 1832. This day closes the twenty-second year of my life. On reviewing the past, I am constrained to say, I have done nothing for the Saviour who died for me. My childhood passed thoughtlessly away. The days of my impenitency were spent in such a manner that I cannot think of them without shuddering, and even since I hope to have loved Jesus, I have continued to disobey his just commands. As to my own enjoyment, it is so much obstructed by sin that my course is very much retarded,— still, can but love Jesus and put my trust in Him. "He is my soul's bright morning star,"—and "He my rising sun." And on Him my hopes depend.

CHAPTER V

CONTINUATION OF LETTERS AND JOURNAL—THIRD YEAR AT HAMILTON—THE MISSION FAMILY

Hamilton, Nov. 11th, 1832.

This day I have been reading the Journal of *Elder Judson*,[1] and while I have traced him over hills and across rivers, now walking until his worn feet prevented, then rowing his little boat up the *Salween*[2]—here preaching in the open air—there in a shed—writing his journal in the canoe and sleeping on the ground—I have almost thought I was accompanying him. I would gladly be with him, and trust I shall yet retrace his steps. The heathen appear to be willing to hear concerning Christ, and who can withhold the gospel from those who are seeking to know its influence? Surely not those who have the spirit of Christ. Gladly would I exchange these exalted shores for the delightful forests where *Burmans and Karens*[3] rove. How pleasant to point them to Jesus. Surely I should want a thousand tongues that all might hear of His lovely name. When reflecting on this subject I almost forgot my own unworthiness—but Jesus is worthy and in his name I hope to go. I have promised the Lord that I will wear out this mortal frame in Africa—yet let his holy will be done. "Here am I Lord, do with me as seemeth thee good."

Hamilton, Nov. 18th, 1832.

Dear sister,—Yours of the 25th Oct. came to hand yesterday. I had been waiting for it with deep anxiety. When I think of the hand that wrote, as

[1] *The Rev. Adoniram Judson was born in Massachusetts in 1788 and one of the organizers of the American Baptist Missionary Union. In 1811, he undertook a mission to Burma (now Myanmar), and in 1834 he completed a translation of the whole Bible into the Burmese language. During the Anglo-Burmese War, he spent 21 months in prison. After 34 years in Burma, he spent two years in the U.S. He returned to Burma in 1847 and spent his remaining years there working on his English-Burmese dictionary until his death in 1850.—Editor.*
[2] *Today the Than Lwin River.—Editor.*
[3] *Ethnic groups in Burma.—Editor.*

being where I have long prayed that it might be, I feel in a measure happy. Last spring, when you wrote that you were sick, my sweet anticipations forsook me. It appeared that the door was forever closed. I wept and prayed, but how could I willingly submit that you must die before you had done any thing for the perishing heathen. But how good the Lord was, for He showed by that affliction that without his assistance we could do nothing. Blessed be the name of the Lord, that He has ever given you a heart to labor for Him, and more especially, that He has humbled it sufficient to make you willing to labor among the Indians. I doubt not, you often feel when looking over some delightsome forests to say, "where is the lamb for sacrifice." Your feelings accord with mine in this respect, but let us not be discouraged, for Jesus Christ is interested in this work, and He will raise up men after his own heart who will gladly be sacrificed upon such an altar.

As regards my own views and feelings on this all-absorbing topic, I can only say, I delight in praying for the heathen and I hope to wear out this mortal body in laboring for their good, but in what part of our world, (if God should spare my life and make me humble,) I shall labor, is known only to him. When I read of the benighted Africans, I almost vow to render them my services. The islands of the sea, Burma and the Indians are often called to mind, and I think of their wants and degradation with feelings indescribable, but cannot as yet do any thing to help them. I trust the Lord will keep me through his truth and make me willing to go where the cause shall most demand. You are aware how persons feel when they take a religious publication and read that assistance is wanted in Greece — Oh, say they, I will go and help them. They read again, that France is ready to receive the gospel, — they say within themselves, can I not help them, — and as they continue to read, other places are presented to view, until at last the *world* appears before them with all its wants. Then they cry "here Lord am I, send me where thou wilt." When I enjoy the presence of the Saviour I have similar feelings. I have received two letters from mother since you left home. She says, sometimes I feel as though I cannot part with my children; at other times I commit them into the hands of Jesus that they may work in his vineyard. Her heart, she says, was rent when you left her, but she feels reconciled to the will of heaven. When we think of the situation of our parents, we feel that it would be desirable to continue with them and comfort their hearts; so also the glories of heaven were inviting to the Son of God, yet He did not refuse to leave them for a season, even that He might die on the cross. May we not then gladly leave father, mother and all friends, for so glorious an object as the extension of our Redeemer's kingdom, and when the resurrection morn shall come, may we not hope to meet our friends in a world which knows no change, forever to dwell in the home of the blest.

With reference to his brothers he remarks:

You know that when the Lord called me to leave my business, it was with many tears that I gave up the idea of educating my brothers, but God has been better to me than either tears or fears. How unsearchable, &c. But dear sister, they have no hope in Christ.

Come my Cynthia, let us pray God for them and don't ask anything less than that He should make them faithful ministers of Jesus Christ. I find, God is just as willing to do great things for us as He is small, and the more we ask, if we ask a night, the more He loves us.

In looking forward to the work in which I design to labor, I tremble at the thought of appearing before the bar of God, there to give an account how I preach. Not less fearful is that also, of addressing in the name of Christ my fellow men. Had I the views of the apostle Paul, I could cheerfully go forth with the assurance that God would bless my efforts; but who can do any good in preaching with such a heart as mine. I feel that all I am and all I possess is the Lord's, and that my life is to be sacredly devoted to his cause. I am aware that I can do nothing without the assistance of divine grace, and that I have abused all the blessings which God has bestowed upon me. Still, I cannot think of going back — and if I stand still, I shall only be a curse to the cause, therefore go forward I must or perish. The subject of self-denial, has occupied my mind very much since my return from Massachusetts. The great majority of professing christians appear to have just as much self-denial about them, as they can have and gratify all their selfish desires and appetites. Many say, what I have, is mine, I therefore have a right to eat, drink and wear what I please. If religion does not consist in loving God with all the heart and our neighbors as ourselves, and if these affections do not manifest themselves by our actions, I know not what evidence we have to think we are christians. It seems to me also to be very inconsistent, for christians to talk about loving Jesus and yet have no *desire*, consequently put forth no *effort* that others may enjoy the same blessings. Many say, that I err, in carrying the principle of self-denial to so great an extent, but if I am in an error I am with Judson, with Paul, and I think I may safely say with Christ. When I mention the name of our Saviour as an example of self-denial, I blush and am ashamed of my own. Oh Jesus, are there none to walk in thy footsteps? Help me, Lord, to follow Thee.

It seems from his own account that the same abstemiousness of living still marked his course, only more rigid if possible — boarding himself, &c. With reference thereto, to his sister he remarks — "never have I enjoyed better health, never was more thankful, never, if I am not deceived, felt so much for the cause of Christ, and never was permitted to come so near the mercy seat as at the present time."

> 1833, Jan. 6, Sabbath morning — I have for the week past been collecting some Missionary intelligence to present before our christian friends, and it sets my soul on fire, to go forth and bear the toils of a Missionary life. What a poor world this would be to live in, had we not the privilege of laboring for Jesus. What are all the social enjoyments of friends compared with the blessedness of preaching the gospel to the heathen.

Again, he says, "God in his providence has so ordered that I cannot go far hence to the Gentiles, unless He sees fit to remove the obstacle now in the way."

In referring to his views and feelings respecting those with whom he was called to labor, it seems that *the obstacle* preventing him from turning his attention directly to the "heathen world" was found in the obvious and therefore imperious necessity of laboring at home in his own native hand. Still he held himself ready and willing to obey the call of God wherever it might lead him. It is perhaps enough that he possessed the spirit of a missionary, for God only requires the heart with submission to his will.

> Feb. 18, 1833. — I have of late felt more anxiety about being filled with the spirit than ever before in my short life — I have seen many ministers who appeared to know and say many things in themselves excellent, while the spirit of God seemed not to be with them, — and I have observed that all such men do not seem to have their labors blessed of God, while the more ignorant and unlearned who possess piety of heart are blessed abundantly. These with some other things have been visible witnesses to me that unless one is endowed with the Holy Spirit, he can be of no use as a servant of Christ. Then follow his hours of retirement and study in his little Bethel (as he was wont to term it) into whose sanctuary I would not farther intrude. Suffice it to say, such was his idea of preparation in rendering himself able to "impart the word of life skillfully" and with success to others, aside from mere technical theology.

> Hamilton, Feb. 28, 1833.
> My Dear Absent Sister, — I have this P.M. received your letter, and while I have been reading and thinking where the person who wrote it labored,

I have felt to say with the Psalmist, "Oh that I had wings, then would I fly away" *not* to "be at rest," but to lead the poor heathen to the Lamb of God.

Never, my dear, did you appear so precious to me as at present. I loved you when we thought not of God, because you were my only sister,— but now I love you because I see you putting on the image of Jesus. I love you as a sister, a christian, and a missionary. Believe me when I tell you, I esteem you too much to wish you even here. Every time I think of you, I feel more and more to say, Oh Jesus, spare her and permit her to labor for the Indians, and bring us at last to dwell with Thee.

Relative to separation from home and friends, he adds:

There is a consolation in the thought, that Christ will help us to overcome those affections that would debar us from his service. True, we must pray much and "wrestle with the angel of the covenant"— but soon he will say, your name is Israel, for you have prevailed with God. In view of the work of the Missionary, we need neither fear nor despond, for it must and will prosper. The more we become like Christ, the more the powers of darkness will rally their adherents to obstruct our way, but what are all the wicked men and devils and evil passions combined, to hinder us when we have an Almighty Christ to intercede for us. In view of the agonies in the garden who would not labor, and with a bleeding Jesus before our eyes, who would not deny self and suffer all that earth and hell can inflict, for the privilege of telling the poor heathen about so dear a Saviour. Dear sister, go on,— my soul says go. Keep the glory of Christ and the worth of deathless spirits in view, and God will nerve your arm for the conflict while on earth, and at last receive you to his embrace in heaven.

Mar. 3d, 1833. I sensibly feel my unpreparedness to write you, and were it not that you are my only sister, and were you not expecting me to write I should lay aside my pen, but bear with mine if I am not as much like Jesus as yourself. Realize that I have not loved Jesus as long as you have, and if we had grown in grace every day — you would have been at an immense distance in advance. But sister, the more I see of the loveliness of Christ the more I long to be like him. I do not desire so much to go to Heaven now and be clothed in his likeness, but I want the humility, devotedness, self-denial and self-control, and love for dying sinners which he possessed. I see so great a want of personal piety in myself, and in far too many of the servants of Christ already in the field, that I almost despair ever being of any use in the vineyard of my Master. We must feel as did one of old when he said, "rivers of water run down mine eyes because men keep not God's law," and then when we address sinners we shall see the effect. Jesus could weep — and Paul could weep in view of the condition of sinners, and cold must be the heart that refuses to feel when called to address those who are more than eighteen hundred years nearer the judgment seat.

During a temporary visit of his sister home, he writes the following:

Hamilton, July 4th, 1833.

Very Dear Sister, — By your letter of the 26th, I was happy to learn that you were at home, but happier to know that you are soon to return to the wilds of the forest. You say you would be happy to see me, and I assure you I should be happy to spend a few weeks in your society, yet I know not that it will be consistent for me to gratify that desire. Believe me, when I tell you it is not because I love you the less, but a sense of duty alone keeps me from my parental abode. Dr. Bolles from Boston was here, when I received your letter, and after knowing your situation and that of brother Meeker and wife, said that if brother M had prepared a new alphabet for the Indian language, he would have to stay in Boston until a new font of types could be cast, which would probably detain him five or six weeks, therefore, as you doubtless know what brother M is expecting to accomplish, you can easily judge whether he will be detained longer than you wrote me or not. Brother and sister Wade are here teaching four brethren and five sisters the Burman language. Brother and sister W appear to live as they have so often (by their letters) said that others should.

My Dear Cynthia, bear with me if I raise a warning voice, for I assure you I do it with the best wishes of my heart. I do not imagine that you have overcome all the inclinations of the natural heart, even though you have become a Missionary, — neither do I think you are above temptation, therefore just permit me to say, that as you have seen the vanity of the vain trash of earth, so I hope you will show by all your intercourse with others, that you esteem it of too little worth to have your attention even for an hour. Manifest the same self-denying spirit, whether among heathen or sitting amid the splendor and pomp of an enlightened society. You may perhaps be presented things, which would not be consistent for you in your present situation to receive or use — in such a case try to act the part of wisdom. I sometimes think, that many christians think more of seeing and pleasing Missionaries than of pleasing the Saviour — to such, say with one of old, "*Behold the Lamb of God who taketh away the sins of the world?*" There is one other way in which, if I mistake not, the devil will try you —

and that is, by getting persons to intimate to you, or tell so that you may hear of it, that you are very pious and Christ-like — but I pray you listen not to such insinuations, for if you do, I can tell you by sad experience, you will be deceived. Do not understand me by these remarks, to think you are destitute of piety, — for this is not the case, but I do not think you are as free from sin as our Master Jesus. With very little piety we may be called pious by a majority of professing christians, but let us ever remember, that it is vastly different with us in the eyes of a holy God. Whatever be your situation my dearest sister, live so near the Saviour that you can say, "none of these things move me." And now I commend you to God, hoping and praying, that through his grace you may be enabled to live above the flatteries or frowns of this deceitful world, and that while on earth you may ever be found faithful in the service of our Lord Jesus Christ.

Concerning the reasons, for denying himself this last and only privilege of seeing his sister in this world, he thus writes:

I am extensively engaged in Sabbath Schools in Madison, and if I should leave they would doubtless lose their interest in such a degree that many children who have been taken from the paths of vice would again return. We are also preparing the most flourishing school for a public examination, and I cannot leave should our object be accomplished. There are other young men better qualified to conduct Sabbath Schools than myself, but there are none acquainted in that town to whom I dare resign my place; furthermore, some of MY CHILDREN begin to feel that they are sinners, and how can I leave them? I know that I should receive much benefit from a personal interview with you, but I cannot go unless duty seems to require, and this is what I know you wish me to consult. Weep not, sister, for if we deny ourselves this gratification for Christ's sake, He will gratify us with the blessed influences of his spirit, which is far superior. I say then, my dear sister, go on and labor for the good of the perishing heathen, and if I never see you again on earth, may I meet you in heaven with the fruits of your labors and the crown of your rejoicing.

THE MISSION FAMILY.

Having received instruction from the Board to leave St. Mary's and remove west of the Mississippi River, Cynthia had embraced the opportunity, while preparing for the expedition, of returning home. After spending four weeks, (in the words of her mother) "she then took her last and *final* farewell of us all," and joined her co-laborers at Cleveland.

They left that place during the summer and directed their course to the Shawnee Mission, N.W. Frontier of the State of Missouri. On the last of October, 1833, Mr. Merrill and wife with Cynthia proceeded on their route for the purpose of visiting new tribes for the same benevolent end. With two young men for guides, they pursued their way through a trackless prairie inhabited only by wild beasts and Indians. They were out a number of days longer than they anticipated, and consequently became reduced to a very scanty allowance of provisions. They lay at the Platte river four days before they could cross, on account of the wind and ice, with nothing but their tents to cover them, and those afforded but a slight protection. On the 5th day they crossed and arrived at the settlement of the Ottoe Indians, where they formed a *new* station.[4]

In allusion to these circumstances of trial and suffering he is led to exclaim, how sweet must be the cold that is endured for Christ's sake. Oh how luxurious the hunger that is felt for the sake of carrying the gospel to the heathen.

EXHORTATION TO HIS SISTER.

> Be not faithless but believing, for "it is through much tribulation that we enter the kingdom of God," and although "clouds and darkness are round about you," yet retain an unshaken confidence in God, and He will provide. Lift up your head and rejoice in the God of your salvation, and continue to go on cheerfully in teaching the perishing Indians. Flesh and blood may fail, but only to give life immortal to the soul. Let others do as they will, but may we labor and die to bring the souls of men to God. *Farewell.*[5]
>
> ABEL BROWN, JR.

---

[4] *South of the present day Omaha, Nebraska, near the intersection of the Platte River with the Missouri River. — Editor.*

[5] *Abel's comments during this period of idealistic youth are often romantic and unrealistic. It also may be judged by some that Abel neglected his family and put his vocation ahead of them. However, Abel was a man who put his ideals and ethics above all else. Certainly, he loved his family, but he loved God more. It was this obligation to God that he put above all else, and to which he would adhere for the rest of his life. — Editor.*

CHAPTER VI

LABORS IN WESTERN AND CENTRAL N. Y. FOR THE PROMOTION OF SABBATH SCHOOLS—LEAVES HAMILTON AND STUDIES AT HOMER—BECOMES A LECTURING AGENT IN THE CAUSE OF TEMPERANCE

In addition to previous efforts in the cause of Sabbath Schools, he now labored continuously for three successive years in the same benevolent enterprise — pursuing his studies at intervals as time and opportunity would allow. He seemed to deem it sufficient in his Theological course to have entered the school of Christ, whose matchless example was illustrative of the principles he taught — and as His disciple, he endeavored to conform his life thereto, receiving the doctrines of inspiration as of literal import and direct application in all the walks of life — when with many, those same truths were received as accompanied by great difficulty, sacrifice and self-denial; these, however, he never looked at except to brave. He therefore went forward as one having a divine commission to preach wherever and in what way the indication of Providence might lead him. Preaching on the Sabbath relative to the utility and practicability of S. Schools — then surveying the ground of operations, visiting families, conversing with children in the highways and byways, and indeed, in these actual observations, he found ample scope for missionary effort, even in the enlightened state of N.Y. A few citations from his well-stored journal will suffice in relation to this part of his career.

Hamilton Institution, —
Nov. 4th, Sabbath Evening.
Have just returned from Brookfield where I have been engaged in efforts to promote the welfare of the youth in that section. The parts visited are

destitute of S. School instruction and most of the people are willing to
remain thus. Had the opportunity of addressing the first church on the
subject of S. Schools. Soon as I mentioned my intention of speaking in
behalf of this cause, some began to gaze with a jealous eye — and when I
commenced the subject, eight or ten left the house, unwilling even to hear
concerning the nature and object of this Institution. Those who stayed gave
good attention, and before the close of my remarks many wept, and others seemed to say, I will do something to relieve the dear children in our
land.

    Nov. 10th. This day have again visited B_____, and there rode from dis-
trict to district, and ascertained the situation of the children residing within
those limits. The whole town, a few districts excepted, is a moral waste.
Professing Christians are cold and indifferent. My heart is pained, in looking at nearly seven hundred children in that place, growing up without
any of the restraints of the gospel.

His sermons show him to have been well furnished to the good
work, and should have met with the hearty response of every professed
lover of Christ. And this was the case in those places where the subject
was fully understood and appreciated. But the ignorance and prejudice
attending the introduction of this system form a strange contrast to the
zeal and enthusiasm with which this institution was hailed at a *later*
period in almost every portion of Christendom.

    When wearied with exertion, and faint with toil in the arduous
duties of his calling, he says — "there is a happiness in retiring to the forest and there rolling off the burden which my soul feels for the youth of
this country upon the Saviour."

    Nov. 24th. This has been to me one of those days of hard labor to which
    every person who is engaged in the cause of Christ is subject. Have been
    at Nelson, Cazenovia, Eaton, and Woodstock. In these towns there are
    hundreds of children growing up destitute of religious instruction. How
    long it will be thus, time only will determine; as for myself, I cannot cease
    my efforts, until they are differently situated.

Institution — Sunday Eve, Dec. 8th.
Last Sabbath I spent in Smithfield and had the pleasure of tarrying with
Mr. G. Smith.[1] I had seen the man in public and in private, in both of

---

[1]*Gerrit Smith was one of the nineteenth century's foremost social reformers and philanthropists.
Son of a wealthy landowner, Smith used his father's fortune to espouse his social causes, mainly*

which places he is to be admired and beloved; but far more in his family does he exhibit the father and the christian. His conversation was replete with interest and instruction, and his singing was "with the spirit and understanding." He read the Scriptures with reverence and godly fear, and prayed as if filled with the spirit of Christ. With delight on Sabbath morn he went into the S. School, and with the simplicity of a child, did he talk to the children of Jesus and urge them to repent without delay. Mr. Smith is one of the few men who possessing great natural and acquired talents is equally at home in the councils of State and with the little child, as

ENGRAVING OF GERRIT SMITH PAINTED BY E.W. GOODWIN, IMPROVED BY J. SARTAIN (SPECIAL COLLECTIONS RESEARCH CENTER, SYRACUSE UNIVERSITY LIBRARY).

with a paternal hand he would lead it to the fold of Christ.

The S. School in Peterborough is well conducted, and where many souls have been born of God.

Dec. 19th. This day has been one of deep anxiety for the impenitent. Have had free access to the mercy seat and some faith in God, that he was about to pour out his spirit without measure upon this place (Hamilton). Visited S. School at 9 o'clock A.M. and had the privilege of talking to the children. Many wept over their condition, others seemed thinking deeply,

antislavery but also temperance. A leader of the Liberty party, Smith was elected to Congress under its banner in 1852; he also was the Liberty party candidate for president in 1848, 1856, and 1860. After 1848, however, the Liberty party had become little more than a regional entity. Smith was president of a number of important antislavery organizations, including the New York State Anti-Slavery Society, the New York Committee of Vigilance, and the Organization of Radical Abolitionists. He gave freely to Frederick Douglass's newspaper operations and to John Brown's militant campaign to end slavery, as well as numerous other individuals pledged to the cause of ending slavery. In 1846, he gave away 120,000 acres of land, mostly in the Adirondack region, to 3,000 free temperate black men. His home in Peterboro was ever a sanctuary for freedom-seekers and African American leaders who were in the forefront of the movement to end slavery.—Editor.

and eight or ten have lately given themselves up to Christ. The female teachers especially are agonizing for the souls of their Scholars. Attended church at eleven, and this evening — and have preached to an assembly about two miles distant, — a deep solemnity seemed to pervade the audience and I felt as though God's spirit assisted me. Jesus seems more and more precious, the closet a paradise, and praying a casting off of my anxieties upon Jesus — *there* I find peace indescribable and faith which takes hold of the promises of God.

Again he was led to view himself as expressed in the following extract from his journal:

God has seen fit to teach me that I have not even had the form of godliness. I have labored by night and by day to benefit my fellow men. I have prayed for them with a feeling of sympathy even unto tears, but that I have had any thing more than *human* sympathy in trying to pray, I do not much doubt — or that the glory of God in these exercises has been my object, I do as much doubt. I have prayed, because it was a privilege — and I have labored, because I longed to see my fellow beings in a better condition, and could not bear to see them following the downward road to perdition. True, I have not wished to engage in any thing but the service of Christ, but my views of a holy consecration have been as great as the heathen have of the true God. But blessed Saviour, I thank thee that the spell is broken, and that Thou hast raised my mind and enlarged my views of thyself and word, and that I now no longer see Thee at a distance, but that I can dwell in thy presence and feel thy spirit pervading my inmost soul. I am less than nothing — Christ is all in all. Thou hast taken the clay and used it thyself, whilst the vessel has been striving against Thee — but here am I — form, Oh form me to the image of Christ. Oh Saviour, drive from my soul everything but Thee.

Oh how heavenly is the place of prayer — for certain it is, that God is there.

At another time he seemed to himself:

like a man who stands at the entrance of a delightful garden, gazing with supreme delight upon its pleasantness, but is not prepared to walk in its beautiful alleys. The christian often feels the necessity of consecrating himself anew and anew to the love and service of his divine Redeemer, and as he passes on "from perfection to perfection," the former seems nought to his present attainment. But the true idea of consecration as here presented, was an entire renunciation of *self* to the will of God, and a feeling of utter helplessness in himself alone, and reliance on Christ, not only as the Author but Finisher of the work of grace commenced in his heart to his complete and final salvation.

So much more vivid were his conceptions that he felt that he had entered anew the divine life, "a life of giving up all to God, and living for Him." He says:

I have for years thought that the gospel of Christ demanded that men should deny self, but never have so fully realized it as at present. It appears to me that if the spirit of God is to dwell with me, I must eat, drink, sleep, talk and think, and act with direct reference to his glory. God not only demands that I should preach for his glory, but that in the smallest trans-actions of my life I should have his glory in view. God has so far enabled me to overcome evil that I can, in most instances, govern my words and actions, but these sinful thoughts disturb my peace.

In these seasons of delightful communion with God, which He so graciously condescends to vouchsafe to the children of men, he was led to the following reflections:

This world has no charms, the society of friends is not inviting — every thing but Christ and his cause has dwindled to a point. Those who wish for worldly honor, can have it, but to me it is vain and contemptible.

Of his friends he says,

dearly as I love them, could I sit down with my father and mother and brothers in family converse, or were I permitted to see my sister in her Indian hut, they could yield me no comfort, for they could not hold inter-course with God for me, which alone can render me peaceful and happy. Christians are prone to think too much of themselves and too little of their fellow beings.

In one of these delightful exercises of contemplation, he suddenly exclaims —

but why should I allow myself to be thinking so much of my own enjoy-ment, while this earth is filled with misery. Oh ye who seek after honor, pleasure, ease or riches, how low and debasing are your joys. You despise the joys of the drunkard, in like manner do I despise your foolish pursuits. Oh how pitiable is your condition, seeking pleasure where misery alone dwells Why will you thus debase your noble powers? You think yourself rich, but oh how poor. For you I weep, and for you will I pray and labor.

About this time he left Hamilton (having received a regular dismission from the Institution) and removed to Homer, to pursue his studies under charge of Eld. Whiting. In view of the responsibility of his calling as a minister of Christ, he was often led to exclaim, "if it be possible, &c." Still (he continues):

I dare not cease, but how can I see men reject the gospel and meet them at the judgment seat and witness against them? Yet who could "hold his peace," while men all around are so unlike even the RESEMBLANCE of holiness. One thought has very much occupied my mind, namely, how I can bear to say "amen" to the sentence of condemnation pronounced upon my fellow beings, without having made the mightiest exertion to turn them from sin.

Extract from a letter to his brother Lyman under date of *Aug.* 24th, 1834.

... Thirteen years of your life are gone — and every moment of them which you have spent in idleness is lost — and you never, no never can live them over again. If for a moment you will reflect on the amount of time you have spent in play, I think you will very much regret that it was not better improved. Had you been as industrious as many boys of your age, you now would have been able to read the Greek Testament with as much fluency as you can your Virgil. Can you not see how much time you have lost? Make then every possible effort to improve what remains. Every moment, is a part of all the time which God has allotted you. Therefore, let each moment be spent in preparing for future usefulness. Do you inquire how this object can be accomplished? *This*, my brother, is what I wish to tell you. You remember that from our earliest days, our dear Father has daily commended us to God in prayer. He has done this because he has ever known that we could not live unless God sustained us — that we received our breath from God; also that he daily gave us our food, health and all the blessings of which we were the recipients, — and he also knew that God could take away these blessings and our lives, at any time. God also numbers even the hairs of your head and watches over you when asleep and when awake — and has preserved you from a thousand dangers, of which you knew nothing. He also sees you when you are studying your lessons, and at all other times; you indeed cannot see God, but He is nearer to you than any thing you can see. Now, as God is all around you and hears all that you say — and sees all that you do — and knows all your thoughts, how careful you should be to *think and act* in such a manner as will please Him. If you would thus meet His approbation and be useful, you must study your lessons; not that you may be a great man, a fine poet or an eloquent orator, and thereby gain applause — but that you may improve your mind, and obtain knowledge, and thereby, be able to learn more concerning God, and better serve Him. Study to fill your heart with the love of God, and the love of those beings of His creation around you, and be satisfied, to be no greater scholar or finer gentleman, than these tempers will make you.

Consider, that every ignorant person and wicked boy that you see, is your *brother*, — and instead of despising, love him, for he was made in the image of God and if you hate him, you also hate *God* who created him. Never think or study how you may obtain the most money or be the most honored, but how you may *do the most good*. There are many other things, concerning which, I wish to write you, but I must omit them for want of time.

From your Brother,
ABEL.

To his mother, he writes the following: —

I received yours, of the 10th inst., and read it with pleasure. I am glad you are so careful to correct every seeming error of your sinful son — but rest assured, all your fears are groundless. H. must have received his ideas from the fact that Prof. Whiting and myself sometimes hold a controversy upon a subject, concerning which, we think alike — sometimes *he* takes the wrong side and sometimes I do — just for the sake of argument and better preparing myself to advocate the truth. I have at times advocated the doctrine of Universal Salvation, that I might thereby be shown its errors. Concerning the doctrine of the sinner's coming to Christ, we have the same opinion, only I do not know but that I am the strongest Calvinist.[2] I am very far from believing that the sinner can or will believe on the Lord Jesus Christ, unless the Holy Spirit enlightens his mind and changes his heart. I never advocated the doctrine only as above stated....

---

[2]*The Calvinist doctrine, which held that salvation is predestined for only a select few, was in disfavor among evangelicals of the Second Great Awakening.* — Editor.

Why should I pray, if "I had renounced the Holy Spirit?" Concerning my plain manner of preaching, I have only to say, that to God I stand accountable. I hope, my Dear Mother, you will not regard every report that the impure breezes waft along, but first try to ascertain the truth, and then make me pay one and six pence for a good and kind reproof. I hear many stories concerning myself and others, which I know to be false, but they do not trouble me in the least. I have heard that I was expelled from Hamilton — when I have a regular Dismissal in my pocket — but I never even take pains to contradict such reports; and now my dear parents pray much for me.

Yours, in the hope of Heaven,
ABEL.

In studying the New Testament in its original language, he remarks, "There is an excellency in the Scriptures discernable only by those who possess the spirit of their Author." From his dissertations also it is obvious that he valued the Scriptures as the medium of communication between God and man in making known His will and character, and therefore *claiming preference, over any other "moral science," to his attention.*

With reference to his feelings for the impenitent at this time, in comparison with those at a former period, he says:

Then I could weep profusely over the condition of men — though much of this was a sympathy not the entire fruit of the spirit — but now, the distress of my soul is such, that I cannot weep; tears indeed might prove a momentary relief, but their flowing will not unburden my soul. I think, I can say with Paul, "a constant heaviness of spirit," &c.[3]

Since gratitude is ever coupled with true humility, he was led to exclaim, in view of his unworthiness — "It seems as though God was about to humble me with His mercies." At another time, he says, "I have so much confidence in God, that I think, severe afflictions would prove the most kind blessing, yet I may be mistaken. Still, if I would only 'get low enough in the dust,' blessings would flow through rough channels."

Dec. 7th, 1834, Sunday Evening, 9 o'clock.
This day has been to me one of some labor — have rode about 28 miles to ascertain the condition of the children in this county. Christ's gospel seems

[3]*From Romans 9:1-2. As Paul, a Jew, was distressed that most Jews did not accept Jesus as the promised Messiah, Abel felt likewise that most of those to whom he preached did not renounce their sinfulness. — Editor.*

very precious tonight. The path of self-denial is also desirable. I would have the privilege of walking in it. Oh may I die daily, to every thing but Thee and Thy cause.

Passing over similar accounts to the one above stated, I will myself give a compendium of his labors, from his S. S. Journal.

Homer, Apr. 20th, 1835.
Spent from 7 until 10 o'clock, in collecting money and adjusting accounts, for the examination of the Board — from 10 until 4 o'clock in visiting poor families in Courtlandville — saw much misery — met the Board at 4 P.M.

Of one place visited, he says, "the inhabitants appear to be given up to *cursing.* From thence I went two or three miles N. W. through a part of the town where I am glad no one lives."

In writing of one congregation, he says,

I became convinced that some of them were opening their eyes about half way to the importance of the subject. Their pastor, Elder P., is really engaged in the good cause, but having formed his habits and manner of action in a different age from this, and having other excessive labors to perform, he can do little more than talk to his people in favor of the object. He will encourage any cause, calculated to make men better.

Among the obstacles in his way, he says, "There being such a multiplicity of denominations, that think it not proper to unite with any sect except their own, renders it exceedingly difficult, for the friends of S. S. to advance the good cause."

Truxton, Sunday, Apr. 26th, 1835.
Addressed the Presbyterian Church in A.M., and the Baptist in P.M. — met the friends at 3 o'clock, and formed S. S. Teachers and friends of S. S. Association in the town. The Officers are, — a Methodist, President, — Secretary, a Presbyterian, ... Treasurer a Baptist, and the Directors, were also from the different sects; all of which Officers constituted an Executive Committee.

In his excursions he did not fail to visit the most obscure villages, seeking the abodes of vice, poverty and wretchedness, that he might impart the words of instruction to the ignorant, administer the kindly warning, gently reprove the erring, and alleviate the woes of the suffering. Many affecting cases of the last named class are given; one in particular of an elderly man who lived with his daughter — she "dependent on the care and protection," and he on the hospitalities, of a drunkard, (her husband). After united prayer and conversation, the old man gave glory to God for the friendly call, and the woman disconsolate and weary with watching beside the sick among her little ones felt her hopes brightened and her strength renewed, by the unexpected visit.

Thus in visiting families to ascertain their condition and want of religious instruction, he was led to see the misery of intemperance, and immediately enlisted in the warfare to extirpate an evil so direful in its consequences, proving alike destructive to man's moral nature and to the relations he sustains to his Maker and to his fellow beings, [and] thus forming a mighty obstacle to the progress of truth and Christian effort. He accordingly sought every opportunity to portray the evil in the light of its own hideous deformity, by detailing facts from his own personal observation, and urging the necessity of reformation. Pledges of cooperation were often given by devoted individuals to sustain and forward this noble undertaking. In rallying those to be soldiers of the cross, he seemed to say, as Lord Nelson[4] inscribed on the banners of his army — I expect every man to do his duty; and something was done (the Lord be praised) in the deliverance of thousands of poor, ignorant, and even degraded children in those sections of country wherein he labored, raising them from the paths of immorality and vice to respectability and usefulness in society. It is hoped that, to many, such efforts extended even to the salvation of their souls. These were beneficial results, to say nothing of the reflex influence on parents and S. S. teachers in the work of instruction.

As a sample of his usual manner of rest, the following is an indication:

May 20th, 1835.

Returned to Homer and found myself so much fatigued that it was necessary to rest one day. Spent it in writing a report for the board and in reading general intelligence. Attended temperance meeting in Cortland Village in the evening.

[4]*English admiral who died in battle while vanquishing the fleet of Napoleon at the Battle of Trafalgar in 1805.—Editor.*

From a general survey of S. Schools throughout the country, in one of his Lectures he remarks:

> The destitution of the 458 counties upon the Atlantic slope may be learned in some measure, from the fact, that in the counties of Madison, Cortland, Cayuga, Erie and Chautauque, there are about 80,000 children, and only about 18,000 of them were in S.S. one year ago, and as many as 30,000 of them were destitute of either moral or religious instruction. Having been through all the counties except Erie, I am sure, that there are as many as the 30,000 who do not attend meeting or S.S., and have no religious parents to instruct them.

From his Journal, it appears also that he visited places in other counties contiguous to those mentioned. During the entire period of his labors in this cause, he also engaged in various agencies for the dissemination of books and periodicals ... collectively forming a valuable auxiliary to the institution of S. Schools, wherever established.[5]

As a licentiate preacher, he labored in Oswego, during the Summer and Autumn of 1835. Under date of Sept. 21, he writes:

> ... Attended a prayer meeting at Eld. Sawyer's. Brethren and sisters seemed to pray anew. My own soul was more deeply roused than ever, to pray for sinners here. Oh, how precious the souls of men appeared. Brother Norfleet, a colored man and minister, was present. He sung and prayed in his good negro slave style. Sunday morning, preached in the Baptist church. In the afternoon the house was filled and all in a mass, looked me direct in the face and perfect stillness pervaded the audience. Eternity was the subject. They all thought for the moment, and then I fear the world rushed in again. The dear old man seemed filled with Jesus' love, and all were interested in him personally, if not with his subject.
> "He whom the truth makes free, is free indeed."[6]

[5]By 1827, the American Tract Society in New York City alone had printed 44 million pages of religious literature, the bulk of which were circulated in New York State. In the next ten years it published 30 million tracts, nearly a million Christian Almanacs, and over 2 million miscellaneous magazines, books, and pamphlets. More than three-quarters of these were circulated in New York State.— Editor. (Cross: 24.)

[6]This is a paraphrase of John 8:36: "He whom the Son makes free is free indeed." It refers to Jesus and salvation. There is also a scriptural passage: "You will hold to my teaching, and the truth will set you free," John 8:32, spoken by Jesus to Jews who believed in Him. Generally, Brown was saying that so long as Norfleet or any black man who faced daily oppression and prejudice believed in Jesus, he was free because he would obtain salvation.— Editor.

In a subsequent letter to his sister, (then a Missionary at Bellevue)[7] a particular friend of the subject of this memoir, writes the following [to her], under date of

Sept. 16th, 1834.

I received a letter from Abel a week since. He was well, and in his usual good spirits. Perhaps, it may not be wrong for me to say to you, that your brother is tenderly beloved by me. Four long years since, when I was a child, I gave him my heart, with a promise of my hand when I should be old enough; and never for one moment, have I repented of that promise on my own account, and a fearful change must come over me, ere I ever shall. I never have spoken to you on this subject, for I dared not begin, but have many times wished you would ask me, had the subject occurred to your mind, and then I should have told you all. If I have done wrong in speaking to you so freely, or if it seems to you unmaidenly, forgive me, and think it an error of the head and not the heart.

After relating her recent experience in religion at that time and her joyful anticipation of seeing Abel, she remarks, I can now appreciate his worth.

From her superior education and intellectual endowments united with her disposition to serve God, she was eminently qualified to unite in any benevolent enterprise destined to elevate and bless her fellow beings, or raise the fallen from the paths of vice amid degradation. In this devoted lady (Miss Mary Ann Brigham), Mr. Brown found a valuable assistant in the cause of Temperance, in the collection of facts, visiting families, &c. Accordingly in the autumn of 1835 she accompanied him to Auburn, on his agency in behalf of this cause, and was kindly received and sustained by the friends in that place.

The following letter will serve to show the light in which her labors were appreciated:

Albany, Oct. 15th, 1835.

ABEL BROWN, JR.: My dear Sir — I have just received and read with the most lively interest, the narrative of facts signed by Miss Brigham. Allow me to thank you both, in the name of our Society and of our common humanity, for this labor of kindness and love. May you both hear the welcome plaudit — "I was sick and in prison and ye visited me." Oh that the

[7]*In Nebraska, just north of the intersection of the Platte River with the Missouri River.*

healing and restoring influence of the Temperance reformation, could be borne into all those abodes of consummate wretchedness! Oh that woman, wherever dignified and elevated and blessed by the heavenly influence of Christianity, would lend her aid, to bear that influence onward, until all the dark places of the earth shall have been enlightened, and all its miserable sinks of sin purified! To this end let us toil without ceasing.

I remain yours truly, EDWIN JAMES, Cor. Sec. N. Y. Tem. Soc.

While no feeling but that of gratitude was felt and expressed on the part of friends in the cause of Temperance, a very different sensation was produced among those vendors engaged in the ungodly traffic of selling spirituous liquors, and those who were made victims to this degrading vice and sold those spirits of beastly intoxication.

A short account of the affair is found in his journal, penned some months after the occurrence in connection with that of similar treatment at a subsequent period:

> I was whipped by a grocery keeper, last Fall in Auburn N. Y., also assaulted and seized in the street, and an attempt was made to drag me from the house or cowskin[8] me in the same, and at last was forced to leave the place or submit to the fury of a mob, headed by a number of grocery keepers; among whom were Jonas Brown, Frederic I. Chute, Thomas Munroe and others of a similar stamp.
>
> My "crime" was that of visiting about one hundred Drunkards' families, and telling to the community their wretchedness.
>
> The Mob pursued me about eight miles. I left my conveyance and fled to the *woods*, and was hunted for until ten o'clock at night. At one time they came within thirty feet of me. I often prayed for them and felt confident, that God would deliver me, yet I felt deeply the impotency of every thing but God to sustain me. I trembled, and often found myself saying, 'they will have you yet.' I never before could sympathize with David, when persecuted by Saul.

In a description of these scenes to me, he said that about 11 o'clock A.M., the mob collected, consisting of some five hundred persons who surrounded the hotel where he was. In consequence of a man rushing into the house to seize him, the innkeeper became alarmed for the safety

---

[8]*A cowskin is a kind of leather whip about as hard as a piece of oak. It is of various sizes, but usually about three feet, and it tapers to a point, making it very elastic. A blow with it will readily cause bleeding. — Editor.*

of his house and ordered Mr. Brown to quit. Consequently, he was
obliged to make his way directly through the assembled multitude. Yet
on account of his smallness in stature and swiftness in running, passed
unobserved and succeeded in reaching the conveyance in wait for him.
On reaching a certain distance, as previously stated, he was overtaken by
a man on horseback, who was employed for the direct purpose of taking
his life. Those who were with Mr. Brown had taken the precaution to
fill the vehicle with clubs, &c., as weapons in case of an assault, and Mr.
Brown said he thought how easy it would be for him to take the life of
this highway assassin; the next thought that struck his mind was the
awful fate attending such a soul in Eternity. The man thus employed to
commit the deed of violence seemed also to relent. Mr. Brown, therefore considering him as a hireling in the business, offered him five dollars to leave him, and then fled for the woods and was pursued, as before
stated, until 10 o'clock at night, making it a twelve hours chase from the
starting point at eleven in the morning.

Rev. C. Van Loon,[9] in allusion to the affair, told me that in taking
lodging for the night at a house, Mr. Brown was received by the inmates
as a supposed convict from the State Prison, and harbored with the intention of returning him the next morning to Auburn. A satisfactory explanation probably averted the design. Friends were not wanting at this
juncture of events to assist and sustain Mr. Brown in his efforts thus to
advance the cause of Temperance. Among the numerous letters of sympathy addressed to him at this time is the following:

Albany, Sept. 9th, 1835.

MY DEAR SIR:— I rejoice, that you have been persecuted for righteousness
sake. It is one of the instruments God uses to advance His own glory, and
we should rejoice to be His instruments, no matter how much we suffer.
You can with great propriety congratulate me on this point. The persecution, I am now enduring is tremendous, and I have to withstand it almost
singlehanded, except that I feel that God is working for me, and will support me in the opposition. I am now enduring from wine drinking Chris-

[9]The Rev. Charles Van Loon, a Poughkeepsie native, was a young Baptist minister devoted to
the causes of antislavery and temperance. He was plagued by poor health throughout his life, yet
lectured throughout New York in support of these causes, and was highly respected by African Americans. Van Loon, who had not yet reached his twenty-ninth birthday when he died, was a vice-
president of the Eastern New York Anti-Slavery Society.— Editor. ("What Death has Done!" Albany
Patriot, 15 December 1847; "Eastern New York Anti-Slavery Society Organizational Meeting,"
The Emancipator, 12 May 1842: 7.)

tians, rum sellers, beer makers, &c., &c. I pray God for counsel constantly. We must all seek direction from Him. But to the subject of your letter. Send us, my dear sir, your manuscript at once. We dare publish any thing that is true, avoiding personalities, and if these tales are of the character you name, they may be made a blessing to the nation. Should we conclude to publish them, we shall scatter them to the four winds. The time has come for increased effort, and we are prepared to increase our labors in any way and every way to promote the great work. We are now circulating almost millions of documents gratuitously, and we are trusting to Providence for the means — we never yet have trusted in vain. Should we publish your documents, then I suppose those who have desired their publication, and have subscribed, will help us.

I am, dear Sir, Your Brother in being persecuted, E.C. DELAVAN.[10]

An address to the public was also issued, commendatory of the course pursued by Mr. Brown, and relative to the attendant circumstances of those riotous proceedings from which the following is an extract:

Mr. Brown, of whose good moral character we have sufficient testimonials, came to this village a few weeks since, with a view of making it a temporary residence. Being warmly enlisted in the principal benevolent operations of the day, and particularly in the Temperance reform, and Sabbath School institutions, he determined to exert himself in the promotion of these two philanthropic objects in our village. Accordingly he proposed to visit personally the groceries, where, in open violation of the law, spirituous liquors are daily sold, to investigate their character — company, — and amount of sales — and from thence, by correct estimate, and actual observation, to trace directly the influence of the traffic on the families of their customers, and indirectly on the inhabitants of the entire town. And having obtained these facts, he designed at a general meeting of the citizens to lay them before the public, in the hope that these details of the misery and vice existing in our midst, would excite more activity in the cause of temperance, and thus remove, or mitigate that most fruitful source of evil, to our beloved country and village — intemperance.

Whilst visiting the abodes of the poor and wretched, he also proposed

[10]*Edward C. Delavan, a wealthy resident of Ballston, N.Y., was a nationally known temperance advocate. His Delevan House temperance hotel in Albany was a notable location. A friend of Gerrit Smith, Delevan also participated in the New York Anti-Slavery Society and, according to Wilbur Siebert, was a conductor on the Underground Railroad. — Editor. (Wilbur H. Siebert,* The Underground Railroad: From Slavery to Freedom, *New York: Macmillan, 1898: 414.)*

to procure relief for the suffering and destitute — to secure the attendance of children at some one of the village Sabbath Schools, and enlist the feelings of the parents in the support of these institutions.

These were the objects, and these the motives that prompted Mr. Brown to enter upon a work so arduous and self denying — to seek out and visit in their own wretched hovels the sons of poverty and distress. The very objects and the very motives, though exercised upon a diminished field, that prompted the immortal Howard to trace to their miserable habitations the loathsome victims of vice and debauchery.

He made known these intentions to a few individuals, who encouraged him to proceed, and accordingly he had been engaged for weeks in prosecuting his labors — when on Thursday the 27th of August last, being then prepared to lay the facts he had obtained before the public, a paper was forcibly taken from his hands in our streets by certain individuals, and publicly read: Which paper, being a private memorandum, contained a list of drunkards, of grocers, names of families upon whom he designed to call — in relation to the objects he had in view. To which actual enumeration, rumor and misstatement added the names of other citizens, all of whom were represented as included in the same catalogue of confirmed inebriates — which names also it was confidently affirmed were designed to be published. Such rumors and false statements having soon gained general credence, an extraordinary commotion ensued, and Mr. Brown without trial was held forth and denounced as a libelous scoundrel and disturber of the public peace. A few who considered themselves particularly aggrieved in the heat of the temporary excitement, not mindful of the salutary laws of our land, attempted to inflict summary punishment by a resort to personal violence, from which attempt however, we are happy to say, he providentially escaped unharmed. And we are still more happy to be able to state, that some of his most determined opposers have since in a spirit of commendable candor and honesty, acknowledged their error, and expressed a regret that by a momentary ebullition of passion they were betrayed into so great an excess.

The above is a correct and unprejudiced statement of the grounds of the recent disturbance — and we are therefore prepared to make the positive declaration, that the excitement originated in no sufficient cause, but sprung solely from false and erroneous representations. That he designed to collect and publish facts in reference to Intemperance, we have said — and to *this* no friend to the general cause of humanity could object — but that he intended to publish *names*, we deny upon his own authority and assertion previous to the disturbance. He refused repeatedly to give the names to his most intimate friends — declaring that he considered himself honorably bound to some poor families from whom he obtained facts not to reveal names and that he never would be guilty of such a breach of faith—and of this determination his friends at once saw and acknowledged the propriety. Should any think that the mere fact of having in his possession such a memorandum, is an evidence of his intention to publish it—we would simply ask how any person, being a stranger, could collate and properly arrange a mass of facts relative to individuals without a memorandum?

Thus, then it appears manifest, that the charge instituted against Mr. Brown, of an intention to libel our citizens, and create an unwarrantable excitement, is groundless.

Should it be said, that the manner of obtaining these facts is highly objectionable, as it is a disingenuous method of prying into the secret concerns of families, and an officious intermeddling with the affairs of others;—we would observe that the character of such procedure depends, very materially, upon the motives which prompt to the investigations in question. What patriot, what philanthropist can object to the efforts of benevolence for the relief of misery, how delicate soever the circumstances, with which it may have relationship? All our sympathies, the spirit of benevolence, and the word of God, in which that spirit breathes pure and heavenly from the Throne of the Highest, urge us to the abode of wretchedness and woe, to weep with those who weep, to sooth the anguish of broken hearts, and to guide the young and helpless into the paths of virtue, respectability, and usefulness.

A sample of the facts were also given of the most thrilling description, and the report was signed by eighty individuals, whose names will be held in everlasting remembrance by the lovers of Temperance.

Some months subsequent, he writes the following letter.

Fredonia, Feb. 1st, 1836.

MY DEAR AND ONLY SISTER:—You still share in the affections of my heart, although I was married to Mary Ann Brigham on the fourth of December last. I am laboring in the Sunday School in this County—during the present winter.... Mary Ann's health is better than formerly, and my own is almost perfect—heat and cold, winds and storms are alike to me.

... The churches generally, are declining in piety, but God is raising up some Ministers, valiant for the truth, and there will be a reaction....

All my S. S. efforts seem to be blessed. There is good coming out of the Temperance, anti-slavery, and moral reform society. The cause of Christ is rising in our land; there are a noble few who fear none but God, who are marching boldly on. We expect opposition, but God sustains us. We have mobs, &c., but all does not deter us. I have been publicly mobbed, cowskined, knocked beside of the head, and assaulted five or six different times during the year past, but God delivers me, and puts all mine enemies to confusion. Our laws here are not our strength —"God is our refuge and strength," &c. Some of the whiskey manufacturers talk of whipping me, but I fear them not. All goes well with me, long as I pray. I have been talking Temperance during a part of the summer, and have endeavored to show the manufacturer and vendor, that they are chargeable with the sins of the drunkard, and this makes some repent and others to gnash their teeth. There are a host of children, coming under the influence of religious instruction. The cause of anti-slavery has very much opposition, but it is advancing and will soon prevail. The truth will always prosper. I am an abolitionist in the full sense of the word, yet I have found little time to say or do much in the cause.[11] Labor on, my dear sister. My dear wife sends her kind regards, and all send hearty love. Adieu. ABEL BROWN, JR.

[11] *This is Brown's first mention of the antislavery cause in the book; however, his obituary in the Jan. 19, 1845, issue of the* Albany Patriot *stated that he took up the cause as early as 1829 under the tutelage of the Rev. Elisha Tucker.*

CHAPTER VII

PREACHES AT WESTFIELD, N. Y. — TRIALS
AND PERSECUTION — IS PUBLICLY WHIPPED, &C. —
LABORS IN PENNSYLVANIA — LECTURES IN BEHALF
OF THE AMERICAN ANTI-SLAVERY SOCIETY —
AN EPISTOLARY ADDRESS TO THE SENIOR
CLASS OF HAMILTON INSTITUTION

The ensuing summer, Mr. Brown was located at Westfield in the work
of the ministry, some account of which is found in his journal at this period.

Westfield, July 23d, 1836.
... For a few days past, have been in deep distress. Have before been
whipped and pounded and hunted like the fox, by men more savage than
wild beasts, and have had afflictions of various sorts, but never any thing
that took hold of my very life, like the present. In prayer all is light, but
elsewhere, all is dark. I have almost wished for death.

Have this day been making some enquiries relative to a religious newspaper. The Pulpit and Press, with few exceptions, are silent, in reference
to the sins of Adultery, and to *Intemperance,* in many cases, and Slaveholding — and but few men, do or say, more than what public opinion will sustain. As for real and entire consecration to Christ, there is little, except in
name even among those who preach. Alas! Alas! Too true. For myself, I am
ashamed, also for my Country and People. If I preach and live according
to the truth, all men will hate me. I seem to be known and hated now, by
many — or men seem to hate to hear about their own sins.

After giving an exposition of Bible truth in reference to prayer, at
a preparatory lecture, he remarks — "The truth was highly commended,
but I fear, a very few, if any, will obey it. Enough are always found to
commend the truth, but few to live in accordance thereto."

July 28th.

In the morning, Elder Zenas Freeman called. Had a pleasant interview. Brother F. informed me of the speculation now in progress among the Ministers. The churches and leaders seem to be going after the world. The minister who spends a portion of his time in business transactions cannot spend the same time in preaching *"Christ crucified."* The Apostles thought it not fit for them to leave the ministry (or preaching "Christ crucified") to even serve *tables* for their brethren, although some were neglected — and can it be best for ministers who have most talent, to devote so large a portion of their time to this work of gain? How would Paul have appeared attending auctions to buy land, and how do ministers appear *now* in pursuing a course directly opposite to that of Paul. The right course seems clear — "a single eye to the glory of God," in the conversion of sinners.

Sunday, Aug. 21, 1836.

Preached in A.M. to Baptist and Presbyterian Churches in Presbyterian house in Westfield. Text — Luke 3:15.[1] Pleasant state of mind during the exercises. All heard.

Aug. 23d.

Attended the Anniversary of the Chautauque Co. S. S. Union at Maysville. Talked temperance in the evening. As I went from the house to my lodgings, saw ten or fifteen men around a poor drunkard. The tavern keeper had sold him liquor until he could not walk alone, and then thrust him into the street. I could get neither house nor place for a long time, where any one would take him; at last, found a barn to which I led him, and he was laid on the hay until morning. He repented and confessed in the morning, and went home.

Sunday, Aug. 28th.

At 5 o'clock, lectured at Portland Harbor. At half past 7 o'clock lectured at Westfield. Congregation large and solemn. Text — Eternity. A drunken man hallooed in the street, and disturbed the congregation until the cause was ascertained. He had been whipping his wife.

Westfield, Sunday, Nov. 6th, 1836.

Having received an invitation from the Presbyterian Church to preach in their house, the brethren of the Baptist Church thought proper to accept

[1] *The people who were anxious for the coming of the Messiah were wondering if John (the Baptist) might possibly be the Christ. John disavows this, and says one is coming whose sandal he is not fit to tie. John says he baptizes with water, but Christ will baptize with the Holy Spirit. Perhaps Abel is comparing himself with John and reminding the congregation that there is someone far greater who seeks their repentance and offers genuine love. — Editor.*

the same. In A.M. used as a text, "Rebuke a wise man and he will love thee."[2] Showed the duty of Christians in reference to rebuking sin, and rebuked the sin of Gambling, Whiskey making, and other public sins.

Nov. 9th, 1836.

This evening while walking through the streets of Westfield, was attacked by Doct. C. Jones, who struck me about thirty or more times, with a rawhide.

I felt while he was inflicting the blows, calm and composed. Christ held my spirit, as quiet as when sitting by my own blessed fireside. My eye was injured by the end of the whip. The Doctor cursed and swore awhile, and commenced whipping again, but the blessed spirit kept my heart and lips. After my return home, had an hour of sweet communion with God, and could pray with a sincere heart, for him who inflicted the strokes. I have not even an unkind thought, although I was rather severely whipped.

There were ten or fifteen of the most enlightened haters of God about me, while I was receiving the lashes. They all seemed thunderstruck, and one (a Lawyer) who has threatened caning me, became as gentle as a lamb, and said to one of his fellows — "I should not think it possible, for a man to endure thus, and not become enraged!"

The reason assigned for whipping me was, that I had slandered him in the pulpit. I had been preaching against gambling, and the Doctor considered himself slandered.

Sunday, Nov. 13th, 1836.

Being earnestly pressed by the Presbyterian minister, (Mr. Gregory) preached in the Presbyterian Church, to the congregations united. The house was filled. The text — Rom. 2:19.[3] The congregation listened attentively. A class of Infidels, Gamblers, Adulterers, and Rumsellers, and Haters of God, having banded together, passed resolutions to whip, tar and feather, and otherwise abuse me. Bro. Gregory felt anxious to identify publicly his interest with mine — and after service, said — "Together we live or die."

Mr. Brown continued to preach in Westfield and vicinity for the space of several months, notwithstanding the opposition he was obliged to surmount, often being threatened with similar treatment in other places by those who gloried in his having been whipped.

[2]*Proverbs 9:8.— Editor.*

[3]*"If you are convinced you are a guide to the blind, a light for those who are in the dark, an instructor to the foolish, a teacher of infants, because you have in the law the embodiment of knowledge and truth, you, then, who teach others, do you not teach yourself?" The Rev. Gregory is apparently chiding those in the congregation who profess to practice Christianity and yet have come there to act in an unchristian manner.— Editor.*

ABEL BROWN BEING WHIPPED IN WESTfield (FROM ORIGINAL PUBLICATION OF *Memoir of Rev. Abel Brown*).

His sermons were not harsh, bitter, or invective, but scriptural, full of point and seasonable rebuke.

The solemnities of eternity afforded him a theme of warning and instruction to his hearers, in view of the final retribution of the wicked. "Christ weeps over Jerusalem," one evening formed the subject of his discourse. In accordance with which, he says, "my heart was deeply impressed."

Westfield, Dec. 9th, 1836.

DR. C. JONES: VERY DEAR SIR—"Prepare to meet thy God" is a warning given by God himself, and that I may not be found unfaithful to one, who has, unintentionally perhaps, caused me to hate evil and love Christ more ardently, I remind you of this awful, awful injunction. Since the unhappy evening, in which you were left to sin against God so openly, I have felt extremely anxious that you should be converted and become as a little child. You have not injured me in the sight of God, and whatever man may say, is of little consequence. It will be but a few days, before you and myself will stand before the judgment seat of Christ. Are we prepared? For myself, I frankly say, that the thought of meeting a holy, holy God, causes me to tremble. The sacrifice of Jesus, affords me the only consolation. "The blood of Christ, cleanseth from all sin." Therefore, I have some hope, yes, I have a perfect hope, that I shall eventually dwell with Christ.

Will not you, my dear Sir, repent of your sins and ask pardon through the blood of Jesus. "Though hand join in hand, the wicked shall not go unpunished."

Your sincere friend, ABEL BROWN, JR.

(Dr. J. whipped me November 9th, 1836.)

North East, Pa . Aug. 9th, 1837.

Have been laboring at Westfield until 1st of May, when I expected to have gone to Ohio — even marked and started my goods — but those who owed me could not or would not pay me, therefore, was compelled to stop. The brethren at this place, entreated me to settle, and sent for my goods and brought them about the 1st of June.

While in Westfield, enjoyed some of the love of Christ. Mr. G. forsook me, when my cause became unpopular. Poor man, may the Lord have mercy on him.

When I came to this place, I found about thirty hearers upon the Sabbath, Church divided, and every thing but real *heart piety* abounding.

Have usually talked to four congregations on the Sabbath, and at present superintending two S. Schools beside.

... I feel myself, a poor vile sinner, unfit to do anything, and deserve to be condemned for not saying or doing much more.

His preaching was of that stamp, that his hearers could not easily occupy a neutral position. Concerning them he says — "Some professors greet me with apparent delight, others are very outrageous, and leave church before I hardly begin to speak, &c." A revival of deep and extensive interest (through the blessing of God) seems to have been the result of his labors at this period.

He writes:

Aug. 17th.

Visited Erie, saw Brethren Bakers, and made arrangements for forming a County Domestic Missionary Society.

On the 30th September (following) attended the Annual Meeting of the Erie Co. Domestic Missionary Society. Preached the opening sermon. "Behold the Lamb of God."[4]

North East, Pa., Nov. 16th, 1837.

This day was ordained. Father Geo. Sawin made the Ordaining Prayer. He appeared to pray in the spirit. Felt calm during the exercises. Eld. Win. T. Boynton preached the Sermon. It was such as the occasion required.

Sunday, Nov. 19th, 1837.

In the morning attended S. S. at half past 10. At noon baptized. In P.M. lectured two hours, in behalf of the American Anti-Slavery Society. In the evening, preached at Freeport.

From his correspondence at this time, it is obvious that he was much engaged in devising plans, &c. to forward the cause of the slave.

The following epistolary address will serve to illustrate, in some measure, his views and feelings relative to the duty of Christians in the upholding and sustaining the sin of oppression and robbery in the form of human slavery.

North East, Erie Co. Pa., Oct. 30th, 1837.

Messrs. Ira Corwin, E. E. L. Taylor, Wm. Everts, and others, late members of the Senior Class, in the Collegiate department of the Baptist Literary and Theological Institution at Hamilton, N. Y.:

DEAR BRETHREN— The acquaintance which I have enjoyed while a classmate with you, has given you a place near my heart; and in thus publicly addressing you, I would honor the cause which we all profess to love, and if I speak of what I think your errors, I will endeavor to do it with kindness.

You are watchmen upon Zion's walls. You are to hear the word from God's mouth, and faithfully deliver the same to the people. You are not to shun to declare the "whole counsel of God." You have finished a Collegiate course of study — received the approbation of your Professors, and applause of the denomination of Christians, to which we hold membership.

---

[4]*John the Baptist's words when Jesus came to him for baptizing: "Behold the Lamb of God who takes away the sins of the world!" (John 1:29)— Editor.*

ILLUSTRATION FROM ORIGINAL PUBLICATION OF *Memoir of Rev. Abel Brown.*

You are now about to enter upon a course of Theological studies, under the guidance of those Divines whom we have been accustomed to venerate.

My object, in addressing you, is to endeavor to persuade you to leave that Institution immediately; I do this, because I think you will sustain American Slavery, by continuing [as] members of the Institution in its present condition. My belief is founded upon the following reasons:—1st. That Institution courts the support of Slaveholders and their apologists.

Slaveholding ministers and laymen frequently visit the Institution — great pains are taken to obtain their favor. Nothing is said to them respecting the *sin* of Slavery, or if it is mentioned, it is only to say that the circumstances justify its continuance. The contributions of Slaveholders are received. In return, your Professors go to the South, talk and pray, but hold their peace in reference to "the peculiar Institution"—Slavery....

... Your Professors neglect to cry against the sin of Slaveholding. These men profess to be Teachers of the pure Religion of Jesus Christ. Their station gives them an extensive influence. I learn from the minutes of the last Triennial Convention of the Baptists[5] in the U. S. held at Richmond, Va.,

[5]*On May 18, 1814, 33 delegates from Baptist churches in North and South met in Philadelphia to form the General Missionary Convention of the Baptist Denomination in the United States for Foreign Missions. Because the convention met every three years, it became known as the Triennial Convention. This was the first Baptist organization of national scope. It was formed to facilitate missionary work. It raised financial support for missions and missionaries, the first of whom were Luther Rice and Adoniram Judson.—Editor.*

that two of them were among the Speakers on that occasion. In the State
of N.Y., their influence is almost boundless. Indeed, it may be said, that
the teachings of the Hamilton Professors are exhibited in almost every town
in the State. If they neglect to hear the cry of the poor, ministers, less
informed, readily think themselves excusable. Your Professors preach in
behalf of the heathen, and correctly charge that man, who neglects the call
of God through them, as lacking the essentials of piety; and a prominent
argument, presented by the Agents of your Institution when soliciting
funds, is that young men are trained within its walls to preach the Gospel
to the benighted nations of the earth. And is it true, that those very Professors hold their peace, when two and a half millions of Americans are
forbidden even the Bible!

You are forbidden *speaking* against the sin, or the right of free discussion. The evidence of this is, that an Anti-Slavery Society formed by yourselves and fellow students in the Institution, "was dissolved by the Official
request of the Faculty."

You are permitted to form Temperance, Moral Reform, Missionary, Colonization and other Societies, and their merits have been freely discussed.
You doubtless recollect, the public discussion of the merits of the Colonization Society,[6] when our departed brother, Ralph J. Brown, exposed its
foolishness, yet the Professors entered their protest against his arguments,
and sustained the ignoble enterprise. These various societies prosper, and
their continuance is thought to be advantageous; even weekly and semi-
weekly discussions are not only permitted but considered useful. Time rolls
on a little, and a few brethren form an A. S. Society. The Professors hear
the news, and "post haste," one of that venerable body, is sent with a
stiffnecked request, that the infant A. S. Society be immediately dissolved....

The reasons for dissolving that Society were, I suppose, simply these.
Anti-Slavery principles were rather unpopular. The South universally hated
them, and the North did not fear God sufficiently to preach what they must
admit to be true. If the Society prospered, its members would be ranked
among the Fanatics, and as the Professors were known to control the inter-
nal operations of the Institution, they of course, must be considered as sanc-
tioning the Society, and thus they also, yes, even the venerable Board of
Professors of the Hamilton Baptist Literary and Theological Institution,
with a double D. D. at their head, would be reckoned among the reckless
fanatics. Methinks, such thoughts as these filled their mighty minds. There
are Garrison, Tappan, Birney — good men — but overzealous, called fanat-

---

[6]*Many commentators, both historians and contemporaries, among them William Lloyd Garrison, have exposed the racist origins and intent of the American Colonization Society, which formed
in Washington, D.C., in 1816.—Editor.*

ics by the world, and madmen by the Church. Our venerable names, noted for our candor and consistency — "cool heads" — our reputation will be gone, if it is once known that we sanction abolition. Again, it is not practicable. Slavery is a sin. It cannot be right to make property of a man, but it cannot be stopped all at once. Then, Abraham had servants. Again, there is the Baptist Denomination, just getting into lovely Union. Let the Presbyterian body fight Slavery. The Baptists have been contemptuously looked upon long enough. There are our Southern brethren, excellent men, good Christians. Our beloved Baptist Zion, it must not be distracted. Our Institution, just insuring the confidence of the Churches. Our candid and stable friends will leave us. "The gospel will destroy Slavery." O Lord, Thou great Head of the Church, direct us. Give us wisdom to check this abolition spirit in the bud.

Whatever might have been the reasons assigned, causing your Faculty to dissolve that Anti-Slavery Society, it is certain that it was a worldly policy, a bending of the truth for the sake of gain, and to win the confidence and favor of the votaries of this system of oppression, in violation of the dearest rights of humanity.[7]

Yours, &c., ABEL BROWN, JR.

[7]*Hamilton College was one of a number of colleges during this time where students formed antislavery societies in opposition to faculty and administration. Perhaps the most famous was Lane Seminary in Cincinnati, where in 1834 students led by the renowned antislavery lecturer Theodore Weld were expelled from the school for their activities, then moved on to continue their studies at Oberlin College. — Editor.*

CHAPTER VIII

SETTLEMENT AT BEAVER—RECEIVES APPOINTMENT
OF AGENCY FROM THE A. S. SOCIETY OF WESTERN
PENNSYLVANIA—PERSECUTION—AN ATTEMPT TO
THROW HIM INTO THE RIVER OHIO—"DELIVERS
THE SPOILED FROM THE HAND OF THE
SPOILER"—EFFORTS TO ADVANCE THE CAUSE
OF THE SLAVE IN HIS OWN DENOMINATION

While at North East, a church was established through his instrumentality on reformatory principles. Soon as this was accomplished, he left the pastoral charge of the church and received an invitation to settle at Beaver, a city pleasantly located on the Ohio.[1] The call was accepted, at what date I am not informed. He chose rather to itinerate, fearlessly preaching the truth, than to establish himself in any one place by a time serving policy. Neither can it be expected that a minister will long be tolerated in openly rebuking the sins of a people in such a manner that they cannot fail to make the personal application, for his preaching was of that character that it seemed to speak like that of Nathan to David — "Thou art the man."[2] He continued to preach throughout that section

---

[1]*Beaver is located less than 13 miles from the border of West Virginia, about 30 miles west of Pittsburgh.—Editor.*

[2]*2 Samuel 12:9-7. After David had lost his infant son conceived with Bathsheba, Nathan, a prophet, pointed out to David the reason for his loss was that he had committed a sin in taking Bathsheba, who had been another man's wife. David had contrived to take her by putting her husband in harm's way in a battle that cost him his life. Nathan showed this through a parable of a poor shepherd who only had one little ewe lamb, which he raised with his family (it was like a daughter to him), and a rich man who had many sheep and cattle who took the poor man's one lamb in order to feed a guest. David responded that such a man should pay four times over and die, because he had no pity on the poor man. Nathan answered David, "Thou art the man." Like Nathan, Abel is pointing out the sins of his brethren.—Editor.*

as opportunity offered. Additional sketches from his journal, sufficient
to show the assiduity and zeal with which he labored, are given.

Sunday, 15th, 1838.

In morning attended Sabbath School at Bridgewater. At 11 and 2 o'clock
attempted to preach. Prayer meeting at noon. Communion at 3 o'clock.
At half past 4 went to Old Brighton, to lecture in the evening at Fallston.
Felt very little in comparison with Christ, yet felt like warning men in view
of the approaching judgment...

Sunday, April 29th.

Have preached four sermons and attended two Sabbath Schools. At the S.
School at Fallston, 9 o'clock A.M. Some large boys gathered from the fishing
places, came in and were instructed with interest (to myself at least), and
more apparent interest is manifested in all congregations than on last Sabbath.

I feel delighted in presenting the sublime truths of the Gospel, to the
children of men, and although so vile and unworthy myself, yet I hope
and expect a revival in this region.

Sunday, May 6th, 1838.

In the morning superintended the S. S. at Fallston. Good attendance and
interesting. Children many of them gathered from the "highways and
hedges." Some quite large, twelve or fourteen years old, who could not read.
Others quite intelligent. Tried to plainly warn these young immortals. At
11 o'clock preached in W. Bridgwater. At 2 P.M. in Freedom. Congregation
full and attentive. At 4 P.M. preached in East Bridgewater. In the evening
at half past 7 preached at Fallston. Visited a number of destitute families.
Retired at 10 o'clock rather fatigued and feeling myself miserably vile and
sinful, in view of my own heart.

Monday, 7th, 1838.

Spent most of the day aiding my wife. In the evening attended and lectured at a Temperance Meeting in Bridgewater.

Sunday, 13th.

Spent the day as usual. Attended five services — at 11 A.M., and 2, 4, 6 and
8 P.M.; also a S. School at 9 A.M.

The following days of the week attended an Anti-Slavery Convention
at Pittsburg. Lectured each evening to large assemblies. The same spirit

was rife, that caused the burning of Pennsylvania Hall,[3] whose walls resounded to the motto, "Virtue, Liberty, and Independence," from the 14th day of this month, until the evening of the 17th witnessed its destruction by a lawless mob in that "city of brotherly love" and state so dear to the memory of Franklin, Rush and others, among the earliest advocates of human liberty.

On the 25th succeeding, Mr. Brown received an appointment of agency from the Western Pa. A[nti] S[lavery] Society. Soon after, he relinquished his charge as pastor of the Baptist church in Beaver, and as "a Minister in good standing" received a cordial recommendation from the same. He now devoted his time and talents almost exclusively to the cause of the Slave, zealously endeavoring to arouse and incite his

BURNING OF PENNSYLVANIA HALL IN PHILADELPHIA (JOHN SARTAIN, 1838). ON MAY 17, 1838, THREE DAYS AFTER THE DEDICATION OF THIS BUILDING, AN ANGRY MOB GATHERED OUTSIDE WHILE INSIDE MORE THAN 3,000 PEOPLE LISTENED TO ANGELINA GRIMKE ATTACK THE INSTITUTION OF SLAVERY. THE HALL WAS BUILT AS A MEETING PLACE FOR ABOLITIONISTS. TWO THOUSAND SUBSCRIBERS CONTRIBUTED MORE THAN $40,000 FOR ITS CONSTRUCTION. THE MOB BEGAN SMASHING WINDOWS AND, AFTER THOSE INSIDE EXITED, BURNED IT TO THE GROUND (THE LIBRARY COMPANY OF PHILADELPHIA).

[3]*On May 17, 1838, Pennsylvania Hall, a large, new classical-style stone building built with the contributions of 2,000 people for the purpose of hosting antislavery functions and other reformatory meetings in Philadelphia, was burned to the ground by a mob after a female antislavery society meeting. The building had been open only three days.*—Editor.

brethren of the Baptist denomination to action. He was also employed as corresponding secretary and agent of the Home Missionary operations of that section.[4] He seemed ready to act at once and determinately on any subject involving the duties of himself and co-laborers with reference to the question of that "sum of all villanies" — American Slavery. The following letter on a subject previously entertained and suggested by himself is full of interest, and was perhaps the dawn of a brighter day, both to the denomination to which he belonged and the slave of our country:

Pittsburgh, Pa., Feb. 5th, 1839.

REV. JOSHUA LEAVITT[5]: Dear Brother — In the Emancipator of last week I see a proposition for holding a Baptist Abolition Convention. I think it very important that such a convention should be held in the month of May or June.

The alarming demands of a slaveholding church require that immediate and mighty efforts should be made lest an avenging God overwhelm us in deep destruction.

The Baptist churches in the South hold property in slaves, buy and sell men for the sake of gain, — even Baptists sell Baptists — part husband and wife — parent and child — advocate and sanction polygamy — rob the poor to replenish the treasury of the Lord — withhold the scriptures from those whom God has required to search them, — and then say that God has given them this liberty and requires it at their hands. Ministers, D. D's commit these crimes, and even leave men and women to be sold at auction after their death. Baptists have been found on lynch committees, who have beat innocent men contrary to the laws of God and man. Northern Baptists have quietly beheld these things, have fellowshipped and are still fellowshipping these "dear southern brethren" — have sent their agents to the South, asked and received a part of the profits of these Christian robbers — received men-stealers into their pulpits — asked them to preach, pray and commune with them. The leading Baptist periodicals have been silent under the command, "Open thy mouth for the dumb," have excused slaveholders and censured those who "rebuked them sharply," have seen their own brethren driven from the house of God by brutal mobs, have opposed a faithful edi-

---

[4]*The American Baptist Home Mission Society was organized in New York City on Friday April 27, 1832, "to promote the preaching of the Gospel in North America."— Editor.*

[5]*Joshua Leavitt, editor of the nationally prominent antislavery newspaper* The Emancipator, *also was an active antislavery lecturer. He became widely known for his role in aiding the release of the Africans who overthrew their captors in the* Amistad *incident of 1839.— Editor.*

tor until he was shot down at his post,[6] and then rejoiced that the martyr
was not a Baptist minister. Baptist ministers, D. D's, and Theological professors, have limited "human responsibilities," expelled young men who
feared God more than mortals from their "Schools of the Prophets," uttered
gag laws,[7] and defended practices at which hell itself would shudder. These
statements may appear harsh to many, but they are true, and even this is
not all the truth. Transactions far more degrading have been exhibited by
Baptists. Many good brethren are not aware that slavery is thus sapping the
very foundations of truth in our churches. They have supposed that such
papers as the N. Y. B[aptist] Register, Gospel Witness, and Cross and Journal published weekly a true account of all affairs of importance occurring
in the denomination. They have never once thought that they were upholding slavery. Very many professed abolitionists have voted to send delegates
to the Triennial Convention, without even suspecting that they were sending them as agents to welcome men-stealers into the bosom of our Zion,
and thereby bidding them "God speed." How can the Baptist churches be
aroused and enlightened upon this infinitely important matter? Can it be
done more effectually than by calling and attending a National Baptist Abolition Convention? In such a meeting the whole subject could be canvassed,
at least as far as human power is concerned,— many of the Baptist papers
would publish the proceedings — new papers could be established if necessary, and thus this subject would be brought before most if not all the Baptist churches in the North. The result would show whether the Baptists love
slavery more than truth. My abolition brethren in the church, upon whom
rests the responsibility of calling such a convention, if not upon us? Most
surely God hath committed this blessed work to US. Why should we delay?
Fifty thousand of our colored brethren in bonds ask us, *Why?* 3,000,000,
who have never heard of Christ, will soon meet us before the throne of God,
and in the silence of eternity ask, *Why?* Will not an insulted God ask, *Why?*
And shall we, while the blood of Jesus is interceding for us, delay?

The place of holding such a convention is not very important. I pro-
pose Albany, New York, Utica or Philadelphia. Certainly many would meet
at either place. Will not brethren Galusha, Tucker, Carpenter, Grosvenor,
Ide, Colver, and others, immediately issue a call?

I have no apology to offer for thus presenting this proposition to the
public. I almost daily see the poor heartbroken slave making his way to a

[6]*The Rev. Elijah Lovejoy, who was murdered in Alton, Illinois, on Nov. 7, 1837, following a
vendetta against him after he publicly rebuked a mob that had lynched a black man in St. Louis,
Missouri, on April 28, 1836.— Editor.*
[7]*A reference to the infamous "Gag Law" ruling of 1835 in the U.S. Congress that prohibited
the discussion of slavery.— Editor.*

land of freedom. I saw a noble, pious, distressed, spirit-crushed slave, a member of the Baptist church, escaping from a (professed christian's) bloodhound, to a land where he could enjoy that of which he had been robbed, during forty years. His prayers would have made us all feel. I saw a baptist sister of about the same age, her children had been torn from her, her head was covered with fresh wounds, while her upper lip had scarcely ceased to bleed, in consequence of a blow with the poker, which knocked out her teeth; she too was going to a land of freedom. Only a very few days since, I saw a girl of about eighteen, with a child as white as myself, aged ten months; a christian master was raising her child (as well his own perhaps) to sell to a southern market. She had heard of the intention, and at midnight took her only treasure and travelled twenty miles on foot through a land of strangers — she found friends. I gazed upon her intelligent countenance — I thought of the immortal but crushed intellect. That body which should have been the "temple of the Holy Ghost," had been, and was still intended by her master to be a source of profit to him, realized even by the raising and selling of its fruit as would best promote his interest. But why should I write? Have not the Baptists hearts? Do they not hear the wailings of millions? Does not the wintry blast echo their howlings? Will they neglect to act? Will they forget the slave? Forbid it, slumbering justice! Forbid it, indulgent mercy! Forbid it, Almighty God!

Will the editor of the Christian Reflector please publish this communication?

ABEL BROWN, JR., late Pastor of the 1st Bap. Ch., Beaver, Pa.

From a Report to the Executive Committee of the A. S. Society, under date of December 3d, 1838, I make the following extract:

I have been laboring during the two past weeks in Beaver, Bridgewater, Old Brighton and New Brighton, Fallston, Freedom and Chippeway. I have been in close action with the enemy. Friday, Saturday and Sunday was one continued row. A mob drove me from the house on Friday night. Saturday night I could not get to the house unless through showers of stones, and Sunday, the house was found nailed up, and during one hour the friends could not open it; after it was opened, it was found too late to address the people without infringing upon the appointment of the Methodists, which must not be done, even to save all the souls of the slaves. The mob in Bridgewater was headed by ... of the firm of ... forwarding merchants, ... merchant, ... and ... butchers.[8] There were others concerned

---

[8]*Apparently, Mrs. Brown has omitted the names of these individuals for reasons of privacy. — Editor.*

in the matter, but the two first named gentlemen, gave the "character and standing" to it. I suppose, perhaps, some went even greater lengths, than was anticipated by the leaders. Who threw the stones, I am unable to say, but stones were thrown. The house of a friend of mine was stoned, and his wife barely escaped being hit in the head, as the mob threw at me. The door was accidentally left open. It is hardly safe for me to walk in the street after dark. The cause of these things, is simply, because there is no minister in the place who opens his mouth for the dumb. The presiding Elder in this region, is one of those haters of abolition, of which the Devil should be ashamed. There has been a great "Revival of Religion," among the Methodists in this place. I mean the religion of this age, not the religion of the Bible. I shall be heard even here, before many weeks, I am quite sure. I wish to state to the Committee, that it will be utterly impossible, for me to support my family with less than $700 per year. I am obliged to give my whole and undivided attention, and the best days and energies of my life, to the cause. I only regret, that I cannot do more. I must now be absent from home (if the northern county meetings are held) until the first of Feb., with the exception of only one or two days. In the month of February, I hope to be obliged to attend four or five county meetings. My family are so situated, they think it impossible to "board out." This is a matter, however, that I leave with the Committee. I cannot think it my duty to leave Beaver, until I find a more needy and wicked place. I would give up the cause in this region, and seek the retired spot from whence I came (which is proffered me), if I was not sure that it would be running away from duty. I know the truth will ultimately prosper, even here. Indeed, even the leaders of the mob, who on Saturday evening stoned me, are afraid to look me in the face. I have had a personal interview with one of them this day; he turned ghastly pale, and even these God defying ministers seem ashamed of themselves, although I have not uttered a word, for or against them....

Of further riotous proceedings, he writes the following letter, without date:

REV. ROBERT CROOKS: Very Dear Sir — I cannot express all the satisfaction and grief, I have felt in reading your short, instead of long, as you say, letter. I thank God and take courage. Be assured, that it will be of vast benefit to our common cause; this, I know, is all the reward you desire. I intend having the three articles published in an extra sheet, and scattered through this region. It will probably be as well to omit your name and residence, as the effect here will be the same.

Last night, I came home in deep distress. This morning I received your letter, and it is indeed refreshing. While lecturing, on last evening, a ruffian rushed into the house, seized me by the collar, and started to drag me from the house. His associates who were in the house followed, but the friends of truth were too strong for them. As I went from the place I was stoned. There are a few such men among us at present. It was I think the enemies last struggle in that place (Brighton, Beaver Co.). I drop my pen, to return to the same house this evening and lecture.

Some additional circumstances are found in another account, probably referring to the same event during a series of meetings in Old Brighton, in the month of Nov., 1838:

... Returning from the schoolhouse after lecturing, I was egged, &c. Sabbath following, preached to a large assembly in this place. On Monday evening, a respectable audience convened. There was considerable excitement. I saw the mob as I passed up the street, and most of them soon followed me into the house. They exhibited their wrath, by tearing down a picture, posted for the evening's use. After prayer, I commenced speaking. The mob kept quiet, perhaps ten minutes, when a person entered the room in disguise. His face was either painted or false (probably both,) with large false whiskers. His savage appearance rather surprised me — quick as thought, he rushed towards me with a hideous yell — seized me by the collar, and in connection with some associates, attempted to drag me from the house.

"Making no resistance," the interference of his friends alone prevented the merciless treatment in store for him, as the victim of their [the mob's] rage and malice.

While residing on the Ohio River, it is said that Mr. Brown aided slaves in their escape from bondage. Indeed, all those who had been in the prison house of slavery and were in the act of fleeing from the tyrant monster, ever found a welcome at his door and safety from the grasp of the pursuer.

From a verbal statement given me by a gentleman from Va., I have the following account, (omitting names not essential to be given[9]), pertaining to the case of a young girl in Alexandria, District of Columbia:

---

[9]*Because Mrs. Brown wrote this memoir in 1849 when the Underground Railroad was in operation, she did not want to incriminate or indict individuals by publishing their names. — Editor.*

Mr. R. (who gave the facts) was with Mr. Brown, and both labored to help her off. Mr. B. went to Baltimore — met R. there. He had previously written to him (Mr. B.) at Beaver. The girl was conveyed to _____ at Baltimore, through Mr. B's influence.

The advertisements were ahead of them, for her apprehension. Officers were watching at the cars, and also at the steamboats. Mr. B. was in a very critical situation. Suspicion rested on Mr. B., by one of the principal slaveholders. He was detained there three days, concealing himself; then Mr. B. obtained a carriage, took the girl in, and drove off about 7 o'clock in the evening, and went on to Little York. He was there arrested, and taken on trial. He disposed of the girl previous by putting her under the care of Mr. J. A trial was held, but no evidence being found, and Mr. B. not being obliged to confess against himself, (in the eye of the law), he was consequently discharged. Mr. Brown contrived to have her (the alleged slave) conveyed on, during the trial, and she proceeded to Canada. Mr. B. was engaged also in a case in Kentucky with Mr. K. A slave was conveyed from Louisville to Cincinnati, Ohio through Mr. Brown's influence. Many might have been aided, through his means, from the adjoining States, as his location afforded peculiar facilities for thus "delivering the spoiled from the hands of the spoiler."

An attempt was made while [he was] residing in Beaver to throw him into the river, by twelve men assembled for the purpose of thus taking his life. Mr. Brown had been lecturing on the evils of intemperance. In relating the circumstances to myself, he said the mob surrounded him on the Ohio — that he stood fearless before them, looking them directly in the eye and talking to them of the "judgment to come." They all quailed and faltered from their purpose, except one who was very determined in his purpose but was restrained by his fellows from committing the act. At a meeting in the evening of the same day, those ungodly men presented themselves directly in front of him as listeners to the preaching of Mr. Brown, whose life a few hours previous they had essayed to destroy.

CHAPTER IX

RECEIVES APPOINTMENT OF AGENCY FOR THE
WESTERN EDUCATION SOCIETY—LEAVES
PENNSYLVANIA—VISITS MASSACHUSETTS—
CONTINUES TO LABOR IN THE CAUSE OF THE SLAVE

April following, Mr. Brown received the appointment of agency for the Western Education Society, formed the year previous, and in which he had taken part in devising plans and forwarding operations to carry into effect.

The leading design of the Society was to form "an Institution for the instruction of youth in all the various branches of a collegiate and theological course of studies" on the basis of a free, moral, and enlightened sentiment involving the reformatory movements of the age.

The location of the Institution in view to be established at some eligible point on the river Ohio, communicating by the canal with Lake Erie and regions of the west.

The College itself, to be instituted, controlled, and sustained by a body of men actively engaged in purifying the church from the contaminating influence of Slavery.

How successful in the result of their efforts I am entirely unacquainted, but presume from the nature of the object and the state of public sentiment linked as it is with a proslavery conservatism (in this "Republican age") that the project was never fully realized. Or even if as was the fact that the auspices under which it commenced were favorable, would there be found principle, self-sacrifice and perseverance enough to sustain such an enterprise. Certain it is, however, that a joint stock company was formed with a capital of eighty thousand, about one half of which (thirty-eight thousand) was taken up and the remainder offered to the Eastern and Middle States.

Writing on this subject, Mr. Brown remarks:

> There is a great necessity for a wholesale business to be done, in educating pious young men and women for the work of the Lord in the west. A small number will not answer. At least, ten thousand teachers of common schools are now wanted to instruct over five hundred thousand children, now destitute in the valley of the Mississippi. I am overwhelmed with the thought — and that a *nation* is almost *sleeping* over this subject, fraught with such momentous consequences.

One reason for starting a project like that under consideration may have been found in the alarming tendency not only of a corrupt Protestantism, but in the increasing population of the Roman Catholics at the west with all their auxiliaries in the form of churches, colleges and missionary points of influence.[1] The subjoined article written by Mr. Brown contains an account of some of the obstacles in the way of progress to advance the cause of emancipation and kindred efforts:

> The missionaries employed by the Catholics are men who easily ingratiate themselves into the affections of a community, composed of such materials as are found in many sections of the west; and Jesuits as they are, they pass for kind, tender hearted and pious ministers, of our Lord and Saviour Jesus Christ. They go into villages inhabited almost entirely by Protestants, and obtain Protestant churches and congregations, and there defend their religion with such cunning craftiness, as to cause multitudes to admire. Some churches which are denied to Baptist ministers and Anti-Slavery lecturers, are readily opened for Roman Catholic Priests. The Methodist Episcopal church at Wellsville, Ohio, has been repeatedly refused to Baptist ministers, also to the friends of the slave to hold a prayer meeting, and yet this church was opened last year to a Catholic Bishop, and such was his defence of the Catholic *Church,* and her blessed effects upon the nation were so skillfully portrayed that apparently all apprehension of evil results were allayed. From facts that have come under my observation, I am quite confident that many ministers in the west would sooner aid and assist the Roman Catholics in their efforts to subdue the nation to the will of the Pope, than to suffer the Baptist Church, with its republican government, to be established upon that extensive field. The Catholics are taking possession, as far as their means will permit, of all the strong points, the large

---

[1] *For the most part, the Catholic Church did not concern itself with the cause of antislavery.* — Editor.

cities, the seats of government, &c. in the western States. They are at present, making a mighty effort to command the influence of the State of Illinois. They are erecting a College at its seat of government, thus preparing to win its Legislators to aid them in corrupting the morals, and debasing the minds of its future inhabitants. There are many other influences, which hinder the progress of enlightened Christian efforts in the west, but the most potent of them all, is that of an aristocratic and domineering priesthood; that by their ecclesiastical power and personal influence would prevent the people from hearing every sentiment, but such as they approve. The leading men in the Methodist Episcopal church, and too many in the Presbyterian and Baptist churches, are of this stamp. These men, knowing that the truth would uproot them, make every possible exertion to keep it from the people. There are ministers who are known by reputation in this commonwealth, as pious, devoted servants of God, who do not hesitate to connive at, and by their influence sustain mobs, rather than have the Truth, as God has revealed it, proclaimed among them. *Would to God, the Baptist church was free from such men!!*

Leaving Pennsylvania, on his way to the Eastern States, Mr. Brown, in a communication to Rev. C. P. Grosvenor, writes the following under date of

> Rochester, May 16th, 1839.
>
> DEAR BROTHER:— Since receiving your last letter I have been very busily engaged in forwarding our cause, on my way from Pittsburgh to this place. I have visited many warm friends, and not a few stern opposers. Many influential Baptist Ministers are determined to shut the discussion of the subject of Slavery out of the church....
>
> I was told yesterday, by one of the most influential opposers of abolition in the Baptist church, that the Faculty of the Hamilton Literary and Theological Institution had resolved anew, that the students should not form A. S. Societies or discuss the subject of Slavery in that Institution....

In reference to the appointment of Agents for the Christian Reflector, he says:

> They will all do something. There is, however, a determination on the part of many in this (N. Y.) State, to keep all Anti-Slavery Papers, especially Baptist, away. Some men go on as if determined to die opposing the cause of Emancipation.
>
> Your brother, amid scenes of strife.

To The Same.

Ballston Spa., N. Y., June 3d, 1839.

... I have conversed more with that class of ministers, who oppose the Anti-Slavery cause, and find most of them determined to sustain their ground. They say slaveholders shall not be excluded from the church. They are also determined to sustain the "gag laws" at Hamilton and Granville Institutions, and the Baptist Register & Co. in their neutrality. The ministers say, they are the servants of the Church and must preach what the Church says. This is especially the doctrine of the Hamilton Faculty. A.M. Beebe, editor of the N. Y. B. Register, denies me a small place in his paper, even to state the principles upon which the Education Society intended to act.

He said that Institutions that permitted students to form Anti-Slavery Societies should meet with no encouragement from him, and denounced us as a set of ultraists, doing more hurt than good. I see, we must as friends of the slave go on alone. Church and State have united with the devil to oppose the freedom of the slave, but go on, dear Brother, and in God's name you shall triumph....

CHAPTER X

COMMISSION FROM THE MASSACHUSETTS
ABOLITION SOCIETY—SETTLES AT NORTHAMPTON—
PRIVATE CORRESPONDENCE—DEATH OF
HIS SISTER—LETTER TO C. P. GROSVENOR.

While in Massachusetts, he labored unitedly in the ministry and the cause of the slave. In the month of July, 1839, he received a commission from the Massachusetts Abolition Society, and subsequently settled as pastor of the Baptist church in Northampton. A few extracts from his correspondence at this period are given.

TO REV. ELON GALUSHA.[1]

Sept. 5th, 1839.

... I see by the Christian Reflector of yesterday, that through your instrumentality, a number of worthy names have been attached to a *call* for a National Baptist A. S. Convention. I wish to inquire, whether the persons whose names appear in the Christian Reflector, as far as you have been instrumental in obtaining them, are believers in the doctrine —

1st. Of the sinfulness of holding men as property under all circumstances?

2d. In the duty of immediate emancipation without compensation?

3d. That Slaveholders should be excluded from the fellowship of the Christian Church?

You will understand the reasons of this inquiry, when I say, that some of the persons whose names appear with yours, were bitter opposers of Anti-Slavery efforts, only a few months since. Will you tell the readers of the Reflector whether they have been converted or not.

Yours for the Slave, A. B., Jr.

[1]*Brown apparently is addressing Galusha through the medium of the newspaper, whose editor, the Rev. Cyrus Grosvenor, is referenced following the letter.*

Bro. Grosvenor—You can attach my name to the above if necessary. I fear that many of the names are of the "prudent sort."

Quotations from family letters at this period:

... Our dear Walter is very well. A noble little fellow truly as we think. Mary Ann is usually well. She has been lecturing for the Moral Reform Society. She now has an invitation to labor for the New England F. M. Society. She will, if she can have time, do something in the cause I trust.... I was lately invited to address a large audience in Boston upon this degrading vice (licentiousness)—five hundred houses of Infamy in Boston. We hope to accomplish something through the press &c., if time is not otherwise occupied.

... I attend, upon an average, about ten meetings per week. My health is good, very good.

... There is now a tremendous opposition from these old Congregational churches, and the open haters of truth, but all to no purpose. The Lord is with us, I trust. The Church[es] are all united. Our religious denominations are becoming more and more conformed to the world, and filled with the spirit of human expediency. Consequently we must be the more faithful in rebuking and reproving their hypocrisy.

I have very few attachments on earth. Yet, I love my friends, but I dare not spend time to visit them. Indeed, it renders all society irksome, when I am not benefitting my fellow men. It is also hard for one to attend to my business transactions. Indeed, there are such multitudes perishing, that I cannot do less than labor without ceasing for their conversion. I do not expect that the old superstitions of N. E. [New England] will last very much longer. They are withering before the truth.

I have no expectation of continuing here, longer than the Church can be sufficiently advanced to sustain the gospel.

To his sister (Mrs. C. B. Mercer) then resident of Missouri:

... The cause of Anti-Slavery is marching onward. This is especially true in all the northern States. The slaves must be free. Yes, they will be free or *death* will overwhelm the nation. There are many abolitionists who will labor without any relaxation of effort, until slavery dies. I hope you will not be contaminated by that vilest of all abominations—American Slavery. Touch it not, but pour the burning fire of truth upon it, whenever in your power. Make no terms with it whatever.

ON THE DEATH OF HIS SISTER.

Northampton, Mass. Nov. 30th, 1840.

MR. REUBEN MERCER: Very Dear Brother — A letter from my parents informs me that my dearly beloved sister Cynthia, is no more. She was my only sister, and much I loved her, and earnestly did I labor to aid her to that place where you first knew her. Indeed, I feel the loss. Not that I mourn, for why should I, since God has thus appointed it. It was not because I loved her less that I aided her to depart to a land of strangers, but because I felt that I could not see her live without being useful to this lost and fallen world. I thought then, and still think, that I did what was duty, and I would that I had another sister to live and die, if God designed, under such circumstances. Yours has been the lot to enjoy the society of her, whom I loved as I did myself, and I am quite sure that you have appreciated it. She was indeed, worthy of the society of a kind and generous friend.

I have not been able, on account of an overwhelming pressure of duties, to hold a regular correspondence with you or my sister, but have heard regularly by my parents. I hope you will not give yourself to grief and over much sorrow. Death is common to us all, and we should daily be so conversant with it, as to be able to meet it with calmness and reconciliation. There is nothing about death that should really make us afraid, since Jesus Christ has been with us in life — he certainly will not forsake us in that trying hour, and if He is with us all will be safe.

I should be very happy to see you, and it would give me great pleasure to visit you. Should be very happy to have you visit this State.

Permit me to say, that inasmuch as you have found pleasure in the society of one who is now taken from you, be not given to melancholy, but commit your cares to the Lord, and think it not criminal to secure the friendship and society of another, who may go with you through this wilderness world. I am sure I shall not think you loved my sister less. I make this remark and leave you to make your own choice, whether to live single or otherwise. I shall ever think of you as brother.

But my brother, your dear and interesting wife is not dead. All there was about her that made her interesting, and that filled your mind with joy and satisfaction indescribable, still lives and will eternally live. That wife, who made your home an earthly paradise, has lost none of her sweetness. That which made all her form lovely, that which made her eyes to you more precious than gold, and her voice the music of heaven, still lives. All that is dead would never have been loved by us, had it not been the abiding place of that which never dies. You only think of that body, and of its loveliness, as enclosing the intelligence which made it all that was to you desirable, and you never would have wished its stay, if it had not possessed that intelligence. *That is not dead,* and that *only* was your wife. While that form was with you, there was a constant struggling within it, a desire to look beyond, an *indescribable something,* which was constantly seeming to say, *"unbind me, take off these fitters, cut me loose, let me expand and be with God, and dwell with Him — see His glory and know His greatness. This temple is too small for me. I am immortal. I cannot thrive in mortality."* God has heard those groanings after *life,* — has struck off the dog and set the prisoner free, and now she is where there is nothing to retard her progress. She is beyond every influence that affects mortal life. She is lost in the boundless contemplation of God. You would not bring her back. How calmly she watches all your ways. *Yes, she lives. Lives* did I say? Poor word, it does not half express the thought. *She reigns with God.* I can almost hear her saying, husband weep not. Dry up all your tears. I am happier than you could make me. You were overwhelmed with grief when I left that body which you so much loved, but to me it was the beginning of life. It raised the curtain which introduced me into this state of happiness, which to mortals I cannot describe. I cannot come back, but you can come here. Gabriel is here. Jesus is here, and is constantly saying, Father see my hands, my feet, my side. Forgive! O forgive. Could you but see him once, certainly you would love him, for he is beyond expression lovely.

Your Brother,
ABEL BROWN, JR.

P.S. I should be happy to have you preserve the writings of my sister, as I desire to write a small volume for the S. S. library. Therefore, any writings of hers which you may possess, and any account which you may give of her life, sickness, and death, I should be happy to obtain, especially her journal. You will, of course, be willing that her friends should thus prepare a short token of remembrance, of an only daughter and sister. If you concur in this request or suggestion, I wish you would be so kind as to send such writings &c., as may be of service to me to Northampton, Mass. If you could copy what you think would be of some interest on to two, three, or four large double sheets, you would be at liberty to send it by the mail. If you cannot, please retain them until I can get them, or you have an opportunity to send them to this place, or to my father at Prairie Village,[2] or send by mail, if the postage is not more than two or three dollars. Please write me soon. Yours, &c., A. B.

---

[2] *In Wisconsin.*

In reference to the Annual Conventions of the County A. S. Societies in the western section of Massachusetts, under date of January, 1840, he writes:

TO C. P. GROSVENOR.

... The Hampshire county meeting was attended by about 150 delegates. There were a number of ministers present, among whom I recognized our aged Father Nelson. He made a thrilling speech in favor of withdrawing fellowship from all slaveholding churches, and benevolent associations. The Missionary, Bible, Tract, and other societies, which ask and receive robbery for burnt offering, were shown to be unworthy of confidence, almost all of which are directly upholding slavery. The duty of Christians, and especially abolitionists at the polls, was freely discussed. It was distinctly shown that God requires us to regard this cause when we vote. The wickedness of sustaining such papers as the Boston Recorder and Christian Watchman, was clearly portrayed.

In Hampshire county similar resolutions were discussed. That respecting withholding contributions from those benevolent associations, which ask and receive the "price of blood" into their treasuries, occupied about half of the time. It was stated upon authority which will not be disputed, that the A. B. of C. for F. M. [American Board of Commissioners for Foreign Missions] held slaves only about two years since — that their missionaries had remonstrated with the Board, and had attempted to appeal to the churches, respecting the wickedness of slaveholding, and against the reception of money kept back from the slave by fraud, and that the A. B. of C. for F. M. had suppressed the communication. Also, that the abolitionists had remonstrated with these servants of the church, and yet they were conniving at the robbing of the poor. The A[merican] Tract Society was begging for aid, professing to supply the destitute with the gospel, yet amid about 400 volumes of publications, not a word had been said in behalf of the poor and oppressed bondmen in America. The A[merican] Bible Society was and is still, do. [the same]

The A[merican] Baptist Board for Foreign Missions had not only asked robbery for burnt offering, and through their corresponding Secretary, apologized and defended the Baptist slaveholders, but had sent a bold defender of slavery and an unrepenting slaveholder in heart, not in practice, to preach the gospel to the heathen — had made a notorious slaveholder president of the Convention, and still manifested no repentance for their evil doings. I heard all this and more also stated in a public meeting of hundreds. Are these things so?

The Baptists in this region, are awaking to their duty concerning the slave. I hope the "watchman" will sound the alarm. May wisdom from above guide us all, is the desire of your brother in Christ.

A. BROWN.

CHAPTER XI

HIS ANTI-SLAVERY POSITION—THE POLITICAL
CONTEST—CORRESPONDENCE—LEAVES
NORTHAMPTON—SUBSEQUENT SETTLEMENT AT
SAND LAKE, N. Y.—CONTINUATION OF LETTERS

From the correspondence of Mr. Brown, it is evident that he had
no sympathy, neither could he have had participation, in the origin of
the secession movement in 1840 in opposition to the original Anti-Slavery organization. He, however, firmly believed and sustained a system of
political action, which formed the *second* issue of the *new* organization,
but not alone the ground of their separation. In the right, duty and privilege of *women* to act, speak, and vote in the cause of the slave, he ever
believed and maintained.

In a letter addressed to the Massachusetts Anti-Slavery Society, January 27, 1841, he writes that:

> the Hampshire County Society became auxiliary to the Massachusetts Abo-
> lition Society the winter previous, in order that it might get rid of that
> "pestilent fellow, Garrison,"[1] and his (or rather *Christ's*) more humble doc-
> trines of "Peace on earth and good will to men." A few of the more influen-
> tial Abolitionists, were very anxious to be where their influence at the polls,
> and at the church, might not be retarded, by Garrison and his true-isms.

This ground assumed, seemed less objectionable and even *justifiable*
at first in the mind of Mr. Brown, who entertained a high respect for the

[1] *William Lloyd Garrison was the nation's most prominent antislavery spokesmen. His newspaper,* The Liberator, *launched in Boston on January 1, 1831, ushered in a movement calling for
immediate emancipation and led to the widespread organization of anti-slavery societies in the
North united in this cause. Garrison's national prominence continued until* The Liberator *ceased
publication after the Civil War.—Editor.*

piety of the churches, and especially of his ancestral town. In reference to which, he says of Northampton:

> It seemed that "the place where I stood was holy ground." But alas, my confidence for once was misplaced.... The time came for the exercise of that mighty instrument, political action. The Committee of this same County, not only did not sustain their professed principles, but used every effort to defeat those who were desirous to remember, (even at the polls), crushed and bleeding humanity; many of them previously gave their names to secure the election of pro-slavery candidates....
>
> ... With one or two exceptions, the committee sustain ministers, who do not open their mouths for the dumb, and who are among the neglectors of Anti-Slavery efforts. Some members of the Committee, receive their spiritual food from, belong to, and *sustain* a minister, who is an open reviler of the Anti-Slavery cause at large, and a slanderer of the friends here, in particular. The church where they worship, is forbidden to those who plead for the slave.... Yet there are a few, who have not bowed the knee to Baal.[2]

In the political contest of 1840, Mr. Brown found occasion for open and decided reprehension. And to the people of his charge in the ministry, he did not fail especially to warn and dissuade from attendance on those conventional exercises in which log cabins, hard cider, and loud sounding hosannas in favor of "Tippecanoe and Tyler too" [3]were the prominent features, and the only visible arguments of partisans of that period. He also engaged in endeavoring to correct the false impressions of the public mind with reference to the artifice employed to ensure the votes of abolitionists. Such a course in opposition to the popular current of the times called forth the most severe opprobrium, not only from private foes, but from the public prints — professors of Theology and Politics, among whom were Prof. Stowe[4] and J. C. Calhoun[5] — noticing a speech delivered by him in Boston, bearing on some points relative to this eminent statesman.

[2]*A heathen deity.— Editor.*
[3]*In the presidential election that year, the Democrats fielded a ticket of William Henry Harrison for president and John Tyler for vice-president. As Harrison won a prominent Indian battle at Tippecanoe, Indiana, in 1811 and his running mate was Tyler, the slogan was introduced. That U.S. presidential election, incidentally, was the first to use such slogans.— Editor.*
[4]*Calvin Ellis Stowe, the husband of Harriet Beecher Stowe, who in 1840 was as yet unknown and unpublished.— Editor.*
[5]*John C. Calhoun, U.S. senator from the state of South Carolina.— Editor.*

The following letters from a correspondent contain an exposition of Mr. Brown's course at this crisis of political excitement:

Fredericksburgh, Va., Aug. 17th, 1840.

REV. AND DEAR SIR:— I have seen in the newspapers, a letter addressed by you to "Mr. B. F. Hallett," upon the subject of a letter, which had been circulated privately at the North, written by a member or members of Congress "by authority from Gen. Harrison," &c. And I have also noticed since, in some of the papers, accounts that a *wanton outrage* had been committed upon your person — that you had been insulted and abused, &c., in consequence of some statements, which you made in the correspondence above referred to; which correspondence, it seems, grew out of some remarks which you made in a public meeting, in relation to the letter, which was written and circulated by authority from Gen. Harrison, to aid in his election. Being myself a minister of the Baptist denomination, and an ardent friend of human rights and liberty, I have taken the liberty to address you this letter, and to ask you to give me a full account of the whole matter. I am prompted to this by no one, but for my own satisfaction. I wish to know, if we as a people and nation have come to this, that ministers of the gospel, in their persons and effects, are not safe from the brutal assaults of the Sons of Belial[6] upon publishing without reserve their own views, or in giving a plain statement of facts, in relation to any matter, which may have transpired within their knowledge.

I have for some time, been thinking of taking a preaching tour through some of the northern States, and even on this account, I should be glad to know, to what extent the freedom of speech and the press is abridged; or to what extent, an abridgement has been attempted.

I know that the system of *Lynch Law* has been practiced in our country for several years back, to an alarming extent; and which, together with other scenes, which frequently occur under both religious and political excitement, makes me sometimes tremble for the Republic.

In addition to the facts, in relation to the assault, which is said to have been made on you, I should also be glad that you would give me the particulars of the "secret letter," if there is any thing of note, besides what you wrote to Mr. Hallett.

　　　　　　　　　　　　　　　　　　　I am Yours, &c.

　　　　　　　　　　　　　　　　　　　JOHN CLARK.

REV. ABEL BROWN

---

[6]*Satan.* — *Editor.*

From the Same.

Sept. 8th, 1840.

My Dear Brother:— Your interesting letter of the 21st ult., was received, and as it had been intimated in some of our papers, that you had been abused, and also reports circulated, prejudicial to your character and standing, as a minister of the gospel, I have made your expose of the wickedness of the ciderites[7] public, in which, the intelligent will clearly see the true cause of all the abuse and persecution which you have received.

The party now, will no doubt, devise some new mode of attack, as I understand, they have already declared here that you are an impostor, *politically* so at least, and that you only publish those things, to injure the whig cause. I trust, however, my brother that you will feel a *consolation,* in the midst of these afflictions, from the consideration, that "the master of the house," was treated in like manner, and for a similar cause; that of preaching against wickedness. *He* hesitated not to testify of the world, that their deeds were evil.

My principal object in writing to you at this time is, to guard you against any letter or letters, which you may receive from here or hereabouts, unless subscribed to by me; for you have not many friends here, and they would not write to you without my knowledge, and your enemies may, with a view to entangle you, and expose you in the papers. Should your therefore, receive any letter from this quarter, in which I am not recognized, you had better write to me upon the subject; that is, if you shall feel disposed to answer it at all.

This same cider party have been guilty, both in Ohio and Indiana, of the sacrilegious blasphemy of administering the supper, to their deluded followers and converts to Harrison, with parched corn and hard cider, saying, "take this in remembrance of Old Tip!"

I will, if I can, put my hand upon it, and send you the paper containing the full account of these proceedings. I have thought, that certainly, the monstrous wickedness of the time, was without a parallel in the history of the world.

I remain yours, in the Kingdom and patience of Jesus Christ.

John Clark.

The foolish excess to which the people had been transported at this period of political excitement must, in the cool reflection of "after days," appear like anything but a rational procedure to secure the highest gift

---

[7]*Those who favor consumption of alcohol.*— *Editor.*

of the people in the election of its chief ruler, however worthy the candidate of their suffrages might be.

In the midst of the most virulent opposition, Mr. Brown succeeded in accomplishing much good for the prosperity of the church over which he was placed, yet declined an invitation to remain longer as Pastor of the same.[8]

In the spring of 1841 on his removal to New York, he accepted of a call to the pastoral charge of the Baptist church in Sand Lake. He there pursued the same course of faithful teaching, exhortation and rebuke, as occasion required.

An account of the progress of Temperance in which Mr. Brown might well congratulate himself in having helped to achieve, written by that warm and distinguished friend of every good and noble enterprise, E. W. Goodwin,[9] and a few letters addressed to the editor of the *Tocsin of Liberty*[10] indicative of his views and continued course of action, are herein inserted.

[8]*In a letter to* The Liberator, *dated January 7, 1841, he described his disappointment with anti-slavery efforts in the Northampton area that led to his departure:* "The Executive Committee of the Hampshire County Anti-Slavery Society have made direct efforts to defeat the election of men to any important offices, who were in favor of the abolition of slavery.... It has publicly been declaimed that the leading members of the Committee would vote a pro-slavery ticket, and as it was declaimed, so they have done.... These be it remembered, are the officers of a society, who changed its auxiliaryship because Garrison and the Liberator paralyzed their efforts to effect the abolition of slavery by political action.... Some of the committee are members of churches which refuse to take any action against slavery, whose ministers are as dumb as the dogs spoken of by the prophet, who will not suffer an anti-slavery sermon to be preached in their pulpits, especially on the Sabbath, and whose communion is always polluted by the greatest haters of abolition which our country affords.... There has been no effort made to sustain anti-slavery meetings in this vicinity by this committee, but on the contrary its influence has been directly against any agitation of the subject....— Editor.* ("Recantation," The Liberator, *22 January 1841: 14.)*

[9]*Edwin W. Goodwin was editor of the* Tocsin of Liberty, *later the* Albany Patriot. *He worked with Abel Brown and Charles Torrey in the Eastern New York Anti-Slavery Society in aiding fugitive slaves. He also was a prominent portraitist, who subjects included William Henry Seward, New York governor, senator, and U.S. secretary of state; James Birney, Liberty party candidate for president; and President Martin Van Buren.— Editor.* ("The Late E.W. Goodwin," Albany Patriot, *30 Dec. 1846: 30.)*

[10]*The* Tocsin of Liberty *was perhaps the most radical abolitionist newspaper in the U.S. It was founded in Albany by Edwin W. Goodwin and J.N. Tucker in 1841 and in the coming months welcomed the additions of Abel Brown and Charles Torrey. It became infamous for reporting brazen accounts of the aid it was providing to fugitive slaves. After two years, its name was changed to the* Albany Patriot. *In 1847, the* American Freeman, *an abolitionist newspaper in Wisconsin, called the* Patriot *"the most strongly reformatory newspaper in the U.S."— Editor.* ("Albany Patriot," Albany Patriot, *2 Feb. 1848: 47.)*

SAND LAKE BAPTIST CHURCH IN SAND LAKE, N.Y. (PHOTOGRAPH BY TOM CALARCO).

GREAT MASS TEMPERANCE MEETING.

Auburn, Feb. 1st, 1841.

This is the day advertised for a great mass Temperance meeting in this place. Well, it is now, while I write, about 12 o'clock M. [noon], and it really seems as if the great fountains of the deep are broken up among the people. The principal street is one moving mass of men, women and children. In the mean time the great AUBURN HOUSE, (now kept by J. M. Brown, on Temperance principles) is overflowing. Gen. Riley is here, and a host of reformers, ready to take the platform as orators in the different churches, which will be filled to overflowing at 2 o'clock. Then there are bands of music, and choirs of singers, heading the masses as they march in, from the different towns, with banners and appropriate devices and mottos. Altogether it is grand beyond expression. I can hardly realize that I am not dreaming. How strange! A few short years ago, temperance was very small here.[11] Now men are complete enthusiasts for it. Once the grocery interest held the dominion, and swayed an influence over the entire village. Now it is weak and powerless. Indeed all along my journey to this place east of

---

[11]*This was the same Auburn where Brown was attacked only seven years earlier by a mob intent on murdering him because he preached against intemperance.—Editor.*

Utica, men can scarcely think of anything else, talk of anything else or hear of anything else but temperance. They seem almost to have forgotten the ordinary avocations of business and gone to work *en masse* as moral reformers. Tell Abel Brown, that the man Clute — formerly the great embodyment of intemperance and rum selling, who whipped him while collecting facts and laboring as temperance agent, has turned his liquor into the streets and signed the Reformer's pledge, and has become a good citizen. And that the same mob that howled and dogged him from the place before whose ferocity he was compelled to flee for his life, are now, many of them as energetically engaged as reformers. Ah, what an encouragement this for his reflection. What an encouragement for all who may suffer reproach and shame and poverty in the holy cause of moral reform, to endure patiently, with strong hope. The *day* of rejoicing will come.

Albany, Aug. 23d, 1841.

WM. LLOYD GARRISON: Very Dear Brother — I am always happy when writing to you, because I feel assured that you will publish the truth, though it should render you odious. Go on, my brother. Toil here, and rest not, until Christ shall call you to himself. My spirit cannot rest, so long as my brethren are crushed by the iron hoof of oppression.

What follows may strike you with terror, but it is nevertheless true. Mr. Jones affirmed it to be so in the presence of Mrs. Stewart and Miss Briggs of Troy.

Slaveholders are received into the Mission churches; and the Methodist, Baptist, Presbyterian, and Congregational Missionaries among those tribes, are unanimous, so far as he is acquainted, in sustaining slaveholders, as Christian brethren in the churches! That they (the Missionaries) neither preach against this practice, nor use means to put it out of the church. That almost all the Missionaries, either own or hire slaves of their masters to work, and pay the master for their services! That he [Jones] has been obliged in cases of sickness, to do it himself. That the Rev. Mr. Mason, a Baptist missionary, was obliged to leave the country, because he *would* oppose slavery! Rev. Mr. Kellam left, I suppose, on the same account. That the Rev. Mr. Hatch and wife, Baptist missionaries among the Choctaws, left, because they could not conscientiously sustain slavery. That Rev. Mr. Flemming and Rev. Mr. Dodge, M. D., missionaries of the American Board, left on the same account. That the Rev. Mr. Potts, Baptist missionary among the Choctaws, either owns or hires slaves of their masters, that he is open and public in this, and all understand that he sustains slavery, and receives slaveholders into the church, as good, pious Christians! That Rev. Mr. P., a Methodist missionary among the Choctaws, owns a number of slaves, and treats them as such; and that he shot and killed a white man, whom he supposed was stealing one of his slaves, and that Rev. Mr. P. is in full fellowship with the other missionaries! That he (Mr. Jones) has received the communion services from his hands &c.

It would need a man or woman of considerable faith, as they would perhaps mistrust that "a negro stealer," had come among them, and the Rev. Mr. Perry might be appointed to shoot the fanatics; especially, if he should be found among *his* negroes!

ABEL BROWN.

[MORE FROM THE *TOCSIN OF LIBERTY*]

Elder John Peek of Cazenovia, in this State, who is (or was) traveling at the South, as an agent of the American Baptist Home Missionary Society, writing from Alabama to the N Y. Baptist Register, says:

"I saw in this place a colored ministering brother, belonging to Montgomery church, named Caesar Blackmoor, who is owned by the Alabama Association, and is appointed a missionary to the colored people, under the direction of three trustees, and preaches in the bounds of the Association and elsewhere, at their direction. Brother C. informed me that he has been very successful in his labors, and preaches to great acceptance to both white and colored brethren. He baptized last year on his mission one hundred and ten persons of his own color. As a man, a Christian, and a minister of the gospel, his character is irreproachable. He preached on Lord's day in the afternoon in the same pulpit that I had occupied in the morning, but my health would not permit of my going to hear him."

Shameful! AN AMBASSADOR OF CHRIST MADE A CHATTEL! *The Minister of the Gospel of* **one** *color is placed on a perfect level with the HORSE of his Brother Minister!!* One ambassador the *property, chattel,* of another ambassador. The *Representative of Christ,* for such ministers claim to be, is made the personal property of Christ's church, and sent out as a *Missionary* to preach the glad news of salvation, "peace on earth and good will to man," *with a chain on his neck! The Bible in one hand,* and *the other chained to his back,* to keep him from running away! The proceeds of preaching used to send the gospel of peace to the Isles of the sea!

A Baptist Minister gave $100 to a Missionary Society, and asserted as a reason why he was able, that he had made a good sale of slaves!

The Board of the American and Foreign Missionary Society refuse to testify against slavery, because they could not obtain the support of the south if they should.

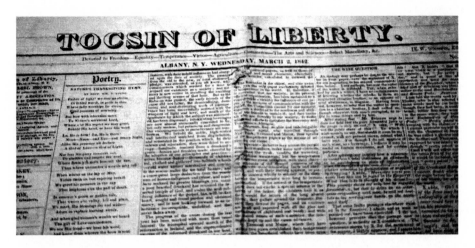

FRONT PAGE OF THE *Tocsin of Liberty*, MARCH 2, 1842 (PUBLISHED: ALBANY, N.Y.: THE SENATORIAL COMMITTEE OF THE 3D DISTRICT. RARE BOOKS E441.M46 V. 285 NO. 32 MAPCASE. COURTESY OF THE DIVISION OF RARE AND MANUSCRIPT COLLECTIONS, CORNELL UNIVERSITY LIBRARY).

We view the church as being in a very wicked position, and as deserving the frowns of offended mercy. We believe the frown of God rests upon American churches, and our *alarm* cry to them is and shall be, in earnest voice:

"Oh, rouse ye — ere the storm comes forth —
The gathered wrath of God and man —
Like that which wasted Egypt's earth,
When hail and fire above it ran."

Sand Lake, June 13th, 1842.

DEAR BROTHER BROWN: — I feel as if I could weep tears of blood over the apparent desolating prospects of Zion. Whether God is about to give up his people, and let them have the desire of their own hearts, or whether his judgments are fast ripening, that will be sent to bring them back to Him, that they may delight to do His will, requires the scrutinizing eye of that God, who alone is able to scan the motives, and trace the windings of the human soul. I feel as though we were called upon to contend inch by inch with the adversary of all good, for the right to our master's territory.

The cloven foot never appeared to me more apparent, and more deformed, than it did yesterday in our church, in the determination of our Deacons, that they would do what they could to prevent your going as a delegate from this church, to the Association at Poughkeepsie. The main objection of Dea. Fox was, that you would agitate the subject of slavery, and it struck him very forcibly, that you had neglected to take a letter of dismission from this church, purposely that you might get the delegation; and this he thought very mysterious. Dea. Gregory had objections, but he did not make them known, and although it was voted that you should go as a delegate, yet the vote was afterwards rescinded.

I hope the Lord will direct you in the way he would have you go, and if it is his will that you should, that all the causes of discouragement will not prevent your being present at the Association. Trust in God — he will sustain you. If means are wanting, I will bear a part of the expense. Yours as ever,

C.H. GREGORY.[12]

[FROM ABEL BROWN TO A FORMER CLASSMATE WHO IS A MISSIONARY IN ASIA]

Sand Lake, Rensselaer Co.,
N.Y., June 28th, 1841.

J. H. VINTON, *MISSIONARY AT MAULMAIN, ASIA:*

Very Dear Brother — You will, doubtless, recognize my name, as that of a brother of your acquaintance, in the Hamilton Institution. I trouble you only to make a few inquiries, as we are in perils among brethren. Whether they are false or not, "God knoweth." You know that American Slavery is upheld and supported by the Baptist churches, I suppose. I will, however, make a few *statements* in order that I may be fully understood.

There are about 125,000, or one sixth part of all the Baptist church members of the U. S., slaves. Almost all the influential Baptists of the Southern States, both ministers and laymen, are slaveholders, and within two or more years past have come out boldly and published sermons, letters and pamphlets, making God, the Father, Son and Holy Ghost, the author and sustainers of slavery. Eld. Fuller, late preacher for the U. S. Baptist Tri. Convention, has just published a document, boldly advocating these doctrines. Dr. Wm. B. Johnson, the President of the Convention, is another. It is known that many of the southern Baptists raise negroes and sell, and almost every southern church upholds this traffic.

---

[12]*C.H. Gregory of Sand Lake, a member of the Sand Lake Baptist Church where Brown was pastor and a member of the executive committee of the Eastern New York Anti-Slavery. He was possibly a relative of Daniel Gregory, one of the owners of the glass factory in West Sand Lake that local historian Judith Rowe claims transported freedom-seekers in barrels between their other locations in Lanesboro, Massachusetts, and Durhamville in central New York.— Editor. ("Eastern New York Anti-Slavery Society Organizational Meeting," The Emancipator, 12 May 1842: 7; Judith Rowe, town historian of Sand Lake, N.Y., personal interview by editor, January 1999.)*

One year ago last April, a convention of Baptists was held in the city of New York to concoct, and carry out measures, for the overthrow of slavery in the Baptist church. The most we did, was to prepare an address to the southern Brethren, telling them our grief, and exhorting them affectionately to cease to buy, sell and hold men as slaves. Eld. Galusha was Chairman of the Convention, and signed the address. We sent them to every church and minister in the Southern States.

The result has been, that the southern churches came out plainly, and justified themselves; said that it was right in the sight of God, to hold property in man; and demanded that the northern churches, should either turn out the brethren who published the address from all and every office in the Baptist Benevolent Societies, and receive and fellowship the southern churches in buying and selling and holding slaves, or they, the southern Baptists, will withhold all money from the Treasuries of the Home and Foreign Mission and Bible Societies. The Boards of these Societies have written letters, and sent their agents to the South, assuring them that they utterly disapprove of the efforts of the Anti-Slavery brethren. The Home and Foreign Mission and Bible Societies have, at their annual meetings, rejected the Anti-Slavery brethren, even put out Eld. Galusha from an office in the F. M. Society, only because he was one of the brethren, who could not conscientiously receive slaveholders into communion and fellowship, in a Christian church. A number of the most strenuous slaveholders (Baptist ministers) have been in Boston, New York, Albany, and have been invited to preach, and received as Baptist Christians in good standing. This has been done by the South, I suppose, to see whether there was any disposition on the part of northern Baptists, to put away slavery.

Again, we are exceedingly grieved, that these Societies should suffer their Boards to send agents to the southern Baptist churches, to collect a part of the money, which is robbed from the blacks, to send the gospel to heathen in other countries. Those agents which are sent South, are particularly understood as being such as will not reprove slaveholders, and indeed they all, I believe, are every month writing home letters to be published, telling what excellent Christians our dear southern Baptists are. They all oppose, and many publicly condemn those of us who are laboring to uproot slavery.

Again, I am exceedingly grieved, that yourself and other missionaries, should suffer yourselves to be supported by money collected from men who rob the poor, and some of the money is actually received from those who sell men, and is a part of the profits, and that too, without offering a single reproof, through the Board for such robbery. The slaveholders make their boasts, that they are sustained by the missionaries in this way, and that the Board and agents sustain them, and condemn the Anti-Slavery Baptists.

Now, my dear brother, I have to ask you if you will not come out, and write letters to the Board, remonstrating against their sending agents South to collect money, robbed from the bleeding slaves, and also refuse to accept support from those who rob the poor. Rest assured one such letter sent home, asking to be supported by money which is not the price of blood, will do much toward arresting the pro-slavery spirit, which is rife among us. And it will secure you and all who take a similar course, an abundant support. I have done paying money to a Board, that helps rob the poor. I cannot send money to those, who, at the same time, ask the price of blood, and sanction the crime of extorting it from my colored brethren under the lash. We sent the last $25,000 last Week. But if the missionaries will come out and condemn this crime and ask to be supported by the earnings of honesty, there are many brethren who would go from house to house and from town to town, and collect money for their support. If you write letters to the Board, please send a copy, to me, for the Board, I fear, will suppress them.

I am having no quarrel with any of these men — have as high a place among my brethren as I deserve. All I wish is, that God may be honored in setting the oppressed free. *Since 1836, I have been traveling much — about two years on the Ohio river and vicinity — for the past three years in Massachusetts, Connecticut and New York. I have been laboring in behalf of the oppressed* [editor's emphasis]. God is fast breaking the yoke, and soon, I trust, I shall have the privilege of preaching Christ to the dying blacks of the South. I have been there and seen their abject heathenism. About two millions of them are as really heathen as those in Asia.

I have often desired to be with you in Asia, but could not, without being sent by a board, that takes the robbery of the poor for burnt offering. I have lived in constant persecution, until within a year past. Three times I have been publicly whipped, once, more than fifty lashes. I have been stoned and mobbed very, very many times, but always in the free States. Very many times have I been stopped by the leading ministers, when I was referring to the heathen at home, as we all do to the heathen abroad. Never, until this year, would Hudson River Association let a word be said in behalf of the slaves; but this year we discussed a resolution about two hours. I was called to order again and again, but the Moderator knowing that I was in order, did not stop me, yet they would not pass a resolution, saying that slavery was a moral evil. However, I think that good was done, and hoping in God, I trust, with his assistance, I shall persevere. The Association appointed me one of their delegates, to attend the annual meeting of the N. Y. State Convention, and the A. B. Home Mission Society, where they must know, I will bring up the case of the slave. The best of all is, God is with us.

My kind regards to your wife, Brother and Sister Howard. And now, may the blessed God help you to do just what will meet his approbation, in consideration of two millions of heathen in this land, and another million that cannot read the Bible.

I shall probably make this my earthly home, for two years or more. The fatigues of myself and family for four or five years past, render it necessary.

When we meet where Jesus is, then we will talk over our trials and troubles, and blessings. I have had the happiness of baptizing about seventy, within the past year.

From your sinful brother, yet hoping in Christ,
ABEL BROWN.

TO N. P. ROGERS, EDITOR
OF THE HERALD OF FREEDOM.[13]

Sand Lake, N. Y., Aug. 17th, 1841.

DEAR BROTHER:— In the last number of the Liberator, I find an article copied from the Herald, headed *"Rev. Jonathan Davis"* In that article you call upon Bro. Murray, and consequently upon all Baptist abolitionists, to renounce the denomination. And you speak of him as having fellowship with the denomination, and as being one of the most worthy among the abolition host, among the Baptists. Bro. Murray is able to answer for himself. As you have cut loose from all denominations, I should be happy to have you point out to me my duty to the Baptist connection, if I am not already doing it.

1st. I am a regular ordained Baptist Minister, and a member of a Baptist church.

2d. I firmly believe that it is my duty to preach that men should repent, believe in Christ and be baptized; and when men or women, black or white, do repent and believe in Christ, I baptize them if it is their request. I then suppose they are members of Christ's visible church on earth, and are at liberty to associate themselves with a body of baptized believers, subject only to the laws and ordinances of Christ himself. They are subject to the laws or authority of no council, association, society, or convention, but elect whom they will, to teach and instruct them in the way of Christ more

[13]The Herald of Freedom, *referred to here, was a New Hampshire antislavery newspaper based in Concord edited by Nathaniel P. Rogers from 1838 to 1846. Rogers was an early supporter and promoter of the Hutchinson Family antislavery singing group.* — Editor.

perfectly. They have power and authority from Christ himself, to ordain or set apart ministers, deacons, or any other officers which Christ appoints; and such officers, when set apart, have no more authority, than any man or woman in the church. Each and every member has one vote, and only one, in deciding any matter whatever, which concerns the church. No sin whatever, is to be practised by them, either in an individual or collective capacity. If a brother or sister fall in sin, and cannot be restored in the spirit of meekness, fellowship is to be withdrawn from them, and the offender counted not as an enemy, but admonished as a brother. Of such a church, am I a member. As their minister, when permitted by Providence to be with them, I do not fail to rebuke and reprove sin, and when abroad I do the same. We would no sooner receive a slaveholder into the church, than we would any other thief; and I would as soon baptize old Satan himself, as a believer in, or a practiser of slavery.

3d. Whenever I am appointed by the church to attend any religious meeting, it is taken for granted, that I will carry out the principles held and practised by the church; that I will not, even by silence, give my sanction to sin in any form. If I am sent to attend an Anti-Slavery, or any other convention, and they refuse (like the National Baptist Anti-Slavery Convention) to obey the whole truth, I am in duty bound to faithfully rebuke them, and use my influence to bring the body to embrace the truth, the whole truth, and nothing but the truth. If after faithful trial, the enemies of God prevail, escape from them; always remembering to bear faithful witness against their evil deeds.

4th. So far as the "National Baptist Triennial Convention" is concerned, I am free to declare, that its last meeting was composed of *thieves* and *robbers,* and *their abettors, as much worse than common horse and sheep thieves, as men are better than horses and sheep.* I fully believe, that those who sanctioned their proceedings, by neglecting to rebuke them, and by giving their votes for thieves and robbers, are partakers of their sins.

5th. These views I endeavor to advocate on all suitable occasions. I have published them to the world. A. Brother was kind enough to take me aside from the Baptist Anti-Slavery Convention in New York city, in April last, and advise me to leave the Convention, and go off along with Garrison & Co., but I expect it will be duty to go back next spring, and rebuke your Bro. Worth, Colver & Co.[14] There is yet some hope that they will come to repentance.

[14]*After several years as pastor of various Adirondack congregations, the Rev. Nathaniel Colver, a native of Champlain, New York, assumed the pastorate at the Bottskill Baptist Church in Union Village, New York, Washington County, fifty miles north of Albany, in 1834. That year he took up abolition in earnest and from that time devoted most of his energies to the cause. While at Bottskill,*

6th. I am not particularly anxious to be called a Baptist, but as I understand the term Baptist to mean "opposition to all sin," and as those who do not practically and really oppose all sin, are only Baptist hypocrites, I think it duty to still belong to a Baptist church. During the past year, amid all the opposition which Baptist hypocrites and their abettors could bring against me, it has been my happy privilege to baptize more persons, than any other Baptist minister in the western half of Massachusetts.

In conclusion, my brother, let me ask you faithfully to rebuke me, if I have not renounced the present Baptist denomination in the U. S., as far as

THE REV. NATHANIEL COLVER (FROM J.A. SMITH, *Memoir of Nathaniel Colver, D.D.* BOSTON: DURKEE AND FOXCROFT, PUBLISHERS, 1873).

duty requires. As you stand aloof from all church organization, you may be better prepared to judge than myself.

I do not patronize any of the hypocritical Baptist periodicals. I pay nothing to their societies, and receive nothing from them. I do endeavor to rebuke their sins, whenever an opportunity presents. In addition to these labors in behalf of common humanity, I still feel it a duty to preach, and baptize in the name of Jesus Christ, all who give evidence of repentance towards God and faith in the Redeemer.

Your brother in Christ,

ABEL BROWN

he lectured in the Adirondacks, Vermont, and Massachusetts as an agent for the New York State and American Anti-Slavery societies. In 1839, he left Union Village and shepherded the Tremont Tabernacle in Boston to national prominence in the cause for emancipation. Nevertheless, he is being attacked by Abel Brown here because of his refusal to condemn Baptist ministers who owned slaves. In defense of Colver, it should be noted that he had close relations with a number of southern colleagues and in 1834 was offered a pastorate at a southern church, but refused after visiting and witnessing slavery first hand. It was this experience that impelled him to take up the antislavery cause. (Rev. J.A. Smith, Memoir of Nathaniel Colver, D.D., Boston: Durkee and Foxcroft, Publishers, 1873: 124.)— Editor.

CHAPTER XII

REMOVAL TO ALBANY—LABORS IN BEHALF
OF REFUGEES—ENGAGES AS PUBLISHER
OF THE *TOCSIN OF LIBERTY*—FORMATION
OF THE EASTERN N.Y. ANTI-SLAVERY
SOCIETY—FUGITIVE SLAVE CASES

Early in the year 1842, Mr. Brown engaged in labors for the slave in Albany: a city which from its location on the banks of the Hudson was the constant resort of fugitive slaves when traveling in the direction of the North Star to seek shelter under the wing of Queen Victoria's dominion, or happily, perchance, to find an asylum in the nominally free states. To effect this, and also to render their flight effectual and speed them on their course to the goal of freedom, it was found necessary that a systematic train of operations be devised by committees formed for the specific purpose of aiding those who thus sought the protection of friends in a strange land. Mr. Brown entered anew into this department of labor with all the zeal and benevolent enthusiasm which had heretofore prompted him when alone on the borders of slave states to pursue in rescuing from slavery the helpless victims of American oppression.

He also engaged as publisher of the *Tocsin of Liberty*, a paper conducted by E. W. Goodwin, whose ability as an editor was equaled only by his philanthropic zeal and devotion to the interests of the slave. It was then that the *Tocsin*[1] rung with the joyful intelligence of the arrival of fugitive slaves from the land of chains — and often too sounded the note of alarm to the *watch*men on freedom's walls, who neither slumbered nor slept in their untiring vigilance to *protect* these "outcasts" of humanity from further invasion of southern manhunters and legalized robbers.

[1]*Literally meaning alarm.—Editor.*

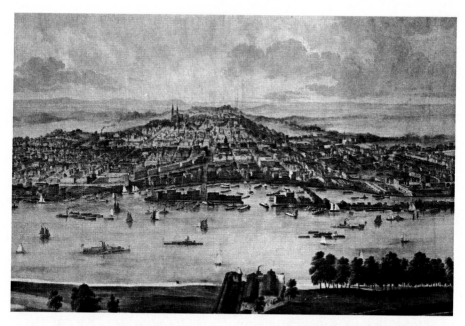

Top: Albany, circa 1850 (collection of the New-York Historical Society, negative #276236). **Right: *Tocsin of Liberty*** Masthead showing Abel Brown as the publisher (Published: Albany, N.Y.: The Senatorial Central Committee of the 3d District. Rare Books E441.M46 V. 285 no. 32 Mapcase. Courtesy of the Division of Rare and Manuscript Collections, Cornell University Library).

The Toesin of Liberty,
Published Weekly, at Albany, N. Y.
BY ELDER ABEL BROWN,
Under the special patronage of the
ALBANY LIBERTY ASSOCIATION.
At $1.50 per annum to Companies of 10,
Or $2.00 the single copy, per mail,
ALWAYS IN ADVANCE.
Devoted to Freedom—Equality—Temperance—Virtue—Agriculture—Commerce—Legislative Proceedings—The News of the Day, Foreign and Domestic—The Arts and Sciences—Trades—Select Miscellany, &c.

Office No. 56 (Up Stairs,) State-Street.

☞ Ministers of the Gospel, Lecturing Agents, and others, are requested to act as Agents.

Clergymen who obtain for us two subscribers and send us Four Dollars in advance, free of postage, or Six Dollars and Four subscribers, will receive our paper a year gratis.

⁎ A liberal commission to travelling agents. Address the publisher, Albany, N. Y.   Jan. 4, 1842.

Those editors who will insert the above, shall have a like favor from us.

FORMATION OF THE EASTERN N. Y. A. S. SOCIETY

Mr. Brown was one of the prominent movers in the organization of this society.

The following is an account of the proceedings of the convention, gathered from the secretary's reports:

In accordance with a call, previously published, the Convention met in Albany on the 20th day of April, 1842, for the purpose of considering the propriety of forming an Eastern N. Y. Antislavery Society, and for doing such other business as might legitimately come before them. The meeting was called to order by Elder Abel Brown, prayer was offered by Rev. Mr. Shipherd[2] of Troy.

The meeting was held at the City Hall and continued in session two days.

There were about one hundred names reported as delegates, representing twelve Counties, viz:— New York, Columbia, Albany, Schenectady, Washington, Saratoga, Schoharie, Montgomery, Fulton, Oneida and Madison. There were also several anti-slavery friends present from three other states, viz: Vermont, Massachusetts and Rhode Island, who by request took seats in the Convention and participated in its deliberations. With the exception of one or two occasions of differences of opinion, wherein some feeling was manifested on both sides, the Convention was characterized with unusual harmony, and a firmness of purpose to go steadily forward, towards the goal for which abolitionists started.

Among the speakers during the series of meetings were Gerrit Smith, Henry B. Stanton,[3] and others whose powers of eloquence and effective address contributed much to the interest of the occasion. John *A.* Collins and Charles Lenox Remond[4] were also present at the solicitation of Mr. Brown, bearing with them the great *Irish Antislavery Address* with its sixty thousand signatures, headed by Daniel O'Connell[5] and Theobald Matthew.

[2] *From 1832 to 1834 and again from 1839 to 1842, the Rev. Fayette Shipherd, an Underground Railroad conductor, was pastor of Bethel Free Congregation, organized for the spiritual benefit of the boatmen in 1832 on the corner of Fifth and Fulton streets in Troy. In 1893 he organized and became pastor of the Free Church there on east side of Seventh Street between Albany and State street. Both his churches in Troy were the site of abolitionist and Liberty party conventions, and the site of lectures by Abel Brown. In his youth, Shipherd was a follower of evangelist Charles Finney, and he came from a family of diehard abolitionists: his father Zebulon, a U.S. congressman, was active in the New York State Anti-Slavery Society; his brother John was the founder of Oberlin College; his son Jacob was a participant in the Oberlin-Wellington fugitive slave rescue; and his daughter married into the Bragdon family, Underground Railroad conductors in Oswego and Rochester.— Editor. (Letter from Fayette Shipherd to Charles Hicks, Rensselaer County, N.Y., 24 Nov. 1840 [Vermont Historical Society]; Bragdon Family Papers, Rare Books and Special Collections, Rush Rhees Library, University of Rochester.)*

[3] *Prominent antislavery leader and lecturer, and husband of feminist Elizabeth Cady Stanton.— Editor.*

[4] *John A. Collins was the general agent for the Massachusetts Anti-Slavery Society and a close associate of William Lloyd Garrison. He also was close to Frederick Douglass during the early days of his career and helped him get started on the antislavery lecture circuit. Charles Lenox Remond, a native of Salem, Massachusetts, was the first African American hired as an antislavery lecturer by the American Anti-Slavery Society (in 1838). He continued as a lecturer throughout the antebellum period, traveling widely throughout the North. In the years approaching the Civil War, he became a staunch advocate of using force to end slavery.— Editor.*

[5] *Daniel O'Connell was an Irish Catholic leader who championed Catholic rights and Irish separation from England. He was the first Irish Catholic elected to Parliament and the most important political figure in Ireland during the first half of the nineteenth century.— Editor.*

Among the resolutions, the following is found in reference to political action. "We pledge ourselves in the words of Gen. Washington, who said, 'Slavery can and ought to be abolished by law, and so far as my suffrage will go, it shall never be wanting.'"

In the election of officers, Mr. Brown was chosen corresponding secretary and general agent of the society. The counties embraced in this division included all those bordering the Hudson, those on Long and Staten Islands, together with Delaware, Schoharie, Montgomery, Schenectady, Fulton, Essex, Hamilton, Washington and Warren.

The field of operations (thus defined) being comparatively new, even at this period of the antislavery enterprise, will account for the apathy and want of interest in some and opposition in other places to the movement. However, there were a few "true and tried friends of the slave," who were neither slow nor weary in well doing in their efforts to upbuild this great and mighty cause, while traversing the valleys and hills of the noble Hudson. Although pledged in the various offices assigned him to sustain the work in this department (involving both his time and powers in no small degree), yet Mr. Brown found occasion still to labor for other objects, alike important to the public weal and to the welfare of individuals.

A few instances on record designate his labors at this period as also some articles published by him in the *Tocsin of Liberty*, concerning his agency for the vigilance committee and fugitive slaves:

> 1842, April 23d. Notified meeting (by writing to all members of Ex. Committee.)
>
> April 28, 29. Spent most of the time preparing for, and getting up a meeting to oppose licensing the sale of spiritous liquors in Albany.
>
> April 31. Sabbath — spent in preaching on dock, and resting.

The following advertisement [in the *Tocsin of Liberty*] from Mr. Brown in behalf of a poor colored brother shows on what conditions many slaveholders are willing to relinquish their slaves:

$1,800 WANTED TO BUY A WIFE AND SIX CHILDREN

Albany, Mon. Morning, May 1, 1842.

E. W. GOODWIN, Esq. — Dear Sir: — There arrived in this city from Washington D. C. during the last week, a man by the name of FREEMEN, a carpenter by trade. He has letters from gentlemen of high standing and respectability, in Washington, and also from gentlemen in Charleston, S. C. He has formerly been a slave of the Hon. Mr. B., late Sec'y of the U. S. Navy,[6] from whom he purchased himself for the sum of $800. The said Sec'y now holds in bondage his wife and six children; and utterly refuses to give them up unless the husband and father will pay him the sum of $1,800, and has promised to retain them nine months, to give the father an opportunity of purchasing them at the expiration of that time: otherwise they are to be sold, and perhaps separated, never more to meet on earth. Mr. Freemen wishes to obtain in this and adjoining places, the sum of $200, which with what he has now in his possession, will enable him to obtain from that *Honored American Robber,* that which now justly belongs to him. He is willing to work for a term of years, for any person who will furnish him means to thus bless his family. Those who love to aid the perishing, are respectfully invited to send donations to the subscriber, No. 8 South-Pearl St.

Yours, in haste,
ABEL BROWN.

A fine opportunity was thus, not infrequently, afforded those who affirm so great a desire that the slaveholder should be paid for his living, though actually dead, "property" in human beings. This is a reward, however, that never should he granted, except, (in the case of no alternative) as a ransom in the liberation of a slave.

[FROM BROWN'S JOURNAL]

May 2d. Visited Poughkeepsie, and lectured in the evening, to a small audience in a corner of the village. The Churches were all closed against lectures from Antislavery Agents.

May 4. Visited Peekskill, but could not find even a hovel, in which to lecture for the slave. The rummies threatened me with a *mob,* if I dared to lecture, and to pull down any house, that should be opened for the purpose. The Washingtonians, got me up a Temperance meeting, and cheered me on, until I was tired. Ascertained that my appointment was not out in Sing Sing[7]—Saw one of the Levites, as also a priest, from that place; but they were as far from doing any thing, as the Priests and Levites of old were, for the man that fell among thieves.

[6]*George E. Badger.—Editor.*
[7]*Sing Sing prison, located along the Hudson River in Ossining, New York, about 30 miles north of New York City.—Editor.*

XII. Removal to Albany

May 5th. Took passage for Brooklyn, and after a long and painful talk with pro-slavery ministers, arrived in New York and from thence to Brooklyn. The dear Christian Churches of that City, shut me out doors. Consequently, my appointment failed. The day following — Spent in obtaining a meeting hereafter, and in consultation with the friends — shall probably obtain a Methodist house soon, and have the assurance of the kind cooperation of the friends of the cause. All appear happy, that the Committee are willing to engage in this good work, and I find a few, to sustain us in all places.

June 3d. Wrote and prepared letters for the Am. & Foreign A. S. Soc'y — aided Fugitives. Watched Kidnappers &c.

[June] 4. Went to Troy, to watch a constable from Baltimore, and aid the friends in Troy, in knowing and watching him.

[June] 5. Sabbath — Preached on the Dock and in the Bethel,[8] four times. (This he usually did on the Sabbath.)

[June] 10th. Spent most of the week in aiding runaways, and in sending off Circulars — Soliciting money and finding solicitors — Went to Sand Lake, and made arrangements to send a certain person there.

Amidst a variety of efforts to aid fugitives, Mr. Brown writes,— "Lectured on the dock, four evenings, respecting Temperance."

A few short sketches (given by Mr. Brown) concerning fugitive slaves, are designed to show the ridiculous position and the contemptible meanness of slaveholders in their pretended ownership of the bodies and souls of men; also, the utter futility of their efforts to regain this species of flying property when once in the hands of a skillful Committee.

FROM THE *TOCSIN OF LIBERTY*

KIDNAPPER, LOOK HERE![9]

Albany, June 20th, 1842.

E. W. GOODWIN, Esq. Dear Sir: — The vigilance committee are up to their elbows in work, and are desirous to have you inform a few of those men who have lately lost *property consisting* of articles of merchandize (falsely

---

[8] *The Rev. Shipherd's Bethel Free Congregation (see note 2).— Editor.*

[9] *These announcements were actually part of a ruse to throw off slave catchers. While the runaway was being hidden in the South, the announcement was published and the paper sent to the slave owner. Believing that the slave was already in Canada, the slave owner called off the search for the slave, and the runaway was able to flee safely north.— Editor. (Harrold, Stanley. Subversives: Antislavery Community in Washington, D.C., 1828-1865, Baton Rouge: LSU Press, 2003: 64–93.)*

so called) in the shape, and having the minds and sympathies of *human
beings,* that we are always on hand, and ready to ship cargoes on the short-
est notice, and ensure a safe passage over the *"Great Ontario."* Please inform
the following persons, that their property arrived safe, (though some of it
was badly worn) and has been forwarded and arrived safe in Canada.

Cheney Hutton is hereby informed that two very large men, the one a
market man and teamster, the other a first rate field hand, came up on the
"Peoples Line" of steamboats, and marched right up to the office and
handed out the following "Bill of Lading."

New York, June 6th, 1842.

"Shipped on board the steamboat R_____, Peoples Line, the bearers, who
are kindly commended to your care," &c.

W _____ _____

Agent.

They confessed that they were runaways and their countenances proved
that they were guilty of being as black as a slaveholder's heart. They did
not appear to be ashamed of what they had done, but a gentleman present said, he was ashamed for them that they had not done one thing more,
and that was, to have driven along the market wagon well loaded, as part
payment for the robbery of about 30 years service. Friend Hutton may as
well give up the chase,—for Benjamin and Phillip, will hereafter sell their
own poultry, raise their own corn and own their bodies, and let Cheney
Hutton do his own marketing or pay for doing if, as honest men do.

ABEL BROWN,
Forwarding Merchant, Albany.

ALBANY KIDNAPPERS.

Mr Editor: *Certain gentlemen,* who take such a deep interest in the welfare of Miss Leah Brown, lately held in servile bondage by Mrs. McDonald, are hereby informed that Leah has no wish to return to the embrace
of the family who have robbed herself and mother, and her brothers and
sisters, of their inalienable rights, from their earliest infancy. Also, that she
is beyond the *reach* of those men who have lately offered *one hundred dollars* for her delivery, to the woman who formerly held her as a slave. She
earnestly hopes, that Mrs. McD. will treat her mother and sisters kindly,
and not sell them to Georgia.

Will you please also, to inform the lovers of liberty, that the Vigilance
Committee are in great want of funds to aid in sending emigrants to
Canada. They have just received a lot fresh from the Southern District.

Please also inform Robert Gilmore of Baltimore, that he need not give himself further trouble about his very intelligent and noble slaves, Marianna, Polly, Elisabeth Castle, and her fine little girl, for they have got safe over the great Ontario, where such men as his honor, would not look very well placing their feet for the purpose of kidnapping. Tell him also, that his slave John Weston left here more than a week since, at full speed, in a fine carriage drawn by fleet horses, and report says, there were not

LETTER OF INTRODUCTION FOR A FUGITIVE SLAVE FROM ABEL BROWN TO CHARLES HICKS, JUNE 9, 1842 (COURTESY OF THE VERMONT HISTORICAL SOCIETY).

less than six well loaded pistols in the hands of John and his associates. The carriage was driven by as fine looking and noble hearted a son of the South, as I ever saw. The kidnappers who came on from Baltimore after John, have great reason to be thankful that they were outwitted and did not overtake the carriage, for most surely they would have met a *hard* reception. John said he would die sooner than go back. I am quite sure that Marianna, Elisabeth, John, and the little girl, have had a joyful thanksgiving in the other land. (I hope Robert will not envy them their happiness.)

Tell the British Consul, that I sympathize with his afflicted wife, in the loss of Elisabeth, and if she will send me her free papers, and give me the liberty of so doing, I will invite her to return from Canada, and make her an inmate of my own family. I will not however, pay the $50 reward which her agent offered for Elisabeth.

Inform Dr. Stewart, that *Mary Ann* had some fears when here, that he would catch her, but that the kindness of *friends* dried up her tears, and she too went over that awful lake, that smiles on slaves, and frowns on slaveholders.

I have a charge against Robert Gilmore of $15 for money paid to the order of John, and $10 for money paid to the order of Elisabeth Castle, and her mother and daughter. I shall charge the British Consul $30 for money and service rendered Elisabeth. I charge the Consul somewhat extra, because he is disgracing the country of his birth, by his American practices.

The kidnappers made it expensive transporting John, and Robert certainly ought to pay the $15 without ceremony. I told him he might go back free of charge, or he might stay in Albany if he chose, but he would listen to no other proposals than such as secured him a passage to Canada; there appeared to be a *charm* in that name. He started on foot, and walked until his feet were perfectly blistered, when a friend brought him back to take a *new* start. Here he found that wretched constable of Baltimore, watching for him, but there were more watching the kidnapper than he could find to watch John, and even the aid of the entire kidnapping gang that hang around a mock *Justice* in this city, could avail nothing after the "Vigilance Committee" had once taken him under their care.

KIDNAPPERS, LOOK HERE!

E. W. GOODWIN, ESQ:— The forwarding business is still good, and a little more ready cash would place us upon a sure footing. We have been making as permanent arrangements as possible, and considering the *"hard times,"* and hard hearts with which we have to do, have succeeded as well as could be anticipated.

Not many weeks since, a licensed exhorter of the Methodist Episcopal Church arrived in this city, and came so well recommended that there could hardly be a doubt but that he was just what he professed to be, a pious Christian man, who had been a slave more than thirty years. He had taken his wife and children, and in the night fled from the land of robbers. The woods and swamps, were the abodes of himself and family for weeks. He found at last a friend, who kindly offered to protect his wife and little ones, until he should flee to Canada, and earn sufficient to defray the expense of moving his family to that land of freedom. He came to this city, and had it not been for a despised abolitionist, he would have come in vain. We will not now, expose the contempt with which he was treated by many of his own brethren in the church. God says, "Vengeance is mine, I will repay saith the Lord." Their wickedness will *one day be exposed*. Then, those who condemned him as a thief, for taking possession of his own body, and of his own wife, and own children, and who turned from him with neglect, will know, that Jesus Christ was treated with neglect, in the person of that dear colored child of his. We helped the man all we could; so did some of the old fashioned Methodists.

There is one Mr. Woodford, living far below Baltimore, whom we wish you to inform at as early a day as possible, respecting that woman, Eliza Wilson, whom he pounded with sticks of wood, whom he stripped naked again and again, and whipped with the cat and nine tails, until her body was completely lacerated, whom he then washed with salt brine, to make the smart worse, whose eyes he also filled with salt and water, whose neck and head my own eyes saw covered with scars, caused by blows from him and his agents, whose back the women say is one complete scar, having been whipped several different times, until it was completely cut to pieces; whose head bears the mark of heavy clubs, in different places, whom he ever treated as a brute, a beast of burden, and whom he has robbed of the Bible and of education, from her earliest infancy; whom he made work on the field, and submitted to be treated like the brutes that perish.

Tell him that he had better repent of his awful crimes, for God's vengeance is out against him, and he will certainly feel even more than he has poured upon the innocent head, of perhaps his own daughter. But she is now beyond his reach. We want money to aid in sending another on the *same road.*

Tell Mrs. Widow Margaret A. Culver, that the reward of $100 which she offered for her slave Levi, put us on the watch, and sure enough, he came pat upon us and handed out his bill of lading.

We told him that the kidnappers of this city, were looking out. That man whom God will bless with a high place in heaven, gave him a piece of money and some food, and he passed on, where Margaret will never go. We refer the poor thievish widow to the letter of Sam Weller,[10] found in another column, for further information respecting Levi.

We trust she will send us forthwith, $25.00, as a reward for telling her where he may be found. We think he is now about half way over the *Great Ontario,* on the steamboat *Freedom,* or at least Levi calls her Freedom, and if Margaret thinks her cause a just one, she had better call in her minister and have special prayer offered to the "Prince and power of the air," that he will drive that steamboat back, and suffer her to take care of Levi.

The forwarding business calls our immediate attention, therefore we cannot write more until next week.

Yours as ever,
BROWN & CO.
Forwarding Merchants, Albany, N. Y.

E.W. GOODWIN, ESQ,—Tell *kidnappers to take notice,* that we have such an amount of business on hand, that we have no time to report progress.

One day last week eight noble persons arrived, all panting for liberty. It only cost about twenty-five dollars to colonize them. A certain knave in New-Orleans owned two of them, and another who intended to have come

---

[10]*Sam Weller was actually Thomas Smallwood, a former slave who worked with Charles Torrey in Washington, D.C. helping hundreds of runaway slaves obtain their freedom.*—Editor. *(Ibid; A Narrative of Thomas Smallwood. Toronto, 1851.)*

with them and who laid the plan for their escape was whipped to death by Joseph Wolcott. That same murderer has sent his sons to a northern college, where they have been educated, and are now following the business of their ungodly father. These sons and their father have been courted by certain *"Doctors of"* who live in the state of _____; yes, they have even given such murderers certificates vouching for their good moral character. But thank indulgent Heaven, Sarah and her little girl of four years old are safe, and her unborn child will, we trust, never feel the curse of slavery. May God have mercy upon the man who killed its father.

More when the shipping season is over.

BROWN & CO.
Forwarding Merchants, Albany.

The history of the slave woman, concerning whom allusion is made in the preceding articles, is as follows:

Mrs. S. was born in the free State of New York; and at an early age went to reside with Mr. _____, New York city. At about the age of ten years, Mr. _____ took her to New-Orleans as a waiter for his wife. At that place he sold her to Mr. Wolcott, who owned a plantation near the city. When Mr. _____ left her, he promised to return within a few months and take her to New York; but he never returned. She bore her toil and oppression with patience, away from home and friends. She was kept as a house girl to wait upon the family.

After six years, Mr. Wolcott brought home a young man by the name of Smith, and gave her to him for a wife. She found him to be a husband, indeed: he was a Methodist, could read and write, and was a praying, Christian man. For six years they lived together, and prayed to be liberated from their cruel bondage. And finally, Smith succeeded in making arrangements with a gentleman to carry them to New York. Previous to the day appointed, it became known that there were certain slaves on the plantation designing to run away; the story was traced to Smith, and he was tied to the whipping post to make him reveal the secrets of the expedition. The lash was applied, but in vain; Smith refused to give them any information respecting it, or to reveal the names of the friends who had aided him in his efforts. They whipped the man until life was almost extinct, and the noble man died the day following the laceration. His poor wife went to see her dead husband, but her grief was so great that the master drove her to the house, with the stern command to "shut up," and never speak again of her husband.

Her grief in secret was indescribable, but it only renewed her desire to get away. Her husband had revealed to her the plan of escape, and when the night arrived, she in connection with two other female slaves, and her little girl of four years, descended the ladder placed at the window by those who aided in her escape, and they, amid the darkness of the night, were placed in the hold of a vessel that conveyed them she knew not where. She was secreted during the day, and in the night was permitted to come out while the passengers were asleep. She did not see the sun from the time she left New Orleans until she found herself on shore a few miles from New York City. They were put to the land in a small boat, with a few shillings of money, happy indeed that they breathed an air free from slavery.

She found friends by whose aid she was sent to the committee at Albany. The master advertised her, which, in connection with other circumstances which she mentioned, found to be correct, was proof positive that she was the slave of Mr. Wolcott, and those who have been most intimate with her, have found her story to be at all times the same. She left N. Orleans about the first of May, a few days after her husband's dreadful death, and arrived in Albany in July. Her situation was such, that the committee dared not send her on, lest she die by the way. A place of rest was therefore provided for her, and after two weeks she gave birth to a son. Her health is restored; she has placed her eldest child with a family near the city, while she is now at work in a neighboring county, and there paying the board of herself and free born child. If the donors of the 'Vigilance Committee' could have been at the office of the agent, when Mrs. Smith came and fell down upon her knees, and with tears of gratitude gave thanks to the committee, for their kindness in providing for her a place of rest during her sickness, they certainly would have thanked God that they had ever been permitted to give to the objects of a vigilance committee.

In another lot of these children of sorrow, was ELIZABETH CASTLE, the slave of Robert Gilmore, of Baltimore. By the wish of her master she took for a husband a slave of the same name. Being a dressmaker, she was quite profitable to her owner, and had reason to expect that she would be permitted to enjoy the society of her family in peace, but it was not so. The birth of her first child convinced her, that her master regarded her as of more value, as every child she bore increased his wealth and caused him to watch her closer than ever. She found to her sorrow that not only herself, but also her children were considered to be mere articles of merchandize, and would in all probability be sold from her as soon as the market would warrant a profitable sale. She resolved, therefore, to flee. Her resolution was strengthened, when she found herself in a situation that would render it less convenient to perform a journey of some seven hundred miles.

ILLUSTRATION FROM ORIGINAL PUBLICATION OF *Memoir of Rev. Abel Brown*.

In connection with her mother, daughter, and two female friends, she started for that snowy paradise a little north of the mighty Ontario, where a *woman* with a heart of flesh sways the sceptre of freedom, and permits even colored women to "bear children, without fearing that their helpless bodies will be torn from them by that American eagle which is ever watching to devour lawful prey."

The company came to this city, but were soon pursued by those hungry bloodhounds who are forever prowling about the kennels of slavery, but the noble women were safely conveyed by the committee to the *happy land*. A few weeks since, they were visited by a member of the committee: all were delighted with their situation. Elizabeth has opened a shop on her own [unreadable word], and is delighted in looking upon her free born infant, safe from the fangs of Robert Gilmore, who sent the constable of Baltimore to seize it, even before it was born. Elizabeth only asks one favor of the ever despicable slaveholder, and that is, that he will liberate her husband, and suffer him to enjoy the society of his wife and children in a land of freedom.

Mr. Brown usually had one or two fugitives from the hand of chains, accompanying him on his agency, and the licensed Methodist exhorter, by the name of James Bulah,[11] (concerning whom, allusion is made earlier in this chapter) was now his traveling companion and exhorter, in behalf of his brethren and sisters in bondage.

Some curious specimens of introduction are found among Mr. Brown's papers, commending to *his* care and that of the Albany Vig. Committee, "certain travellers, going North, for their own accommodation." One is represented as a friend of the Saviour, going to Canada, on an important mission, &c.

A member of the Vigilance Committee of New York, (Mr. Johnson[12])

THE REV. JAMES BEULAH (FROM THE COLLECTION OF THE JORDAN [NY] HISTORICAL SOCIETY).

[11]*James Bulah (Beulah) and his family moved to Jordan, Oswego County, New York, in 1848. They remained there until 1851, after which they moved to Canada because of the threat of slave catchers following the much publicized Jerry Rescue. They returned sometime around 1853 and resettled in Jordan.—Editor. (http://www.pacny.net/freedom_trail/, Website of the Preservation Association of Central N.Y.)*

[12]*William P. Johnson was a leading member of the New York Committee of Vigilance. He is sometimes confused with another New York vigilance committee member, William Johnston, as his name is spelled in some reports as Johnston. For a time, he shared a residence with NYCV secretary Charles B. Ray.—Editor. (Peter C. Ripley, ed.,* The Black Abolitionist Papers, *vol. 4,* The United States 1847–1859, *Chapel Hill: University of North Carolina Press, 1991: 178;* The New York City Directory for 1842 and 1843, *New York: John R. Doggett, Jr., Publisher, 1843.)*

THE REV. HENRY HIGHLAND GAR-
NET, IMPORTANT BLACK CIVIL
RIGHTS LEADER AND UNDER-
GROUND RAILROAD CONDUCTOR.

writing to Rev. *Mr.* Garnet,[13] says: "The bearer is traveling northward, in quest of his wife (who obtained her freedom by operation of natural assumption,) and he is also endeavoring to secure to himself the same advantage. I am under the impression, that she did not go to Troy, but was directed to Mr. Abel Brown, of Albany, to whom I have directed some *forty* or fifty, within a short time.

"You will therefore obtain such information from Mr. Brown, as will enable our friend to find her. If Mr. B. keeps accounts, as a forwarding agent should do, he will find, she was shipped from N. Y. on the 16th or 17th inst."

July 29, 1842

[13]*Henry Highland Garnet was the second most important U.S. black leader after Douglass during the antebellum period. He became well acquainted with Abel Brown as pastor of the Liberty Street Presbyterian (Colored) Church in Troy. A fugitive slave who escaped to freedom as a boy with his parents, who settled in New York City, he came under the influence of the Rev. Theodore Wright, president of the New York Committee of Vigilance. A brilliant orator, he gave his most famous speech at the National Negro Convention in Buffalo in 1843, calling on slaves to resist. After becoming a pastor in Washington, D.C., in 1864, he was chosen by Lincoln to be the first black American to give a speech in Congress shortly after the passage of the 13th amendment. Finally, in 1881, he lived out a lifelong dream and was sent as an ambassador to Liberia, where he died. — Editor.*

CHAPTER XIII

THE SLAVE HUNTER—SCENES OF OUTRAGE—
RIGHTS OF COLORED CITIZENS INVADED—NO
LEGAL REDRESS—INTERFERENCE OF MR. BROWN
IN BEHALF OF THE INJURED—CONSEQUENT
INDICTMENT—PROPOSITION TO LECTURE—MOB
ELEMENTS COMBINED—MR. BROWN IS BURNED
IN EFFIGY, &C.—CLAY INDICTMENT—CIRCULAR—
EXPLANATORY STATEMENTS—INDEFINITE
POSTPONEMENT OF TRIAL

The Vigilance Committee of Albany often found themselves in personal contest with slaveholders and their abettors, on account of the infringement on the rights of colored citizens of Albany by the baboon insolence (I know not what else to term it) of those prowling men and woman hunters to recapture "slaves" under any pretence that might best subserve their purposes. During the month of May, the following occurrence took place.

A lady from Baltimore who has relations in Columbia Co. brought a slave girl with her to this city. Learning that she was free by law, the girl left the woman. The woman and her friends attempted to recover her under the false pretence that she had stolen something. A warrant was obtained for her and committed to constable Charles W. Mink, and he with another tool of slavery undertook to search the houses of the free people of color, violating the just principles of the law which exempts the houses of the citizens from all "unreasonable searches and seizures." In searching the house of Wm. Johnson, a reputable citizen, he was guilty of an assault and battery upon Mrs. Johnson.

The then justice of the police court refused to hold the ruffian to bail, and the Grand Jury refused to indict him in consequence of the false representation of a prominent citizen. But public opinion, as expressed in large public meetings, condemned both the police and the jury, and threw an additional shield around the injured. When a member of the committee exposed the conduct of the police officers and the Jury in the public prints, the servile Grand Jury promptly indicted him (Mr. Brown) for libels upon the jury, and Mink, Loveridge and others. It is a sufficient comment on the indictments, to say that those who obtained them have been wise enough to let them sleep. Another member of the committee, Mr. Goodwin, was brutally assaulted in the street for the part he took in the matter, and when denied redress and outraged by the police magistrate, was promptly acquitted of all blame by an intelligent jury.

The outrage thus committed on peaceable and unoffending citizens in Albany without any power of redress from a civil tribunal — also the corrupt public sentiment that would uphold and sustain the nomination of a slaveholder for the Presidency — called loudly for rebuke. Mr. Brown consequently designed to place before the public an exposition of facts as stated in the following account given by E. W. Goodwin, editor of the *Tocsin of Liberty*.

[FROM THE *TOCSIN OF LIBERTY*]

Grand burst-up of mob elements, but nobody hurt!!

Our staid and quiet Albany was thrown into a most violent commotion on Tuesday evening last, by the appearance of the following handbill:

War! War! War!

Don't be frightened, only a war of words.

The subscriber proposes to give a course of street lectures.

1st. He will comment upon the abominable wickedness of the late gentlemen's Grand Jury, in conniving with kidnappers, and neglecting to indict a slave-hunter of this city. *The names of the Grand Jurors will be given.*

2nd. Show that there is a gang of kidnappers watching for prey.

3d. Will give account of the escape of fugitive slaves, and ask money to aid them to a land of freedom.

4th. Will give a few reasons why that notorious *Sabbath breaker, Swearer, Gambler, Duelist, Thief, Robber, Adulterer, Man-stealer, Slaveholder, &c.* HENRY CLAY! should never be President of these U.S. Lectures will commence on Tuesday evening, at 7 1–2 o'clock precisely, near the Centre Market.

Abel Brown.

Albany, July 18, 1842.

Now in the first place it may be proper to state, that although Mr. Brown is the agent of the Eastern New York Anti-Slavery Society, yet he by no means acted as their agent in the production of that hand bill, as will be seen by his *own* private signature. And further, Mr. Brown did not counsel with any of the abolitionists; as he did not wish that any should share the *responsibility* but himself: "I take the responsibility" was the position he assumed. It is true some of the abolitionists saw the bill before it was posted up, and advised a different course as more prudent: but their counsels did not prevail. Now, what was the sequel? Why, that Mr. Brown did not appear at the time and place appointed, but that the mob to a large number, (as we are told, not being present) did appear with abundance of wrath and cabbage, sheep's plucks, and other missiles, swearing and roaring vengeance on Abel Brown! The Mayor and police were there too, ready as we also *understand,* to take the "street brawler" into custody.

It is true also, that the mob threw a stone against the sash of one of the windows of the Tocsin office, breaking in a couple of lights of glass, and made several efforts to push open the doors, but without success. Here we owe a debt of gratitude to those excellent mechanics, the Woleensack's, for a couple of their excellent and honestly made locks, for the preservation of our property.

Thus much premised; — now for the moral of this business. What was the difficulty? In the first place Mr. B. proposed to give his views or opinions, on the conduct of the grand jury, which refused to indict a man notoriously out of his official duty, in entering and disturbing, and assaulting a colored family, — alleging that he was searching for a slave, which had just escaped — the husband being absent. Was it for this the mayor and police were there?

2nd. He was going to tell the people about there being kidnappers in town! Who doubts it after what has been so publicly made known within a few weeks past.

3d. He was going to give the people an account of the poor fugitive slaves, who are constantly running as for life from a slavery far worse than Egyptian bondage, and ask the benevolent to aid by giving some money to help them on their way. Was this wrong? Oh no: it was the 4th thing he proposed to do that "touched the raw," that entered like seven daggers into the "proud flesh" of pro-slavery politicians — that pierced "like an adder," the very soul and *life seat* of those foul and dark spirits. It was This, that made them "gnash on him with their teeth!!

They were afraid their great Idol, which they had sacrificed so much money and conscience to set up, would be endangered, and like their kindred spirits at Ephesus on another occasion, who clustered around to protect the shrine of Diana, by the existence of which they had their gains, like them we say, they began with one accord to shout "great is Henry Clay of Kentucky:" — "great is Henry Clay of Kentucky;" — and some whig abolitionists were able to sound the loudest bugle in the Babel chorus.

As to the charge Mr. Brown has preferred in his handbill against Mr. Clay, we have nothing further to say at present than this: — We suppose it will not be denied, that Mr. Clay is or has been, (and we have no evidence of reformation or repentance) a "swearer, gambler, and duelist." That he is a SLAVEHOLDER, is notorious. And the Bible decides that "He that stealeth a MAN, or if he be found in his hand, he shall surely be put to DEATH." Are men "found in his (Mr. Clay's) hand?" "All men are created equal, and entitled to life, LIBERTY and the pursuit of happiness," says our admirable declaration. Does Henry Clay deprive any person or persons of their *liberty!*? If so then what is he? What would that man be who in Algiers should deprive YOU of your *liberty,* though he might do it by law! What would you call HIM? You would call him a *manstealer!* Can any doubt then, that, when it is made out, that a man is guilty (morally) of the greater — that he is not also guilty of the lesser crime of stealing? Or in other words does not the greater cover the less?

In reference to the statements in the foregoing notice, Mr. Brown remarked to me that he expected at the time the bills were posted that they would accomplish their own work, and thus save him the necessity of lecturing which, however, he was ready and willing to do, had not the bare announcement proved sufficient for his purpose.

Soon after the production of the handbill, Mr. Brown was indicted for an alleged libel on Henry Clay, and was held to bail in the sum of for his appearance at court. Mr. Brown declared himself prepared to meet the indictment, believing himself able to sustain the allegations rendered by a number of "competent witnesses," who had expressed their willingness to testify to the truth of his assertions, having also secured the most eminent counsel and advice in his friend the Hon. Alvan Stewart,[1] who

[1]*Alvan Stewart was an important antislavery leader from Cherry Valley, New York. Before he took up the cause, he was one of the state's most successful trial lawyers. He was for a time president of the New York State Anti-Slavery Society and is known to have aided runaway slaves. — Editor.*

very generously contributed his services in behalf of Mr. Brown as defendant.

In reference to the alleged libel, Mr. Brown published the following Circular, entitled:

CHARGES AGAINST HENRY CLAY SUSTAINED,
and Albany Grand Jury exposed.

THE CHARGES AGAINST HENRY CLAY.

A subject of some importance to the cause of humanity, and which my position has compelled me to watch over with solicitude, and which now for the first time has compelled me to speak, is the efforts which are making for the election of Henry Clay to the Presidency of this nation.

When these efforts first commenced, I supposed that they were only the efforts of a few reckless and unprincipled men, who wished to get themselves into notice at the expense of the principles of common justice and humanity. In this I have been sadly disappointed, time has proved that men who have heretofore passed as men, of more than common intelligence and honesty, were ready to use their influence in church and state, to secure the election to the highest office in the gift of the people of this union, a man whose public and private character has ever been a disgrace to a Christian nation.

And let it be distinctly understood, that I have made no *new* charges against Mr. Clay. Of the crimes specified in the hand bill, he is not only guilty, but notoriously guilty. He has himself published his own shame, if there is shame attached to these transactions. He has not even waited for political opponents to charge him with these crimes, but has let them shine with all their blighting, withering influence, upon the nation, as if he gloried in them.

In this place, it may be sufficient to state, that his *proofs* were adequate to his statements; and were afforded him by "living and credible witnesses," among whom was Mr. Coffin,[2] a well known philanthropist — then resident of Philadelphia, who authorized a friend of Mr. Brown, to publish, that Henry Clay was not only a gambler, but that he had won and lost *human beings* at the gaming table. This fact, Mr. Coffin pledged himself to establish by the testimony of living witnesses, whenever those papers which are endeavoring to palm the Kentuckian upon the people would open its columns for their presentation. Also, the noted duels, in which

---

[2]*Probably Joshua Coffin of Newburyport, Massachusetts, who was associated with antislavery groups in both New York and Philadelphia. — Editor.*

Mr. Clay had either been accessory or principal, including that with John Randolph, and his influence or second hand in the death of Gilley![3]

Other statements were found in the public prints, such as his oath in the senate, when he said to a distinguished member of that body, when touching some point relative to slavery — Go home, &c. Another light in which Mr. Clay's conduct is considered in this circular, is presented under the following heads; —

"THEFT, ROBBERY, MAN-STEALING, SLAVEHOLDING."

As it regards the charges of theft, robbery, man-stealing, and selling, I have only to remark that the first two are included in the last two. If the writer of this article should meet a fellowman, black or white, in the public highway, and there by violence and force, take from him only the money which he had earned by the labors of one day, that act would be termed *highway robbery;* and for it, this commonwealth would compel him to spend a term of years in the State prison. How much greater would be the crime if the man was robbed of his earnings for life. Henry Clay not only robs the poor man of a single day's wages, but of the services of his *life,* steals his children, steals his wife, steals the man himself, &c. *Any who doubt this, please read the following from James Canning Fuller:*[4]

Having a great desire to see the imported cattle on Henry Clay's plantation, I went thither. On approaching the house, I saw a colored man, to whom I said, "Where wert thou raised?" "In Washington." [was the answer]. "Did Henry Clay buy thee there?" "Yes." "Wilt thou show me his improved cattle?" He pointed to the orchard, and said the man who had charge of them was there. As I followed his direction, I encountered a very intelligent looking boy, apparently eight or nine years old. I said to him, "Canst thou read?" "No." "Is there a school for colored people on Henry Clay's plantation?" "No." "How old art thou?" "Don't know." In the orchard I found a woman at work with her nee-

<hr />

[3] *In addition to his duel with Randolph in 1826, Clay also participated in a duel with Humphrey Marshall in 1809 over a squabble about a resolution he made in the Senate. In neither of these duels was anyone killed. However, Clay is believed to have played a role in instigating one of American history's most infamous duels, the duel between Kentucky congressman William J. Graves and Maine congressman Jonathan Gilley that caused the latter's death. It also resulted in the passage of a national law that banned dueling between public officials. — Editor.*

[4] *James Canning Fuller, an English Quaker, moved to the U.S. in 1834 and settled in Skaneateles. He was very active in antislavery circles and his house was a frequent refuge of freedom-seekers, among them Jermaine Loguen when he arrived in New York. A close associate of Gerrit Smith, Fuller contributed liberally to the Canadian fugitive slave mission of Hiram Wilson and assisted Calvin Fairbank with funds during his incarceration. — Editor. ("Matters and Things," Friend of Man 11 Jan. 1842; Calvin J. Fairbank, Rev. Calvin Fairbank During Slavery Times, Chicago: Patriotic Publishing Co., 1890: 54.)*

dle, I asked, "How old art thou?" "A big fifty." "How old is that?" "Near sixty." "How many children hast thou?" "Fifteen or sixteen." "Where are they? "Colored folks don't know where their children is; they are sent all over the country." "Where wert thou raised? "Washington." "Did Henry Clay buy thee there?" "Yes." "How many children hadst thou then?" "Four." "Where are they?" "I don't know. They tell me they are dead."

The hut in which this "source of wealth" lives, was neither as good, nor as well-floored as my stable. Several slaves were picking fruit in the orchard; I asked one of the young men whether they were taught to read on this plantation, and they answered no. I found the overseer of the cattle with a short-handled stout whip, which had been broken. He said it answered both for a riding whip, and occasionally "to wipe off" the slaves.

Other testimony might be given, but his own confessions, and even boasting of being a slave-holder, render it needless.

APPEAL TO CHRISTIANS

You have before you a synopsis of a few of the many crimes which Henry Clay has been guilty. The fact that almost all southern and many northern public men, participate in them, does not in the least change their moral character. They are sins which God has declared utterly unfit a man for a ruler. God requires us to select such men only as rule in "*his fear*," and he " has denounced his most severe judgments against those nations who select any other." " He that ruleth over men must be just, ruling in the fear of God,"— Is emphatically the mind of that infinite Being. And it is not left for us to decide whether we may or not choose any other. That is a concern which he has settled, and it is trampling the plainest commands of Heaven under our feet to vote for such a man as Henry Clay.

Will you see this nation disgraced? Will you see God dishonored and his word disregarded? Will you see Christ, and his cross, and the holy commands which he died to establish, treated with scorn and contempt, by the election of another man to the Presidency of this nation who *profanes the name of* God,— who *disregards the common principles of justice and humanity,—Who murders his fellow men* to gratify his own ambition,— who *robs God and buys and sells Jesus Christ* in the market as a beast of burden, and who, to cap the climax of his impiety, *lifts up his senatorial voice and warns the nation against any efforts which may be made to stop him in his unhallowed and God-defying crimes!* Be entreated to show yourself worthy of the name you have taken by uttering the commands of high Heaven against the election of wicked rulers. What will sooner call down the tremendous judgments of Almighty God upon us, as a nation, than the choosing of wicked haters of humanity, and God, and blasphemers of his name to rule over us?

THOSE WHO SUPPORT HENRY CLAY.

The eyes of *the* foolish are blinded, and they vainly hope that by the election of a despiser of God and man, to the office of President of this Nation, to secure pecuniary relief. Vain hope! You may succeed in the former, but God will certainly disappoint you in the latter. How plain the case. The party seeking to elevate Henry Clay to the Presidency, assume to be composed of the more respectable and Christian portion of the community. They have designed to pass as the friends of Improvement, Education, Humanity and Religion. Admitting the truth of this assumption; how foolish to anticipate that a holy God will suffer them to prosper through the election of a man who is in principle and practice, directly opposed to the very principles which the party profess. Why not learn wisdom from the past. Only two years since, with the same high pretensions, the party joined hands with despots, and secured the election of their favorite candidates. But where is the promised relief? The answer is short. That God, whom multitudes, even of professing Christians, dishonored by voting for a despot, took away your President, and left us all to the tender mercies of one of whom it may be emphatically said, "*When the* WICKED *bear rule the people mourn.*" That same God still lives to vindicate his own honor, by refusing you relief until you will cease despising him by voting to elevate vicious men to fill offices of the state and nation. It is really to be hoped that the party which is seeking to elevate a slaveholder, duelist and blasphemer, will lay aside all pretensions to Christianity, humanity or even decency.

MINISTERS OF ALBANY.

This city is the seat of all the impious efforts in this state for the elevation of wicked men to office, and you are therefore under special obligation to raise your voices and hold up God's truth before this people. Many of you have warned your congregations against the evil tendency of the various excitements of the age, you have been faithful to the very letter of the *word* upon these minor points, will you not now, when an excitement is arising which if not checked, will overwhelm the nation and call down the just judgments of a holy God upon us — will you not, I ask, give the trumpet a certain sound, that the people may prepare themselves for battle. You that are Doctors of Divinity, I hope for the honor of the religion which you profess, will show that you have a sufficient regard for the Divine Law, to present a few truths like the following, in Ex. 18: Moreover, thou shalt provide out of all the people, able men, *such as fear God, men of truth,* hating covetousness: and place such — to be rulers, &c. Also, 2 Chron. XIX, 7. And He (God) said to the judges, "Wherefore now let the fear of God be upon you; take heed and do it; for there is no iniquity with the Lord our God, nor respect of persons, nor taking of gifts."[5]

MOB.—CITY AUTHORITIES.—EFFIGY.

The mob which made such a glorious display of tar, feathers, eggs, &c., &c. was got up by the Clay and pro-slavery leaders, of this city; and was but the revival of the hard cider and coonskin arguments of 1840. Wonder if the Clayites are confined to such arguments as were exhibited at the Centre-market last Tuesday evening? Those Police officers who stood by and suffered the Effigy of a peaceable citizen to be burned, amid the shoutings of the rabble, are welcome to all the glory of the occasion. It was no more than could be expected from infidel and blaspheming men. It is also in perfect keeping with its object, for the *Daily American Citizen*[6] to honor and puff the mob. We should expect it of any paper engaged in advocating the elevation of a man, who *if a resident of this state*, and guilty of the crimes which have ever disgraced his character, would be condemned to State prison for life. Surely such an editor deserves our pity. We hope he may yet repent and find forgiveness.

The other papers whose editors have so frequently favored us with editorial notices of a certain description, are left in entire possession of the field.

CONCLUSION.

In conclusion, we wish to say to those who favored us with so much advice, that we have acted in this matter from a sense of duty, and as we should have desired another to act, were *we* pining under the lash of Henry Clay.

ABEL BROWN.

Albany, N. Y. July 25th, 1842.

[FROM THE *TOCSIN OF LIBERTY*]

ALBANY GRAND JURY, VS. HUMANITY.

Those Citizens of Albany who wish to obey the Truth.

RESPECTED FELLOW CITIZENS:— My object in appearing before you through the press, is to give an unvarnished statement of facts respecting matters of interest to the cause of humanity and religion. For a proper

---

[5] *These passages from scripture urge the appointment of only good and tested men to office. — Editor.*

[6] *Daily American Citizen, a Whig newspaper published in Albany, 1842 to 1846. — Editor.*

understanding of the motive by which I have been actuated, and the interests at stake, it may not be improper to state, that I am acting as the corresponding secretary of the Eastern N. Y. Anti-Slavery Society, an office to which I was elected by a convention of citizens of Eastern N. Y. a small portion only of whom reside in this city. As the only official and General Agent of the Society, it becomes my duty to watch over its interests, and the humane object which it designs to accomplish, with the fidelity of a faithful servant.

Soon after entering upon the duties assigned me, I was informed that a portion of the Police of this city, were engaged in efforts to obtain unlawful possession of free persons of color, for the avowed purpose of reducing them to slavery. In one case a warrant had been issued by Justice _____ alleging that some unknown person had stolen an article of clothing, and that the same was secreted in a certain house, which the warrant gave them authority to search. The house was searched without any other success than that of being permitted to insult certain innocent women who resided in it. Then all their pretended *lawful* authority *ceased,* even the warrant of Justice was dead. The officers however, without the least authority, (unless that of kidnappers) proceeded to search each and every house "that they in their wisdom saw fit," and that too in the absence of the older male members of the families. They abused, insulted and frightened unprotected women, and in one case committed a gross assault and battery upon an innocent female, wife of a respectable citizen of this city. These facts having come to my knowledge, I visited the police office, and made a few inquiries respecting the conduct of its officers, but immediately learned that they considered me interfering with concerns, which belonged exclusively to themselves. The language used by some of them was too indecent to be recorded here. The constable who had committed the assault, was (upon the oath of the injured woman) arrested, and brought before Justice where the assault was clearly proved, but as a matter of course, the offender was discharged, and the friends of the colored people left to infer that they would receive no countenance from that court. There was however one important fact elicited by the complaint, to wit: that the constable had not the least shadow of authority for searching the house of the complainant. With these facts fully before us, complaint was made to the Grand Jury of the June Term, and the facts definitely proved, that said constable and his associate did without any authority, enter the house of Mr. _____ a colored man of this city, and there pushed and jammed, and endangered the life of his wife during his absence, until she would suffer him to search the premises for a colored person, whom he alleged to be a slave, but who was as free as any reader of this article.

The Jury in their superior wisdom, refused to find a bill.

How they came to such a conclusion is not for me to say, and they probably will never inform us. It looks mysterious that so plain a case of assault was not noticed. It would be insulting their intelligence to suppose that they had the most distant idea that the offender pushed the woman for a lawful purpose, or in a lawful manner.

We should like to inquire of either of those gentlemen who was on that Grand Jury, who has a wife, if that constable had treated *his* wife as it was proved the police officer treated the one in question, whether they would think it justice to discharge the offender?

It may, however, be proper to remark, that had that Grand Jury done its duty, the community would have been put in possession of many important facts, which might have led them to altogether different conclusions from those entertained by the police court of this city, and it might have opened the eyes of too many who are now blindly opposing the cause of the oppressed. The trial might also have brought to light some facts which would have made the slander suit, which Justice commenced against the editor of the *Tocsin of Liberty*, less profitable to the plaintiff. With the Grand Jury I am unacquainted, and that they might have erred unintentionally do not deny, but that they have by this neglect encouraged a class of desperate ruffians, I have daily abundant and increasing evidence. How large a portion of this community will sustain them, remains yet to be seen.

Yours, &c.

A. BROWN.

Concerning this infringement of the colored man's rights in the invasion of his home, Mr. Goodwin makes the following comments.

[FROM THE *TOCSIN OF LIBERTY*]:

The poorest and the meanest white man can fly to our legal tribunals, and justice is swift to punish the man who has dared to do him wrong.

That citizen was a colored man, and such is the coldness and apathy of our courts — such is the perversion of the administration of public justice, that our magistrates can wink at injuries done to the black man, and frown him away from their tribunals. The offender was a *white* man — the sufferer was a *colored* man. The offender was an officer, "clothed with a little brief authority," and his victim was of a *proscribed race*. We, however, acknowledge not the purity of that justice which shields its satellites, and permits them to perpetrate outrage with impunity. We wish in this matter not to be misunderstood. We claim for all men in our state but an *equality of rights*.

We claim that the tribunals of justice should be open alike to all — that the white man should not be privileged to *oppress,* nor the black man compelled to *endure.* Public justice, like the rains and dews of Heaven, should fall equally on all; such is the spirit of our constitution, such is the genius of our laws. The law knows no distinction of color. The black man's home, and the persons of his family, are *as sacred* as those of the white man; and the magistrate who would create or sanction a difference between them, should be hurled from his seat, as a traitor to the principles of our constitution — a traitor to the beautiful system of equality of rights upon which our laws are based — as a caitiff [coward] that would poison the pure streams of public justice, and wield the power of his office, not to redress the wrongs of the injured, but to protect guilt and crime.

The case was continued to another term, at which time, Mr. Brown again appeared as was stated in his Report to the Executive Committee, under date of Oct. 20th, 1842:

Returned to Albany to attend Court, and meet the Indictments against me. After spending a week waiting for the trial to be called, was duly informed, that if the case was ever brought to trial, the District Attorney would give me sufficient notice to prepare for the trial. Thus terminated the contemptible design of the Clay men of this City, to destroy the influence of one, whom they could not meet.

The Report of the E. N. Y. A. S. Society contains an account at the final disposition of this affair, after the following remarks by way of explanation:

These indictments were instigated by the leading whig influence of Albany. They had at the time the sanction of almost the entire whig press. Mr. Brown was denounced as a Reverend slanderer, and as worthy of a place with criminals at *Sing Sing.*

The Judge who presided and charged the Grand Jury was a whig. The Sheriff who had charge of the subpoenaing the Grand Jury was a whig. The mass of the jury were whigs. The foreman was a very influential whig. Others were then and are now whig officeholders. The District Attorney was a whig. And finally, influential whigs have had the entire control and management of the affair. The indictment was pushed with the utmost rigor until it was carried up to the Circuit Court, where whig influences could not be brought to bear upon it. The District Attorney came to the very wise conclusion that the indictment might remain hanging over your Secretary as a kind of *whig rod* to protect Henry Clay from persecution, (as the whig papers termed it.)

The indictment remained in *statu quo,* when a change of Judges made a change in District Attorney, and among the last acts of the late District Attorney we find the following motion:

GENERAL SESSIONS OF THE PEACE, MARCH TERM.

Thursday, March 23, 1844.

Present — Hon. Peter Gansevoort,[7] First Judge. Hon. J. Q. Wilson, Hon. R. W. Murphy, Hon. R. J. Hilton Judges.

The People vs. Abel Brown. — Libel on Henry Clay. On motion of A. G. Wheaton, Dist. Att'y. Ordered that a *Nolle Prose qui* be and the same is hereby entered in this cause.

The People vs. Abel Brown. — Libel on Thurlow Weed[8] and others. On motion of H. G. Wheaton, Dist. Att'y. Ordered that a *Nolle Prose* be and the same is hereby entered in this cause.

Copy. WILLIAM MIX, Clerk.

The county paid the costs in this prosecution of Mr. Brown, instigated by the wealthy and influential whigs of Albany. The cost to Mr. B. for moneys paid out and time spent has been no inconsiderable amount.

The sequel has however demonstrated one fact, to wit: That the whig party, after all their pretended consciousness of the purity of the character of their candidate for the presidency, *dare not* suffer that character to be tested before a legal tribunal.

After the indictment was over (on a refusal of trial), the assertion was still industriously circulated that Mr. Brown was a "Reverend slanderer," &c. His prosecutors had neither the justice nor magnanimity to *retract* the charge or falsify the assertion. His name also appeared in a book entitled *Sargeant's Life of Henry Clay,* in which he is represented as a slanderer of this popular statesman. For these reasons, I feel it my duty, though a painful task, when I recount his sufferings and the persecution he received, to present the facts in vindication of his character from the

---

[7]*Judge Peter Gansevoort, the son of the former slave owner Revolutionary War general Peter Gansevoort, whose family house in Gansevoort, Saratoga County, New York, according to local legend, was a stop on the Underground Railroad. — Editor.*

[8]*Thurlow Weed, editor and publisher of the* Albany Evening Journal, *was an influential player behind the scenes in national politics, first as a Whig and later in the Republican party. A close friend of New York governor and later secretary of state William Henry Seward, he had strong antislavery views and was a financial contributor to the Underground Railroad operation of Stephen Myers in Albany. — Editor. (Peter C. Ripley, ed.,* The Black Abolitionist Papers, *vol. 4,* The United States 1847-1859. *Chapel Hill: University of North Carolina Press, 1991: 410.)*

assaults of his enemies and to give an explanation of the whole affair, not by my own inferences but from the account rendered by Mr. Brown himself.

No person held higher estimation of Mr. Clay's intellectual superiority and ability as a statesman than Mr. Brown. In reference to which, he used to remark, that his influence was proportionably the more dangerous to the interests of the slave question.

As a professed teacher of Christianity and of the God given rights of liberty to man, Mr. Brown could not fail to expose "wickedness in high places" as the only effectual mode of purifying the lesser influences or minor sources of evil.

CHAPTER XIV

SCENES OF DOMESTIC AFFLICTION—DEATH
OF HIS WIFE—THE TWO WHITE FUGITIVES—
REPORT OF VIGILANCE COMMITTEE—LEWIS
WASHINGTON, THE FUGITIVE SLAVE LECTURER—
MR. BROWN VISITS MASSACHUSETTS—OUR
FIRST ACQUAINTANCE—CORRESPONDENCE

In the midst of various and conflicting duties at this time, Mr. Brown was called to witness the sickness and death of his beloved companion—his counselor and friend, and one who when foes thickened around amid the stormy rage of persecution and strife, would bid him "go," saying, "duty is yours, consequences are with God."

The following Obituary notice is taken from *The Golden Rule*,[1] published in Albany.

DEATH OF THE EDITRESS.

Mrs. MARY ANN B. BROWN, the beloved Editress of the *Golden Rule*, died at her residence in this city, on Thursday, the 4th inst., in the 27th year of her age.

The sickness which has thus terminated the life of this excellent woman, was extremely severe, and of about eight weeks duration. The closing scene, however, was perfectly calm and peaceful—it was the departure of one,
"who sinks to rest,
With heaven's approving sentence blest."

Every friend of this paper will feel that the death of Mrs. B. is a great and personal bereavement; for we need not say, she was deeply and truly devoted to the interests it advocates. For the improvement of her sex, in

[1]The Golden Rule, *a family publication in Albany extolling the virtues of Christian charity.*—
Editor.

Front page of *The Golden Rule*, the Christian newspaper for which Mary Ann Brown wrote.

whatever things are pure, and lovely, and of good report, she esteemed no sacrifice too great, no labor too arduous. Both the vigorous and graceful productions of her own pen, and the remarkably judicious and tasteful selections, which have appeared in this paper, will long remain to preserve and honor her memory.

But, beside the important relation in which Mrs. B. stood to the public, there were more sacred and tender ties which bound her to life. She was a *young wife* and *mother*. A husband, and two little children — the youngest but five weeks of age — survive her death. We mourn, but not as them that have no hope; for above the voice of our lamentation, is heard the sweet and earnest assurance of Christian faith — "Blessed are the dead who die in the Lord; yea, saith the spirit, that they may rest from their labors, and their works do follow them." C.V.L.

Among the benevolent efforts of Mrs. Brown, she had succeeded (in connection with the Golden Rule Association) in establishing a home for orphan girls, an asylum for the destitute and unfortunate, which was in successful operation at the time of her death, and there was no subject of reform or enterprise of the age in which she did not feel and manifest the most lively and decided interest.

To his friends, concerning this affliction, Mr. Brown writes:

She talked of death without the least apparent fear, and frequently said, I am not afraid to die. She would not give the least direction relative to the future arrangements of her family, only would say, that God would direct it all better than she could. My own feelings have been indescribable — but I have felt and known that it was all right. I have realized, during her dying hours, the meaning of that sentence — "Motherless children." My dear Walter, felt her death most severely — He would not be consoled. He stood by her bed and kissed her again and again, and cried aloud, "she must not die — Ma must not die." He says, she has gone to Heaven — but then he adds, that dreadful sentence, "she will not come back." He thinks Heaven is a good place, but Ma will stay there — will never visit us again on earth. But neither tears — nor groans — nor prayers — nor sighs, could make her stay another moment. I laid my hand upon her heart and felt it quietly cease to beat — Oh, what an hour was that!

We closed her eyes and retired to our chamber, and there commended ourselves and friends to God, who is ever ready to listen to all our cries. The friends laid out the body. Walter got flowers and placed around that precious face. Often would he go and sweetly kiss that cold cheek. Soon after she died, he wanted me to get the Bible and read about the place where Ma had gone — I read and gave him the Bible description of Heaven. He seemed pleased with it and listened with fixed attention, and burst into tears and cried — "Oh, she will not come back."

Rev. C. Van Loon and Rev. George Storrs[2] attended the funeral, and many went to the grave, although it rained incessantly. The colored people came to weep around her coffin. She had ever been their friend, and they deeply felt that in losing her, they had lost one who felt their dreadful sufferings. There are in the city, many who have been slaves — whenever I see them they express their grief, often in tears. They know and feel that they have lost one whose house was a refuge for the poor and the oppressed, and who knew how to defend them from the attack of their enemies.

Amid these scenes of domestic affliction, when the heart most needs sympathy and the eye turns silently for relief and tenderness of treatment, Mr. Brown was surrounded by men of violence and blood, who, ere the remains of his deceased wife were removed, threatened the destruction of his house. Often he was obliged to seek refuge at night in some habitation of his friends, unknown to his enemies.

[2]*The Rev. George Storrs, evangelical minister, who was arrested in 1835 and 1836 while preaching antislavery sermons in churches in New Hampshire.* — Editor.

From the Reports of Mr. Brown, it seems that he was often obliged to prepare the way in making arrangements for himself and others to lecture, or in other words, to precede his own appointments. He thus performed much incidental business not connected with the official duties of his station. Especially was this the case in the early part of his labors for the slave in N. Y. Much success attended his efforts at this period, and the attention of the community seems to have been effectually aroused to the great question of his advocacy. While in some of the numerous conventions held by Mr. Brown perfect order and quiet prevailed, others presented scenes of violence and outrage.

In the autumn of 1842, a riotous scene occurred in Auburn (N. Y.) at a Convention held by Mr. Brown, concerning which a few particulars are given from an account published by Mr. Hopkins, a well known friend of the cause in that place.

> At the hour appointed, a respectable audience had assembled to hear Mr. Brown's lecture, and the meeting organized by the appointment of a chairman, when the ruffianism, which had been in course of preparation through the day, came in, and began to manifest itself in hisses and continued stamping. When the noise had subsided in part, the chairman remarked that a large majority present were the friends of order, and requested that they might be allowed to hear the lecture undisturbed; when our heroes and their leader, again with one accord, began, "Nine cheers for Henry Clay," &c. Henry Clay was evidently a favorite, and when a voice could again be heard it was remarked that Henry Clay should consider himself under lasting obligation for this devotion of his friends. The meeting, however, was not restored to order, although the Deputy Sheriff was present, and (I am informed) other officers of the peace, and indications of a determination to assault the speaker, and threats of personal violence were made. On the suggestion of the Deputy Sheriff, the chair announced the meeting adjourned — and under protection of that officer, and the friends of good order present, Mr. Brown retired to the store of a friend, followed by a mob apparently anxious to shed his blood. At this crisis, I take pleasure in stating that all political lines appeared to be forgotten by our respectable citizens, both of the Whig and Democratic parties, who seemed anxious to defend the right of discussion, and the reputation of our goodly village; and I am exceedingly mistaken if this disgraceful mob, got up by a few unprincipled Whig leaders here, to prevent the exposure of Henry Clay's robberies of more than fifty laboring men and women, does not open the eyes of good men who have heretofore identified themselves with

the Whig party. Honest men cannot long be used as the tools to exalt such baseness to official station. The Christian portion of this community cannot long remain tied, in their political relations, to the support of a man for the chief magistracy of this nation, who buys and sells our Lord Jesus Christ, in the persons of his oppressed children.

On the arrival of the cars, Mr. Brown, surrounded by a large number of respectable citizens, proceeded from the store where he had taken refuge, to the car-house, followed by the mob, swelled by the accession of many, who, I am informed, had been in attendance at the Whig meeting. While proceeding to the cars, several attempts were made by the mob to assault Mr. Brown, but the firmness of his friends prevented. Some assaults were made with canes, but I am not aware that any blood was shed.

During this season of southern emigration, Mr. Brown frequently invited interesting and intelligent fugitive slaves to accompany him in the work of his agency. Of one who had been a slave more than fifty years, he thus writes, in giving notice of a lecture:

Mr. Ramsay will relate his experience and history while a slave in this *goodly Christian* land; also, an account of the heart rending scenes which occurred at different times in his family, while the ruthless tyrant tore from him his children to the number of eleven, and sold them to the unfeeling traders into the far South, to be worked to death on the cotton and rice fields and sugar plantations.

Concerning another attendant, Mr. Brown writes —

Rochester, Oct. 19, 1842, 5 A.M.

I arrived here about an hour since in company with the *white* slave, Wm. Johnson.

Yesterday we called at Rome, and attended a meeting of the N. Y. S. Baptist A. S. Convention. There were present a large number of delegates, all of whom appeared to sympathize deeply with the slave. In the P.M. Wm. was introduced to the meeting, and gave them a brief relation of his experience. The assembly were deeply interested in his statements, and manifested their interest, by raising eight dollars to defray his expenses from Albany to Canada, whither Wm. will soon go. He will probably arrive in that happy land tomorrow. At Utica I called with William, on Hon. Alvan Stewart, who manifested his interest in his welfare by making him a liberal donation. Mr. S. also introduced him to his family, and it was truly delightful, to see that noble man and his family listening to the tale of sorrow of a poor oppressed brother; to hear and see their expressions of sympathy; to see William take courage as the tears of his auditors rolled down their cheeks. When we left, Mr. S. spoke many encouraging words to the affrighted and distressed fugitive, that greatly calmed his fears, and led him to exclaim as we passed from the yard, "God bless that man! He's a good man! How I should like to live with him! If I ever come back I will call and see him!" From that hour, William began to feel that there were white men who could be trusted; joy beamed in his countenance. A few hours after, he received the kind hospitalities and aid of the Baptist Anti-Slavery Convention. It would have filled you with additional delight, after all you have witnessed, to have seen William after we got into the cars; he was perfectly happy; he sung; he jumped; he thanked God; he blessed the convention; he blessed Mr. Stewart; he said again and again, "God has delivered me." Then he was filled with grief at the thought of his brothers and sisters in slavery. He told us of one[3] who drowned herself upon hearing that she was sold to go to Georgia. Oh that cursed system that has robbed such a man of himself.[4]

Mr. Brown also labored in Western N. Y., "attended by Milton Clark, a white slave who was rescued by the patriotic citizens of the (Ohio) Western Reserve from Kentucky blood hounds, who had caught and bound him, and were carrying him back into perpetual slavery. Mr. Brown held forth to large gatherings, and the people listened with marked attention."

In Nov. '42, Mr. Brown visited Canada, and in writing from Dawn Mills,[5] describes a number of slaves, whom he had assisted in *Albany* to this home of the oppressed, as "well, contented, and happy; and unwilling to return to the kind embrace of their affectionate masters."

At this time a reward was offered by certain gentlemen in Baltimore, to one of the City Constables of Albany, of fifteen hundred dollars for the apprehension of Brown, Torrey[6] and E. W. Goodwin, concerning

[3]*This statement was corroborated by a member of congress (Mr. Gates).—Editor.*

[4]*Seth Gates of Warsaw, New York, a hotbed of abolitionism and an active terminal on the Underground Railroad in western New York. Gates, an Underground Railroad conductor, defied the infamous House gag order of 1835 by mailing wholesale the proceedings of the World Anti-Slavery Convention held in London in 1840, which also resulted in a $500 price on his head being levied in Savannah, Georgia.—Editor. (Letter from Lewis Bishop to Eric Foner, Warsaw, N.Y., February 1963, Warsaw, N.Y., Historical Society.)*

[5]*This community was founded in 1841 by Hiram Wilson, a fugitive slave missionary, who established an agricultural and industrial school. It was here that Josiah Henson came to reside, and a museum with his restored residence is now located there.—Editor.*

[6]*Charles Turner Torrey, a Congregational minister, who was born near Boston, shared a spiri-*

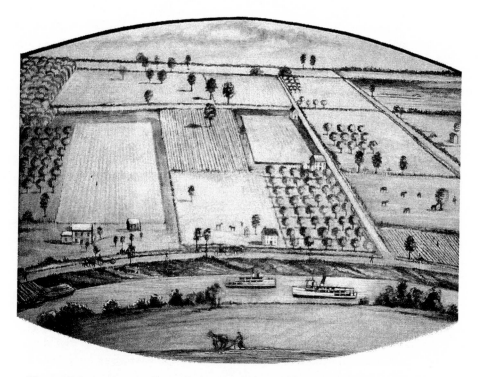

The British American Institute at Dawn Mills, Ontario (courtesy of Uncle Tom's Cabin Historic Site, Dresden, Ontario, Canada).

which information was published that "each of them would go to Baltimore for half that sum, provided the money was only deposited in a good bank, or any way, in which they might be sure that the money would be paid as they were in great need of funds to help the poor fugitives who were escaping from their ungodly man market — Sodomite villanies, and barbarian oppressions.

Dec. 12, 1842.

It appears from the first annual report of the vigilance committee of Albany, that "no less than 350 fugitives had been aided to a place of safety by the committee, at an expense of more than one thousand dollars. Through the efforts of the Committee, every attempt to recover these victims of oppres-

tual kinship with Abel Brown in their passion to end slavery. Both were outspoken and fearless, and Torrey like Brown went into the South to bring slaves to freedom. Torrey organized a trunk of the Underground Railroad leading from Washington, D.C,. to Albany, with the cooperation of Brown, Goodwin, and others. However, he was finally apprehended and convicted for his efforts, and in 1844 sent to prison where he died two years later.— Editor.

sion, on the part of slave catchers in connection with Albany constables, police officers and judges, had proved ineffectual. In one case, the determination in the release of slaves was made on the ground that the United States Court *alone* could entertain the question of slavery. That was by the late decision of the court in the celebrated slave case between Maryland and Pennsylvania,[7] the law of Congress alone founded on the constitutional provision could be applied to the recapture of runaway slaves." — *Vide Peters' Reports.*

At the Annual Meeting of the E. N. Y. A. S. Society,

April 26, 1842.

On motion of C. T. Torrey, the following resolution passed unanimously.

Resolved, That the Executive Committee be authorized to collect and disburse funds for the purpose of aiding fugitive slaves, at their discretion, accounting for the same to the society, as a part of the general duties of the committee.

The propriety of this resolution will be seen from the fact that some of the members of the Executive Committee, were already among the official members of the Committee of Vigilance in Albany. Mr. Torrey had also been instrumental in supplying the committee with this species of merchandize for transportation or disposal in the free states as might best suit their convenience. One who was thus assisted by Mr. Torrey and secreted by Mr. Brown until the time arrived that all suspicion had ceased, or the chase was apparently over, afterward became his friend and traveling companion in pleading the cause of the oppressed. Though unaccustomed to our northern winters, he traveled in connection with Mr. Brown — often through snows impassable, by any mode of conveyance except "on foot." At one time, they were thus obliged to walk twelve miles, or rather wade through banks of snow, to meet an appointment of a meeting. Although a strong athletic man, he could hardly compete with Mr. Brown in this kind of traveling. Yet all this he could cheerfully endure, and more, in view of his brethren and sisters pining under the lash of their cruel task masters on a southern plantation.

In company with this fugitive (Lewis Washington),[8] Mr. Brown visited Massachusetts, in the winter of 1842, when our acquaintance was first formed.

[7]*The Prigg Decision, an 1842 decision by the Supreme Court, prevented states from interfering with slave owners who entered their state to apprehend their slaves. — Editor.*

[8]*Lewis Washington, fugitive slave lecturer and close companion of Abel Brown, was appointed as a Liberty Party agent after Brown's death. Troy, N.Y., directory records show he lived at 153 Second*

A few extracts from our correspondence are given to further illustrate his efforts and character:

The suggestion which is made, respecting the efforts of Vigilance Committees, being only one branch of the subject of emancipation, is equally applicable to any other branch. One person cannot do every thing, yet the individual efforts of one may be the lever, which will overturn the great bastile of slavery. As well might we say, to help Lundsford Lane[9] was only one branch; to help Geo. Lattimore[10] is only one branch; to purify the church is only one branch; to oppose liberty party is only one branch,[11] &c. &c. The facts are these: A

The Rev. Charles Turner Torrey (from J.C. Lovejoy, *Memoir of Rev. Charles T. Torrey*. Boston: John P. Jewett & C o., 1847).

person can make one branch of any subject a "hobby"—can spend all his talk and sympathy on one human being, or if he is capable, can spread out the great subject, and make one slave the representative of millions, as you truly remarked. I have spent half a day in giving the history of a single woman, and when I had finished, I had told all that two or three hours

St. in Troy between 1845 and 1847. He later spent time in Peterboro.—Editor. ("Convention at Troy," Albany Patriot, 29 Jan. 1845; Troy City Directory, Troy, N.Y., 1845-1847; e-mail from Donna Burdick, Smithfield town historian to author, 27 May 2002.)

[9]Lunsford Lane, a slave from North Carolina, who through great industry and initiative purchased his freedom but was banished from the state before he could purchase his wife and children. After lecturing in the North and raising the necessary money, he returned in 1842 to make the purchase, only to be tarred and feathered. In the end, he was able to purchase the freedom of his family, and they settled in the North, living in Boston and Oberlin among other locations, where he became a noted antislavery speaker.—Editor. (Lunsford Lane, The Narrative of Lunsford Lane, Boston, 1842; the Rev. William G. Hawkins, Lunsford Lane or Another Helper from North Carolina, Boston: Crosby & Nichols, 1863.)

[10]George Lattimore (aka Latimer), a fugitive slave from Norfolk, Virginia, who fled with his wife to Boston. His recapture there in 1842 and the activities of the local vigilance committee to prevent his return brought national attention. In the end, the committee was able to pressure Lattimore's owner to accept $400 for his freedom.—Editor. (Wilbur H. Siebert, The Underground Railroad in Massachusetts, Worcester: American Antiquarian Society, 1936: 17.)

[11]Apparently, Brown is being hypothetical and not referring to himself, for he was a member of the Liberty party.—Editor.

would permit, concerning the entire system of slavery, and demonstrated the truth of what I had said, by the example before me

I have not answered all of your enquiries, but my sheet is full, and I am obliged to see a man, who has just paid the last installment for his wife and eight children in Richmond, Va. We hope to make an agent of him. He comes recommended by the Governor of Va. He has worked fifty years, to free himself and family.

In relation to a respite from his labors, on a visit to his children, who soon after the death of *Mary Ann* (his wife) were placed under the care of their maternal relatives, Mr. Brown writes to myself the following:

Fredonia, April 3d, 1843.
... If you had been for nine months, driven by the raging winds upon the boisterous ocean, you would know how to appreciate five days of rest, in the sweet retirement of home....

The foolish think me reckless, and suppose that I rejoice and delight in arousing all the tumults and strife, which it is possible to excite in the community; but these are not the elements on which I live, or which give me any pleasure. In quietude as the stillness of the morning or silence of the evening, I should delight to live. My duty to God and my fellow men, alone urge me on and tear me from the sweetness of retirement and communion with God. Yet as much self-denial as it costs, I am determined, with divine assistance, to not suffer myself to be hindered by outward circumstances, from laboring to bless others with the blessings, which to me, are so dear. God will not suffer me to rest, while others are deprived of the precious blessings designed by our Heavenly Father for all mankind....

ANSWER TO THE LAST COMMUNICATION [BY C.S. BROWN]

... I was glad to find that you were resting at the quiet home of your dear children. Rest again, and again, but not give o'er, till the "battle's fought," the "victory won." I am afraid that you can not live long, amid so much toil and excitement consequent to a laborer, whose whole soul is absorbed in following Him who "went about doing good." Not that I would have you exercise less faith in Him who has said, "my grace is sufficient for thee, and as thy day is so shall thy strength be also." Yet, we should have some regard to our physical constitution and strength of endurance.

The extreme toil to which he subjected himself caused the apprehension of his friends for the safety of his health, and drew from them many a gentle heed of admonition. Neither could they see how he could do *less* with the numerous responsibilities devolving upon him, in a cause, the burden and privilege of sustaining which so few are found willing to share.

In consequence of my own personal efforts in the Anti-Slavery cause, I was suffering much opposition and reproach, and the circumstances of my position in the church and elsewhere were both peculiar and afflictive, and a correspondence with so kind a friend as Mr. Brown was indeed a consolation to my wounded heart.

In one of his letters, he thus expresses himself:

... How kindly this world treats me, when compared with the treatment of the Saviour of mankind. I deeply sympathize with you in your trials and contradictions in H., and I have feared lest they might lead even yourself, to feel otherwise than the Saviour did, when he wept over Jerusalem.

... Oh how noble to rise above every feeling of impatience or hatred, and to look down with the deep feelings of pity and compassion, which possessed the bosom of Him, who, even upon the cross, cried, "Father forgive them for they know not what they do." May that spirit constantly fill our minds.; then and then only, do we become God like. Then and only then, do we assume the place worthy an immortal spirit. How elevated is such a high and holy position.

CHAPTER XV

VISIT TO NEW YORK—SUBSEQUENT MARRIAGE—
ANNIVERSARY OF THE EASTERN N.Y.A.S.
SOCIETY—CITY ASSOCIATION IN BEHALF
OF THE OPPRESSED—LABORS IN NEW YORK—
CONVENTION IN NEW JERSEY—
PHRENOLOGICAL CHARACTER OF MR. BROWN
GIVEN BY O.S. FOWLER

Agreeable to previous arrangement with Mr. Brown, I started from my home in Massachusetts for New York, on May the 8th inst. in a "Car of Emancipation" (literally) inasmuch, as it was exclusively filled with the friends of freedom. We were on our way to attend the anniversaries of the American A. S. Society and other meetings of similar interest, usually held in New York at this season.

Mr. Brown had previously returned to the city, on some preliminary business, connected with the annual convention of the Anti-Slavery Society of Eastern N. Y.[1] In anticipation of my arrival — after giving some directions relative to traveling, Mr. Brown writes, "*I shall be at the Dock without fail,* (Providence permitting) I wish you would stand upon the upper deck of the Boat, as she comes up the dock, and then I will see you." On crossing the Sound, mid the starry brilliancy of night, cheered by the music of the Hutchinsons,[2] like the voice of many waters, we arrived at the Port of New York at break of day, and while admiring the scene on deck, I found my ever faithful friend ready to escort me on

[1] *That the ENYASS held its annual conventions in New York City shows the breadth of the Underground Railroad network it had developed.—Editor.*

[2] *The Hutchinson family singers from New Hampshire were the most renowned antislavery singing group. They traveled extensively throughout the U.S., and their most famous song, "Get Off the Track," came out in 1843.—Editor.*

shore. The week following, on May 15th, 1843, we were married.[3] Our union was based on the immutable principles of truth and love, and therefore indissoluble.

Mr. Brown I esteemed for his zeal and valor in contest with the enemies of God and man. If in the days of chivalric deeds, many a heart was won, and many a song was sung, in honor of the "bravest knight," how much more worthy (to say nothing of the pretended virtue of the former) is he who has contended bravely in defense of the right, not with carnal weapons but through the instrumentalities of the spirit, aiming only at the destruction of evil for the perpetuation of good.

Having received an appointment of agency from the Executive Committee of the Eastern N. Y. Anti-Slavery Society to labor in behalf of the cause, I had left home and friends, and all that my heart held dear in my native state for the fulfillment of this object.

Subsequent to the annual convention of the E. N. Y. A. S. Society, a special meeting was held through the influence of Mr. Brown for the purpose of forming a City Association to facilitate the progress of the cause in New York and vicinity. The platform was free and occupied by speakers irrespective of party organization, and the addresses from fugitives slaves were a living demonstration of the need of such efforts, as were in contemplation in this city. A little white boy of five years old was introduced to the assembly, who had been purchased in Florida at auction by a gentleman who attended the sale for the sum of fifty dollars. Another white slave (a fugitive) was also present, whose master had chased him to this city some years previous. Much interest was manifested on the part of friends in the objects of the occasion. A handsome subscription was collected, and such was the enthusiasm that money was even thrown from the galleries into the desk while Mr. Brown was speaking. One girl, formerly a slave, very modestly gave ten dollars.[4]

On the ensuing Sabbath, Mr. Brown preached at one of the colored churches. The assembly was to me, both a novel and affecting scene.

During our stay in New York (of nearly three months) we labored with direct reference to the objects of the Association — in the dissemination of tracts, public lectures, &c. in short, in every way that the exigencies of the cause seemed to require. A stronghold exists in this

[3]See Appendix I, which includes information about Abel Brown's collaborations with Charles Ray in the Underground Railroad. — Editor.
[4]About $200 today. — Editor.

metropolitan city for the oppressed. Slaveholding interest reigns in the ascendency there, yet faithful hearts are there too, who have pledged their lives to the sacred cause of freedom. One German I remember particularly,—his wife an English lady,—They both devoted their time and money to the cause, and were exceedingly kind and hospitable to us as agents in the enterprise. Some young men were also ardently engaged in the cause. H. Dresser,[5] a leading and efficient member of the Executive Committee,[6] was often called to plead in behalf of the fugitive on a writ of habeas corpus.

Various meetings were held on those summer evenings in behalf of the slave, and occasional interest was manifested. It was our privilege to board at a place in company with a literary gentleman, Monsieur De Cen Tremme, a zealous friend of human rights; and who was ever ready to advocate the cause on all suitable occasions. Many of the ladies of New York were ready and willing to aid and assist in this philanthropic design. An interesting meeting of ladies was held at our rooms; three of the number had been slaves. One of them conversed fluently with the Frenchman alluded to. She had been the slave of a French woman, resident of New Orleans. She had visited France with "her mistress," and had always been a favorite attendant in their journeys. She accompanied "her master" to New York. Suffering under a disease of the eyes, he had come to receive some ocular remedy. Being thus afflicted, he was obliged to walk blindfold through the streets with his slave by his side. He had the impression (she said) that she would never leave him—but he was mistaken; she never left New York!

The stories of all were of an interesting character. One female, who had been a slave, called the same afternoon and showed me her arm, most dreadfully scarred by the whip. Those who were present I hope will never forget the stories related by these daughters of affliction. Yet they seemed cheerful and happy on that occasion, for they found sympathy and were conscious of freedom. Mrs. Lane, wife of an imprisoned husband, seemed alone sad. Much interest was excited in his behalf at this time, a tract in relation to his case, having been written by myself and extensively circulated. Yet this same man, James D. Lane, lies now incarcerated within the walls of Richmond Penitentiary for the alleged crime

[5]Horace Dresser, of New York City, was an attorney who worked with the New York Committee of Vigilance to aid free blacks and fugitive slaves apprehended by slave catchers.—Editor.
[6]Of the NYCV.—Editor.

of assisting fugitive slaves, sentenced for twelve years from 1843.[7] One half of his time only has expired!

A woman called one day to see Mr. Brown, in relation to her husband, whom she suspected had been sold by the Captain of a vessel (in which he sailed) for a slave on the coast of Brazil. She was filled with anxiety and fearful apprehension. Such being often the fate of the poor colored seamen on the Brazilian shores. Petitions have been sent to Congress, signed by hundreds of merchants and others in New York interested in commerce with the southern continent in reference to their detention for the sole purpose of reducing them to slavery. I mention these cases to show how we were employed, and what kind of work is needed in that city. In most cases, we could offer them only our sympathy, which is never lost to their wounded hearts.

On one of our antislavery trips across the river, we called at the house of a colored friend, and there found a white man and his family, who had just escaped from the fangs of the slave monster in South Carolina. The man was about to have been sold by his half-brother to defray the expenses of his wife's last sickness in paying the Doctor's bill. No trace of African blood could we discover; the indication was perceptible alone in his black curly hair. As a proof that his children were quite Anglo Saxon, I need only to add that he took them to a colored school, and the father was told by the teacher that she did not admit *white* children. A little fair white boy, (once a slave) concerning whom allusion has previously been made, was also present at some of Mr. Brown's meetings. He now stood (not upon the auction block) but upon a free table at a meeting for liberty, while Mr. Brown portrayed the features of that vile and abominable system that would thus rob an innocent and lovely child of the dearest rights that God has given.

The amount of good done resulting from our labors is difficult to determine, especially in such a metropolis as New York.

Lewis Washington, the fugitive slave, and laborer with Mr. Brown, was with us part of the time in New York, and also accompanied us to New Jersey, where we spent a week enjoying the hospitalities of Mr. Sayres and family at Elizabethtown. In this place and vicinity, a number of

---

[7]*James D. Lane, of Albany, was a black seaman sentenced to 12 years in prison in 1843 for concealing two female slaves aboard the packet schooner* Empire *during a trip from Norfolk to New York. A check of Richmond census records from 1850 shows no one by his name, so either he was deceased or had been released.* — Editor.

meetings were held at which the colored people (quite numerous) flocked around Lewis with the warmest manifestations of interest and good will.

Many of them had just emerged from the chaos of slavery, and I never shall forget their illuminated faces at our meetings. At one of them, a woman cried out (amid much confusion in the assembly) when Lewis was speaking, and said, "it is true, for I have seen the same in Washington."

Mr. Sayre's family once held slaves, but were now, in view of their former position, humble and penitent abolitionists. Mr. S. was often much affected and would weep like a child over his past sin of slaveholding, and he had sent for us, through the interposition of a friend, to make them a visit.

His aged slave, or at least the one whom he was obliged to retain and support by law, was past the age of release. She was then more than fourscore years. Her name was Kate. Although offered a home by Mr. S. in his family, she chose to live with a little boy, a grandson, the only remaining one of eleven children, of nine or ten of whom she had been inhumanly robbed. Her husband, who was a coach driver, had been sold by his master to meet the loss occasioned by his horses being precipitated into the river through the falling of a bridge. The price of the slave (who barely escaped breaking his neck) was undoubtedly an equivalent in the mind of the slaveholder. She, the wife, had also been sold, and once for an old wagon. Many heartrending accounts were related to me by their weeping wife and daughters concerning many circumstances in connection with slavery within their own personal knowledge. But I must forbear the recital, and return to those incidents more immediately connected with the subject of my history.

During our residence in New York, Mr. Brown was induced to call at the Phrenological Office of the Fowlers, more as a matter of curiosity than otherwise.[8] Being a perfect stranger, his policy was to say little as possible, assuming the most careless, indifferent air (a perfect nonchalance.) The chart given by Mr. O.S. Fowler, is considered by his friends as almost a perfect likeness of his natural traits and character. He pronounced him at once a public man, and engaged on moral subjects, and as an advocate of human rights. His intellectual and moral qualities are

---

[8]*Phrenology was a science of the day that claimed to be able to ascertain the character of an individual by the shape of his skull.—Editor.*

represented as so combined as to constitute a radical Reformer, and as also possessed of those qualities, that rendered him eminently social, as well as an attached friend in the domestic relations of life. His mental activity, or nervous temperament, far superceded his vitality and strength of system.

He [Fowler] remarks in his written character, that he "is called imprudent, but is in fact *cautious*. Does things in an original way — is sui generis and toto celo — mind naturally passes rapidly — possesses *versatility* of talent." With the highest reasoning powers, he also united great firmness and stability of character, yet possessed too little self-respect or esteem. This deficiency was, however, in a great measure obviated by his strong love of approbation and his intense conscientiousness. His organ of benevolence, he states is of the highest order with large ideality and mirthfulness, causing him to argue to the reductio ad absurdum; and the satire sometimes intermingled with his lectures, may have caused in part the ire and opposition of his enemies. Of Brown's propelling or executive faculties, he said, "you have enough high pressure in your composition to build two steam boats and keep them running —[for you] go through every thing with a positive force." He added that Brown "is cautious in commencing, but when he has begun stops for no one and no thing." It was this determined force and resolution in acting that caused many to suppose him reckless and imprudent, but this was not the case. No one calculated results or counted the cost more closely than he did, and the opposition he received in the moral enterprises of the day was what he anticipated in view of past history, the prophecies of Christ, and the present state of public opinion.

CHAPTER XVI

THE SLAVE MUSICIAN—A WESTERN TOUR—
LETTERS—VISITS MASSACHUSETTS—
RETURN TO ALBANY—CONTINUATION OF
EFFORTS IN BEHALF OF THE SLAVE—MR. BROWN'S
POLITICAL VIEWS—HIS CONTINUED INTEREST
IN THE TEMPERANCE CAUSE—LETTER TO
THE MAYOR OF ALBANY

Among the escaped fugitives at this season of our sojourn in New York, two arrived from North Carolina in company with a white man as their assumed master. One of the slaves had been a celebrated violinist, and theatrical player in some of the cities of the south. His musical skill, manners and conversation were such as to evince the truth of his statements.

This summer, Mr. Brown was enabled to fulfill his long contemplated project of visiting "the West." We accordingly started from New York the latter part of June, having made previous arrangements to hold a series of conventions on our route to Wisconsin. The fugitive slave musician accompanied us some part of the way, and his performances as a player added much to the interest of the meetings. He seldom spoke except when interrogated by the audience, and then his answers were always pertinent and to the point.

Agreeable to invitation, on the Fourth of July, we attended a county convention at Canandaigua. An extract from the official report in reference to the occasion, is as follows:

The large court house in the village, was filled at an early hour by the sterling yeomanry from every town in the county, and such firmness and determination as apparently influenced the immense assembly, we have never witnessed in any convention of the kind held in this county heretofore.

After an eloquent address by Abel Brown, of Albany, who in a clear and forcible manner described the influence of the slave power on the North — the sufferings of our enslaved brethren — the inevitable ruin into which slavery is rapidly hurrying the whole country, and the guilt of the North in sustaining this system of cruelty and blood — the business committee reported the following, among other resolutions of a spirited character, which received the unanimous assent of the convention.

Resolved, That the wickedness and hypocrisy of the peo-

SOUTHERN MEANNESS.—The following letter and advertisement were received by mail, with a charge of 56 cents postage, a few days since :

$100 REWARD.—Run away from the subscriber, in Baltimore city, on Thursday, 25th ult. a *Mulatto Man*, named *Robert Hill*. [We omit the description.]

WALTER FERNANDIS.

The letter was addressed inside to "The Abolitionist BROWN."

REPLY.

MR. FERNANDIS—This is to inform you that the noble Robert Hill reached this city in safety, and was safely sent on his way rejoicing. We charge you $25 for money paid him and services rendered, and 56 cents for the letter containing the advertisement. Please send a draft for the same.   ABEL BROWN,
                    Forwarding Merchant, Albany.

P. S.—The business is very good this year. Please inform the slaves that we are always on hand ready to receive them.   A. B.

Representation of advertisement used by Abel Brown to mislead a slaveowner about the whereabouts of his slave. From the *Vermont Freeman*, July 1, 1843, p. 3 (courtesy of the American Antiquarian Society, Worcester, MA).

ple of this country, is fully manifested — in boasting of their freedom and Independence, while they hold 2,500,000 of their fellow countrymen in chains and slavery; and we are loudly called upon today, to humble ourselves before God, to confess our sins and seek forgiveness — by breaking every yoke and letting the oppressed go free.

The convention were much annoyed by the noise of a cannon, which some gentlemen of Canandaigua placed under the court house windows. The motives which actuated those who placed the gun in that position, were duly *appreciated* by the convention.

Thomas Pollock, a very intelligent fugitive, three weeks from North Carolina, gave a very interesting account to the convention, of his sufferings and escape from slavery.

Liberty songs were sung by Mrs. Brown.

"A nobler strife, the world ne'er saw
The enslaved to disenthral;
I am a soldier for the war,
Whatever may befall."

JOHN MOSHER, Secretary.

Canandaigua, July 4, 1843.

A letter from our estimable friend Henry Bradley,[1] addressed to C. T. Torrey, is given in reference to other conventions in that vicinity.

Penn Yann, July 10th, '43.

Great anxiety, is every where felt by the friends of the slave and of humanity, to hear of the advances of the cause and of its triumphs; for it begins to have triumphs: or rather in the midst of the weary and desolate desert of long continued ecclesiastical, political and mob opposition, and violence, we have come to find not only an occasional, but frequently a refreshing Oasis, or what I suppose Alvan Stewart would call — the luxury of abolition. Last Thursday and Friday, we held an Antislavery Mass Convention, at the village of Branchport, in the town of Jerusalem in this county, where no meetings of the kind had ever before been held. The devoted and untiring agent of the Albany Vig. Committee, Rev. Abel Brown, with his young wife, who can both sing and speak for the slave, and a gentlemen from the south, nearly white, the son of a Congressman, who within a few days, has undergone the magic transformation which changes a personal chattel into a man, were present, and contributed greatly to the interest of the meeting. It is due the good people of Branchport, to say that their doors and their hearts were open, the one to receive abolitionists, the other to receive the truths they brought with them. Never was hospitality more generous or unfeigned.

Mr. Brown came to this place from Canandaigua, where he had been invited by the friends of freedom, to address the people on the 4th of July. The cause of impartial liberty was too unholy to be admitted into the church, and was thrust into the Court House, that a shooting, drumming, cold water and patriotic celebration might occupy the meeting house. Not satisfied with this, a cannon was placed under the windows of the Court House, whose arguments were really much louder than Mr. Brown's, but, quite contrary to the intentions of the pious movers, only served to fill the honest yeomanry with disgust for such patrician arrogance. A committee was appointed to wait on "the powers that be," to have the gun removed; but the people interposed and SWORE that their minister and the deacons of the church were the best men in the world, and that if the cannon did not drive abolition out of the place, the church would be divided.

What a change has come over the land! A few years ago, all the demagogue-politicians, and all the vicious and profane, were every where crying "church and state! church and state!" to the top of their voices. Now we hear the same classes expressing the most tender solicitude for the ministers and churches, and often interposing their cannon and their mobs, to secure the former from injury, and the latter from division. Why is all this? Doubtless, God in his all-wise Providence, frequently brings upon ministers, churches and individuals, *tests* by which their *true* character is proved and developed.

In reference to the agitation produced by the conventions, Mr. Brown writes:

The opposers had, of their own free will and accord, placed themselves in a hostile position, and were determined to make one desperate effort to destroy the abolition influence in Canandaigua; thereby rendering it absolutely necessary, either to forsake the field or batter down the fortress of the enemy. With such a systematic opposition I was invited to address the Convention. I was thus placed in a situation which demanded a mighty effort on my part. That I did my duty faithfully, I will not say; that I rebuked as sharply as the case demanded, I do not believe.

That I did my duty, as far as I was capable, I freely confess. That I say hard things, I do not deny, but I never say them for the purpose of revenging any personal animosities, for I have none to gratify.

I regret the circumstances which rendered it necessary for me to talk as I did; I did no more than was necessary to remove the objections, which the men who feel themselves aggrieved had, unasked, publicly made against the cause of abolition. If their objections were futile, the fault was not mine. *Duty to God and his insulted poor, required me to utterly annihilate every objection to the Anti-Slavery cause.*

The occasion was one of deep interest to the friends of the cause in this place (in connection with other meetings held at this period) and was indeed "the ever memorable Fourth," shadowing forth results far in the future, which time has since developed, in the formation of a new church established on those high and holy principles inculcated by our Saviour, who is emphatically styled the Deliverer of his people from sin and oppression.

On giving an account of a visit with me to Niagara Falls, in writing Rev. C. Bradford, under date of July 21st, Mr. Brown remarks:

I have been so overwhelmed with Anti-Slavery duties, that I did not have time to visit the Falls with Mrs. B. Indeed, I did not think she had sufficient health to attend all the meetings, and travel nights into the bargain; therefore gave her three days respite at the Falls. We are in good health, and leave on Monday, P.M. for the "far west." The lake is very fine and the shore inviting. My kind regards to all. Thankful for past favors and hoping their continuance —

I am as ever,

Your Brother,
A. BROWN.

A few sketches of our western journey are given, mostly from the pen of Mr. Brown, written at intervals on our route, as time and leisure would permit.

Steamboat Illinois, Aug. 9, 1843.

DEAR TORREY:

Seated, between Chicago and Milwaukie, on the deck of this noble vessel, enjoying the delightful breezes of lake Michigan, I write you this letter. My wife is also engaged in writing you a letter; and as you are a great favorite among the ladies, and are always disposed to favor them, I shall not write a letter for publication.

I have sounded the Abolitionism of Michigan, and I assure you, that it is as deep as the sorrows of the slave and as abiding as the waters of the "great deep." It would greatly refresh you to enjoy the society of the noble men who compose the Executive Committees of the societies of Michigan and Illinois.

Soon after my arrival at Chicago, a very fine span of horses, attached to a regular yankee wagon, drove up to the door of friend Eastman.[2] The driver was a noble looking man, and there were two or three noble looking men with him, and they politely invited me to occupy a vacant seat, and enjoy a delightful ride to Grove (30 miles), and attend an Anti-Slavery meeting. I soon learned that our driver was no less a personage than — Collins,[3] Esq. one of the oldest and noblest settlers of the city; and that the gentleman by my side was also a lawyer, and that the horses and carriage were owned by Mr. C. and are kept for the purpose of carrying a certain class of passengers, who travel north, for their own accommodation. Just think of it — a *Lawyer* keeps a team and uses it to comfort and bless the slave; and what is still better, this same lawyer, like H. Dresser, Esq. of New York city, defends these same despised slaves before the cruel courts, against the more cruel laws of the slavery-ridden Illinois. But to the ride.

---

[2]*Probably Zabina Eastman, editor of the antislavery newspapers* Western Citizen *and* Free West.— *Editor.*

[3]*James H. Collins, abolitionist lawyer from Chicago, was a close associate of Owen Lovejoy and successfully defended him in 1843 against a charge of aiding fugitive slaves in a prosecution of the Fugitive Slave Law.— Editor.*

We were soon nearly out of sight of land on the broad ocean of a prairie, (surely a splendid scene) with here and there a small island of timbered land, and a yankee residence. After about four hours ride, we stopped at the house of another Vermonter, and found his barn well rigged for a meeting, which assembled in due time, and was addressed by the gentlemen who accompanied me, as also by myself. The women were there and cheered us on by their words and smiles of approbation. The meeting was large considering the sparseness of the population. And the abolitionism was none of the half-way sort — there are no fence men here; but the friends feel deeply and think more deeply than many Eastern abolitionists. They are certainly more decided; they have more to contend with. Almost all of them are subject to indictment under State law, but Lovejoy-like they are unmoved. We rode back to Chicago after 10 o'clock at night.

My sheet is full, and I cannot now write of the very large meeting at Chicago, or of the kind hospitalities received there. However, they were worthy of the great land in which those who proffered them live. May God bless the friends of Michigan and Illinois! Their kindness will never be forgotten. The good will bless them — the slaves will bless them — and God will certainly bless them with life everlasting! Come to the West, if you want to see a people who are full of great hearts and great thoughts. I leave the boat, to go still west, at Milwaukie. I will write you when I get upon the Mississippi.

Yours, as ever,
A. BROWN.

[LETTER OF CATHARINE S. BROWN]

[Editor's note: the following correspondence was written by C.S. Brown and covers the same period as Abel Brown's letter to Charles Torrey, adding a number of interesting details and references].

Milwaukie, Aug. 18, 1843.

FRIEND JACKSON,[4]

Through a kind Providence, we have been enabled to complete our journey in health and safety. Our route has been rather circuitous: for the pur-

---

[4]*James C. Jackson, central New York abolitionist, who came to Albany to be editor of the* Albany Patriot *after serving as editor of the* Liberty Press *in Utica. A Liberty party supporter, he left after dissension within the party and joined the Liberty League. A close associate of William L. Chaplin, he stepped away from his antislavery work in 1851 when he opened a central New York health resort in partnership with Theodosia Gilbert, who had married Chaplin after he returned from prison in Washington, D.C.—Editor.*

pose of holding Conventions at various places in New York, Michigan, Illinois and the territory of Wisconsin and a most pleasant tour it has been, I'll assure you, which is all I can say of it at present, as it would take a port-folio to describe all I could wish, respecting its scenes, the beautiful lakes, and more than all, the enterprise and intelligence of the inhabitants of this western world. I think I now begin to understand a little what is meant by the "Giant West," having seen a small portion of its noble features.

I must now give you a short account of our Anti-Slavery visits, numbering fifty or more, since we started from New York, during all of which we have been most cordially received, and have met with no opposition of a public character, with the exception of meetings at Canandaigua on the ever memorable 4th, and a little skirmish at Buffalo; however, it is hardly worth if the cause is not hindered thereby, which is seldom the case, when Abolitionists are "on duty." At Detroit, we stopped a few days, and were kindly admitted to hold a meeting in the Baptist church. Some few seemed deeply interested for the slave, but from what I could learn, I judged that the community generally were in a quietus; they had received no lecture for some time, and it seemed that the subject was seldom agitated, except in the occurrence of a slave being judicially arrested, when the colored people exhibited no little signs of practical commotion. Anything, thought I, but a "dead calm:" rather give the powder and ball of Canandaigua, and let me hear the cannons thundering voice; then I should know that something was at work (I am a non-resistant you know). The church seems to have thrown the death-pall over the slave's redemption, in that city, for I was told that on the anniversary of Independence day, a Sabbath School celebration was held, and that a delegation previous was sent from the African church to the committee of the three different churches, beseeching them to allow the colored children of their Sabbath school, to join them in the Universal Jubilee — and I cannot but weep while I write they refused! O my God, has it come to this that children who know no prejudice of color, cannot associate together, for an hour or a day, in the joyousness of their hearts, to thank God, and bless his name for the glorious privileges of the Gospel, and for the gift of his Son to save the lost and perishing children of men? And yet said a young lawyer to me, with a very serious air, "the committee thought the parents of the white children would be unwilling that they should associate with the colored children, because of their degradation in *morals*." Query — was it not in condition? and even if it were in morals, was it not owing to the condition into which they had been thrown by their cruel prejudice and neglect for their spiritual welfare?

We next visited Ann Arbor, by invitation from brother Beckley,[5] the able editor of the Signal of Liberty. Here we found quite a different atmosphere, and we could seem to breathe freer, and even the face of nature looked more pleasing, for we had found the liberty-loving spirit ever inspiring and active in the cause. Mr. B. is a preacher of righteousness in that place, and not of sect merely, I conclude, for he now supplies two different churches, the Methodist and Baptist, unitedly. Mr. B. is of the True Wesleyan order, and a seceder or "come-outer" from the Methodist Episcopal body. On the Sabbath, Mr. Brown preached as usual, and in the evening gave two Abolition lectures at the Baptist church, and the evening following at the Court House. The day after, we stopped at Jackson, where we found Mr. Treadwell,[6] author of a highly valuable work on Slavery. Through his influence, we were enabled to hold two entensive meetings; much interest was manifested — and I ought to say, also, that much credit is due to Dr. Willson, the notorious rebel from Canada, who is now the proprietor of a fine Temperance House in that place, and a spirited character in every good cause. He told me that what grieved him most of all, as a "refugee," was the taunts given him by British royalists, saying, that while endeavoring to flee from a land of civil oppression, he had come to a land where a sixth portion of its inhabitants were deprived of all their rights.

On leaving Jackson, we passed through many a pleasant town, and among them Marshall, to which place six slaves had recently escaped, and were overtaken by their inhuman pursuers; but not a person could be marshalled in this noble town "to deliver up the fugitives," — so they were obliged to leave without them. I mention circumstances like these, to give you a clue to the prospect of Anti-slavery in Michigan, or in some of its leading towns, which generally amounts to about the same thing, for what is true of them serves as a kind of index to the whole State.

Proceeding on our way, we passed through the wilds of Michigan, or oak-openings, forming natural parks, where the wild deer roam, with an occasional lake or marsh, adding variety and beauty to the effect, (once the hunting ground of the Indian, whose marks might still be seen upon

[5] The Rev. Guy Beckley was publisher of the Signal of Liberty in Ann Arbor; his house was a stop on the Underground Railroad. — Editor. (Signal of Liberty, Ann Arbor, Mich., 23 April, 22 May 1843.)
[6] Seymour Boughton Treadwell, author of American Liberties and American Slavery Morally and Politically Illustrated (1838), moved to Jackson, Michigan, in 1839 and published the abolitionist newspaper Michigan Freeman. He was active in both the Liberty party and the Free Soil Party. — Editor. (Appleton's Cyclopedia of American Biography, edited by James Grant Wilson and John Fiske, six volumes, New York: D. Appleton and Company, 1887–1889, edited Stanley L. Klos, 1999.)

many a tree.) And here I almost forgot the slave, when I remembered the wrongs of the red man; and as the last glimmering rays of the sun lingered among the trees, so faded his dying hopes, as he gazed a long farewell to his forest home.

On reaching St. Josephs, we took a boat across the Lake to Chicago. This is a fine city, combining all the facilities and advantages of "the West." Here, again, we found Anti-slavery friends, among whom are found some of the most influential citizens of the place. Indeed, we are quite sure of finding some of the very best people on our way, for only such are engaged in our cause. We there held a series of meetings, in the First Presbyterian and Baptist Churches, to crowded and attentive audiences. The tide of public sentiment seems to be rising above their laws, and as a brother remarked to me, to be an Abolitionist here, means something, for we are obliged often to help off a fugitive at the hazard of the law, which inflicts a penalty of a fine for so doing not exceeding five hundred dollars, or imprisonment not exceeding six months in the County Jail.[7] And for this very reason the brother of the martyred Lovejoy, is soon to answer to an indictment for feeding, clothing and comforting a woman named Agnes. Mr. Lovejoy intends to plead his own case, at which time a good convention will undoubtedly be held.

Since coming to this Territory, we have held meetings nearly every evening during the week past, at Prairieville, where the people are in a great measure already abolitionized. Here also we found the same frankness and readiness to hear on this, as on every other moral topic, which characterizes the western people.

Today we arrived at Milwaukie, which name signifies a pleasant place, and indeed it is. The natural scenery exhibits a great variety, resembling that of New England somewhat, in its abrupt declivities, trees and shrubbery, and commanding prospect. The view of the lake is very fine, extending to a great distance. Yet amid all the loveliness of Wisconsin, what signifies flowery banks? A slave hunter is at this moment in pursuit of his prey, with his pistol in his pocket — a slave girl from St. Louis having escaped to this place for refuge. She is now secreted by the colored people, and will not probably be taken, for the simple reason that she cannot be found, though a posse of constables are laying in wait for her, at various points and stations.

At Prairieville[8] we were happy to meet with a brother Abolitionist, by the name of Matthews, an Englishman, and a Baptist clergyman. He was

[7]This state statute in Illinois, which prohibited aiding fugitive slaves, was in addition to the federal law. — Editor.

[8]Now the home of Abel Brown's parents. — Editor.

sent to this region by the Home Missionary Society, but has withdrawn himself from their support, being unwilling to receive the "price of blood" from their treasury. Mr. M. informed me that he had travelled through the greater part of Wisconsin as a revolutionizer on the question of abolition. He says that societies have been established at nearly every part of the Territory, and that in the south-western portion, some abolitionists reside, formerly of Kentucky and other slave States, but who left from their utter abhorrence of slavery, that they might escape its influence.

It seems peculiarly important that the people of this Territory, should be set right in relation to this subject, in its infancy before they have assumed state laws and are admitted into the Union as one of the Confederacy.

We are about to start for home, in order to reach Buffalo on the 31st, to attend the National Convention, and anticipate much pleasure in our journey round by the lakes.

C. S. BROWN.

P. S. I have written at the request of Mr. Brown, as well as from my own inclination, that our friends might hear from us, through the columns of your paper, if you please.   C.S.B.

LETTER TO THE EDITOR OF THE *ALBANY PATRIOT*.

Prairie Village, Wis. Ter., August 18, 1843.

REV. C. T. TORREY,— Here in this land of "great hearts" I write you a short account of the progress of Abolitionism. The evening of my arrival there was a great meeting; the next day two meetings, and the next three meetings, and then one a day until I have now been six days here, and have been permitted to lecture eight times to very large audiences. The people here are wide awake, determined to trample slavery in the dust. The Baptist minister, Rev. Mr. Miner,[9] and the Presbyterian minister, Rev. Mr. Curtis, were not only ready to aid, but prepared the way before-hand for the reception of the truth, and were sufficiently grateful for it to feel in their pockets and make donations to aid those who proclaimed it. Be not surprised when I tell you that where this village now stands, five years ago two log houses enclosed its entire population. Now there are four Churches, an Academy; stores, taverns, flouring mills, &c. &c. The Anti-slavery

---

[9] *The Rev. Mr. Miner was possibly the Rev. Ovid Miner, a Middlebury native, who was an anti-slavery lecturer in the Adirondack region and who later went to Oberlin, Ohio. He eventually settled in Penn Yan, New York, where according to the Rev. Luther Lee he was active in the Underground Railroad. (Flavius Cook,* Sketches of Essex County, *W. Lansing & Sons, 1858: 93;* Luther Lee, *Autobiography of Luther Lee,* New York: Phillips & Hunt, 1882: 331.)*— Editor.*

meetings were cheered by the music of the excellent Pewakie band. It would have made you feel that slavery was dying, to have heard the liberty stirring strains from the instruments of those noble young men, as they died away upon the extensive and fertile plains that surround that lovely village. I heard a slave catcher from Mississippi cursing the Prairieville Abolitionists. He said they were all a pack of thieves, and it was of no use to go there after a slave.

I came here to rest, but a few more such months of rest would send me to my final resting place. Within the last seven weeks, myself and wife have attended fifty-eight meetings, in all of which we have taken a prominent part, and have traveled over 1500 miles. We have everywhere been received in the kindest manner, and every attention has been shown us which heart could wish. I think we ought to call these western men *"great hearted Abolitionists,"* for they are certainly the most noble set of men that I ever saw. Before them slavery begins to tremble, and ere long it will tumble to earth, and probably to the pit

Yours as ever,
ABEL BROWN.

Steam Boat Cleveland, 25th *August,* 1843.

EDITOR OF THE *COUNTRYMAN,*[10]

Dear Sir:— I am now half way between Detroit and Cleveland, on board this noble steamer returning from a delightful trip to Illinois and Wisconsin territory. We left Chicago on Tuesday morning last. Have had a very pleasant passage. This boat is worthy of the patronage of the travelling public.

You will be pleased, I doubt not, to learn that the cause of abolition is rapidly advancing in Illinois and Wisconsin territory. In the Congressional District occupying the N. E. corner of Ill. the liberty vote was over 1200, and that too, without any extra exertions on the part of abolitionists. I think that is the *Banner District* in the U.S. Living, as you do, about 700 miles from that State, you can hardly realize the difficulties which our friends are obliged to encounter. Subject to indictment and imprisonment for giving the poor a piece of bread, and surrounded by a class of men who delight to worry and devour them — constantly harassed with suits at law, and the more dreadful acts of mob violence, yet they quietly and with a firm step carry forward their benevolent efforts for the redemption of their brethren in bonds. I enjoyed a number of interesting meetings with the friends in

[10]The Countryman *was a newspaper published in Perry, New York (Wyoming County) from 1843 to 1845. It continued thereafter as the* Impartial Countryman *and then the* Free Citizen *until sometime after 1846.— Editor.*

Chicago and vicinity. They are usually men of piety and stern integrity, who are even ready to sacrifice their property, reputation and life if necessary to advance the cause.— They certainly deserve the prayers and aid of every friend of the oppressed.— Even at Chicago, I saw a number of men or monsters from Missouri, in pursuit of fugitives. They were armed with pistols and dirks, and have the law all on their side. Still I do not know an abolitionist in Chicago who would not protect the poor fleeing fugitive to the last. *God bless the Illinois abolitionists,* is the spontaneous emotion of my heart.

In Wisconsin Territory I found a noble band of men. I lectured there, and in Illinois to very large audiences. I went there to rest, but a few more such rests, and I shall find my final *resting place.* They flocked to hear in great numbers, and told the slave catchers to their faces, that law or no law, they would protect any and every slave, that came among them. There were men at Milwaukie and in the vicinity, during my entire stay, in search of slaves. The law is on their side, but who can resist the people, when they arise in the strength of the God of Israel.— Sickness and weariness prevented me from visiting Delavan,[11] but I heard a good report of that place. I had abundant evidence that the Devil and all his pro-slavery legions hate its very name. Old Perry may rejoice, that God accounted her worthy to plant a colony like that at Delavan. Those brethren, who went from your place and planted the standard of truth, lived not in vain. They are dead but their names yet live, and their influence is felt for forty or fifty miles around.

During my passage from Chicago, I have had as a companion, Rev. Owen Lovejoy,[12] of Princeton Ill., a brother of the *Martyr.* He is truly one of the noble men of earth. He intends, I believe, to plead his own cause. He has been harassed by the slave power constantly, yet he does not appear in the least discouraged. Meets opposition with cheerfulness; murmurs not that his time and money are torn from him in the cause of the slave. May he long live to enjoy the luxury of doing good, and then rest with the just in that mansion above, where no opposition can disturb his repose.

Yours in labors abundant,
ABEL BROWN.

Cor. Sec.. of E. N. Y. A. S. Soc'y.

[11]*Delevan (Wisconsin) village founded on temperance principles and named after Edwin C. Delevan; apparently, its founders were natives of Perry, New York.— Editor.*

[12]*Owen Lovejoy was the brother of religious editor and antislavery martyr Elijah Lovejoy. In 1836, Owen moved from Maine to Illinois in support of his brother, who was being persecuted for his outcry against the lynching of a black man. After his brother's murder, he vowed to carry on the work of his brother and his home became a station on the Underground Railroad. He also became a prominent voice in the Liberty party and other abolitionist circles.— Editor.*

Illustration from *American Anti-Slavery Almanac of 1838* showing the burning of a black man named Mcintosh in St. Louis in 1836. This lynching compelled the outcry from religious editor Elijah Lovejoy in his newspaper the *St. Louis Observer*, which led to his murder in 1837.

On our return from Wisconsin, we attended the National Convention held at Buffalo, where some six or seven thousand people were present, and assembled within and around the great Oberlin tent transported from Cleveland expressly for the occasion. Mr. Brown was quite anxious it seems from a letter to C. T. Torrey that the *South* should be represented in the delegation of certain fugitives, amply qualified to bear their testimony respecting the peculiar institution in their own persons and sufferings.

There we met our friend and coadjutor, Torrey, and joined together in holding meetings at various places, indirectly, on our route to Albany.

In September, we visited Massachusetts for the purpose of seeing friends and aiding the cause in which we were engaged, Mr. Brown being obliged soon to return to his labors in N. Y., I remained at the home of my nativity, until his return some weeks subsequent. During his absence, he wrote me a constant description of his labors. A few extracts therefrom are given.

Albany, Saturday Morning, Sept. 23d, 1843.

EVER DEAR CATHARINE:— I hardly know how happy I should be to see you this morning, but as I cannot, I forbear to say more respecting it. Well, we had a glorious meeting of three days continuance at Canastota. The large house was filled to overwhelming day and night, and the interest was intense. We had one discussion which lasted twelve hours.

... Torrey made a great war speech upon another resolution, but it was lost by one tremendous "No." So we are no war and no insurrection men and women too

I almost forgot to tell you, that last night, I lectured on the steps of the Capitol, in connection with Torrey and Goodwin. Tomorrow I go to Quaker street.[13]

Sept. 25th, 1843.

EVER DEAR C ... Here I am in an Abolition meeting in the Court House of Schoharie County. Lewis Washington is talking, and all are looking upon him with intense interest He is now making a most thrilling speech respecting the miseries of the Slave; and I am writing to tell Catharine, I really wish she was here... Could I sit down in your society, and have with us those dear, dear children, I should be as happy as outward circumstances would permit. The field that I am called to occupy is not pleasant to my natural taste, but one which I believe God requires me to occupy, and one from which I must not flee, if I would have the blessing of God; and one that I must continue for a space of time to occupy. Lewis talks with so much pathos, that I cannot write.

....

My labors in this state are more appreciated than ever before. They say, I am more prudent, but they on the contrary are opening their eyes wider.

I am desirous of your company in the northern Counties, and think it would greatly add to the interest of all meetings. I also should be happy to have you visit the south eastern part of the State, should it be convenient; as also L. T. and New York, and in the spring we can, I trust, settle somewhere, and find as much leisure as will be proper for us to enjoy....

I wish I was with you. O how pleasant that fire around which you all sit while I am in this cold office, plotting a campaign against the enemy of God and man.

Dear wife, adieu, for a few days only, I hope. May God bless you and your husband and all friends.

Yours as ever,
ABEL.

[13]*Quaker Street was the name of a section of the village of Duanesburg, New York, about 25 miles west of Albany, which was home to Quakers and, as legend has it, a stop along the Underground Railroad. — Editor.*

Chester, Warren Co . N. Y, Oct 11, 1843.

EVER DEAR CATHARINE:— I have today been pent in, by mountains as high as grass or trees can grow, rising above each other in indescribable masses of rugged piles, which make me tremble as I approach — any part of Massachusetts is a plain, when compared with what I have passed to day. One mountain, which I think is located in the town of Warrensburgh, about twice as high as Wachusett, (I cannot spell it) was perfectly bare — a mass of solid granite; enough to build ten, if not one hundred such cities as New York. I had so much Antislavery to attend to, that I had very little time to look up; and it is now of no use, as the rocks are so high, that I cannot see the top. Yet I am now in a very quiet place in a Temperance house,[14] (parlor very neat and comfortable) thinking, what a fool I was, to let Catharine Swan Brown stay in that nest so good and lovely, and I wander off in this land of hills and glens alone....

I received your letter with more than a glad heart, but was so overwhelmed with duties, that I had no time to write.

I was in Albany only from Thursday 3 o'clock P.M. to Friday morning 6 o'clock, and did not get the morning's mail before I left. Went to the printing office, wrote letters for two County Meetings, &c. &c. Ordered a cab to drive me back to my office — took my valise, bag &c., and was driven at a mad rate to the Railroad, just in time to take the cars — went like an arrow to Schenectady; met my noble companion, Lewis Washington, whom I found ready to join me in a hearty laugh. He took the cars at Troy on that beautiful road, and in one of the most splendid cars; and like any other gentlemen sat where he found a seat. The conductor came and ordered him behind the door. But Mr. W. asked if the seats behind the door were any cheaper, than any other seats; and was told, they were not. He then said, he was a gentleman, and should ride where be pleased; and they might help themselves if they could. After considerable wrath, they left him to glory in his conquest alone, once. After hearing this, I went to the office and asked the agent for the company, if they intended to insult a colored man, on the Troy road and after considerable hesitation, was told, that they always required them to sit behind the door. So now for another warfare....

We went on to Ballston Springs — Took our breakfast a few minutes before eleven o'clock — had a great County convention, and next day went on to Corinth, in time for P.M. meeting, where we continued two days; and left, loaded with invitations to return and bring my dear wife with

---

[14]*Likely the Temperance Tavern in Chestertown, N.Y., run by Oliver Arnold, a member of the Warren County Liberty party. The building which housed this former hotel is now a private home.* — Editor.

me. Next morning, (Monday) rode down in sight of a place where the waters of the Hudson river roll in majestic splendor, over a perpendicular rock of from sixty to eighty feet — a grand sight it would have been, for my dear Catharine and sister Clara. Then passed over a road, that made me glad to hope that I was never to see it again; unless I went to do penance — *the rocks, the rocks!* I cannot describe them. Five miles, brought us to the river again, and then a plain, and fine road to Glens Falls. Then to Sandy Hill, where I found my old friend Stephen Lee, an old Revolutionary soldier, with his wife most dear, and his daughter very kind. Good people — Heaven bless them....

Next morning proceeded on our way to Caldwell, passing over a fine road through a beautifully romantic country, amid mountains and winding ravines, crystal streams, and beautiful Lakes, until we arrived in sight of Lake George, which lies with evening stillness, between towering mountains, inviting you to enjoy its sweet breezes and gentle zephyrs, with its beautiful Islands and overhanging and rock bound shores. How lovely, refreshing and enervating, must be its placid bosom amid the heat of summer But the inhabitants of the beautiful village on its banks, are a slavery and rum cursed race; and where I expected to have found a hearty welcome — I was met by cold repulses. The Post Master said, there was no meeting, and only one Abolitionist within five miles; and no steamboat to convey me from such a miserable place. However, after much inquiry, I found a man (who lived twenty miles from there) who told me that an Antislavery Convention was in session at a distance of five miles, in a Baptist meeting house.[15] God bless the Baptists, said I, and hired a boy for fifty cents to carry us on. Being in a great hurry to get his money, he drove his horse in "hot haste," and soon I found myself surrounded by an audience, who with earnest gaze heard me until five o'clock. Then the ministers who were holding a protracted meeting, politely invited my friend to occupy the evening; and I will only say, that we gratified them until eleven o'clock. A friend then took me in a carriage and carried me two miles to Hon. Mr. Richards, who had sent and invited us to his hospitable dwelling.

I slept from twelve until six, and then found the parlor with a good fire, which was graced with the presence of a Whig Representative, a good man, who made us feel at home in company with his intelligent and truly wor-

---

[15] *Likely the Second Baptist Church in the nearby town of Queensbury, also called the West Mountain Church, which was a member of the staunchly abolitionist Washington Union Baptist Association of 21 churches in New York and Vermont. In 1836 this association condemned the sin of slavery, and in 1838 it broke all ties of fellowship with Baptist churches that admitted slaveholders as members.* (Minutes of the Fourth Annual Meeting of the Washington Union Baptist Association, *Union Village: Lansing, 1838: 6–7.) According to local legend, this church also was a stop on the Underground Railroad. — Editor.*

West Mountain Baptist Church in Queensbury, N.Y., probable site of antislavery convention attended by the Rev. Abel Brown near Caldwell, circa October 1843 (photograph by Tom Calarco).

thy appearing wife and daughters. After our repast, Mr. Washington arrived, and we were taken by my friend Leggett,[16] and brought to this place. Dined with him and his Quaker wife, and am now writing at this Temperance house, at five o'clock and twenty minutes. The tea bell is ringing, and I must go to the table — then go to meeting and tell of the slaves' wrongs....

I expect to spend three weeks in [Massachusetts], during Nov. and wish to have meetings in different places. I can if you please, empower you to get them up. Shall send Lewis down to attend them. I wish to hold them

---

[16]*Joseph Leggett was president of the Liberty party of Warren County, New York, in the southern Adirondacks, where the party held regular meetings at least as late as 1851. Family history documents that Leggett also was a conductor on the Underground Railroad.* — *Editor.*

soon after Election, and collect money to aid the poor slave in his escape. I shall write Mr. Snow of Fitchburg, and Mr. Jones of Ashburnham, and you will please confer with Mr. Everett, our good friend in Princeton.[17] Last month, ending first October, I paid out in cash, for the committee at Albany, $75.90 (most of it directly to aid fugitives) beside my traveling expenses and salary. I think, I shall get it again — I know I shall, for I have a note from One, who always pays with interest.

Joseph W. Leggett, Quaker and legendary Underground Railroad conductor from Chestertown, N.Y. (courtesy Dan Leggett).

Bottom: The Temperance Tavern in Chestertown, where Abel Brown took lodging and dined with Joseph Leggett.

[17]*Snow was likely Benjamin Snow of Fitchburg, and Everett likely Joshua T. Everett of Westminster, just north of Princeton Station, Massachusetts. Both were identified by Wilbur Siebert as participants in the Underground Railroad. — Editor. (Siebert,* Underground Railroad in Massachusetts: *13–15.)*

Plattsburgh, 24 Oct. 1843.

EVER DEAR CATHARINE:— Here I am in Clinton Co., in the town where the celebrated battle was fought on Lake Champlain, during the last war. I am in an upper room, that overlooks the quiet waters that bore up the palaces of death, and were made red with the blood of the slain, The old battle ground, was yesterday pointed out to me, and the place in the river, where the armies crossed and recrossed, and where hundreds died. The Lake with its numerous fertile islands is very beautiful, and while the mountains in the distance are covered with snow, and all nature seems bound in its robes of ice, not a ripple is seen to break the quiet stillness of its bosom. Since I last wrote you, I have regretted a hundred times that you and dear Clara were not with me. The beautiful vallies, the immense forests, extending as far as the eye can reach — the huge piles of rocks, the towering mountains and attendant scenery, have all conspired to fill me with reverence and awe, as I have passed over, through and around these works of God. There is one place in Essex Co. called "Poc'o moonshine," where you pass directly along the base of a mass of rocks, about eight hundred feet high; five hundred of the space is one solid ledge, with not a place of sufficient width to stand upon, and during a clear moonlight night is beyond description grand, and from its mighty summit the view is not only sublime, but beautiful in the extreme [see photograph, p. 168). There you can stand and gaze south, until the sight is lost amid the windings of the sources of the mighty Hudson. West, is one unbroken forest of crags and mountain tops, inhabited only by beasts of prey. North, and the eye rests upon the extensive but gentle slope of land, (a plain almost) reaching to the St. Lawrence. East, and the scene is both grand and beautiful, bordering on a god-like sublimity. Beneath your feet is the valley of a gentle stream, passing through numerous lakes, surrounded by overhanging trees — then rising forests, with here and there a farm-house, and its cultivated fields — then the ever inviting Champlain, whose waters quietly sleep in nature's choicest reservoir — then the rich farms of Vermont, spreading from north to south, as far as the eye can reach — and then the snow-capped mountains, whose summits are lost in the infinite expanse above. There you can stand, gaze, wonder and admire until you are reminded of the everlasting truth, that the unbalanced masses, around and beneath you, are only the specimen of a world that is balanced upon nothing; and fall down in the stillness of the scene, and adore the God, whose unseen power created and sustains it all.

Champlain, Clinton Co. Oct. 25.

Ah my dear, and here I am in an upper room beside a warm stove, where one, who I trust, will soon read this, would make me very happy. I left

Pokomoonshine Mountain in Essex County, N.Y. (photograph courtesy of Carl Heilman, http://www.carlheilman.com/home.html).

Plattsburg at 9 o'clock yesterday; rode fourteen miles to Chazy — lectured twice, and then was taken by Mr. Moore,[18] and brought seven miles after 9 o'clock at night, to this, his truly hospitable mansion. I can only say of them, that they are making me very comfortable. I lecture here twice this P.M. and evening. Then I go (God willing) to Moresville, seven miles, and lecture twice to-morrow, and on Friday leave there for Plattsburgh. Thence by steamboat to St. Albans, Vt. where I lecture twice, and on Saturday take the steamboat to Whitehall, and then Packet to Albany.

I intended to have returned to Albany last week, but the continued importunity of the friends altered my plans; therefore, sent Lewis Washington back to Albany; from whence he will go to fill appointments made for me in Schenectady and Schoharie Counties.

I shall, with God's blessing, be able to meet you at home or at Worcester, about the 10th of Nov. I might perhaps be home the 9th, but that is my birthday, and I believe it is fashion to whip truants, upon such occasions, therefore I think I had better wait one day; still I may venture to risk it.

My health is excellent. There are many things truly delightful in this region, concerning which, I cannot find time to write.

Your Ever Dear Husband,
ABEL.

[18] *Noadiah Moore was president of the Liberty party of Clinton County, New York. His home was about five miles from the Canadian border, and according to individuals contemporary with him, he took freedom-seekers to Canada and helped them find work. Interestingly, he had several businesses in La Colle, Canada, only a short distance from the Canadian border.— Editor. (Allan S. Everest, ed.,* Recollection of Clinton County and the Battle of Plattsburgh, 1800–1840; Memoirs of Early Residents from the Notebooks of D. S. Kellogg, *Plattsburgh, N.Y., 1964: 57.)*

Left: Noadiah Moore, legendary Underground Railroad conductor from Champlain, N.Y. (Clinton County) (courtesy Special Collections, Feinberg Library, Plattsburgh State University).

Mr. Brown revisited Massachusetts (in November) and spent some weeks in a lecturing tour accompanied by Lewis Washington and myself, visiting Lowell, Boston, Andover and other places, and returned to Albany the last of December. The following month, we held an interesting series of conventions in Fulton Co. in behalf of the slave. A short account of succeeding labors is found in a letter written for the *Albany Patriot.*

FROM MRS. ABEL BROWN

Poughkeepsie, March 18, 1844.
BROTHER GOODWIN— It is four weeks to-day since we started on our Anti-Slavery tour. During three weeks, we visited Delaware, Sullivan and Orange counties. We have found many kind friends to aid us in our efforts in this section, and a fair prospect seems opening for the advancement of the cause, though violent opposition has been rife to overthrow our labors and defeat our object. At Delhi, the friends contributed liberally for the support of agents in Delaware county. One gentleman on giving ten dollars, remarked that he wished to have it distinctly understood why he gave that sum. He said, previous to coming into the Convention he had thought of giving five dollars, but on hearing of the mob the night before, determined to give ten, and if another disturbance of the kind should take place the following evening, that he would add another five. As the event happened, Mr.— is indebted another five dollars. Among other friends At Delhi, I cannot forbear to mention our brother, the Rev. Mr. Wescott, who has taken a prominent stand relative to the cause in that place. The Convention being over, we were conveyed by our "whole-souled" friend St. John,[19] to Walton, where we held a meeting in the evening at the Presbyterian church;

---

[19] *There were three St. Johns from Walton in Delaware County who were abolitionists. Smith and C. St. John were vice-presidents of the Delaware County Anti-Slavery Society, and A.P. St. John was a vice-president of the Eastern New York Anti-Slavery Society. ("Eastern New York Anti-Slavery Society Organizational Meeting,"* The Emancipator, *12 May 1842: 7.)— Editor.*

much interest was manifested. We were next conveyed by the same brother to Deposit, at which place we held a Convention of two days, though much disturbed by a company of boys and "children of a larger growth," who knew no more than to act as mere puppets of certain "wire-pullers" ecclesiastical and political (according to their own professions,) yet, amid all the storm tumultuous, we trust much good was effected. Here, we also found true friends, who were willing to share with us the contumely and reproach of a "gainsaying multitude." Rev. Mr. Mumford, of the Baptist church, assisted us much in our efforts at that place, as also Mr. St. John, brother to the one to whom I have already alluded. We next stopped at Beaverkill, where we held two meetings, distributed quite a number of tracts, and then proceeded on our way over the Delaware hills and into Orange county, passing through Newburgh to New Windsor. Here we were cordially received at the hospitable mansion of friend Roe.[20] At this place a Convention was held a day and two evenings. Many good friends from abroad were present, among whom was Mr. Kingsley, formerly professor in the Military Academy at West Point and an officer of the United States navy or army. He seemed zealously interested for the slave and spoke of what be knew from personal observation concerning the system, and corroborated many statements made by the speaker, (Mr. Brown.) In conclusion, he said that it was not in his power to labor in the field at this time, he would therefore make a donation for the distribution of tracts and such other efforts as might be made in that section. Since coming to that place, I have endeavored to interest the "colored people" in behalf of the slave; have held two meetings at Zion's church. Universal interest prevailed. Many tracts were taken by them and a subscription given. Several fugitive slaves were present, being resident in this place. One remarked to me after the meetings were over, that the account given of the treatment of slaves (to use his own words) seemed very natural to him. We are about making arrangements for a series of Conventions in Dutchess county, which we shall hope to fulfill (the Lord prospering) in the course of two or three weeks.

Yours,

C. S. BROWN.

Mr. Brown has also visited Ulster county, where he has also made arrangements for meetings.   C. S. B.

---

[20]*Peter Roe of New Windsor in Orange County was a vice-president in both the Eastern New York Anti-Slavery Society and the New York Anti-Slavery Society. ("Eastern New York Anti-Slavery Society Organizational Meeting,"* The Emancipator, *12 May 1842: 7; "Anti-Slavery Society,"* Friend of Man, *23 September 1840: 200.)— Editor.*

In gliding over the numerous conventions held by Mr. Brown, I am obliged to omit many incidents of interest blended with the intercourse of friends on those genial occasions. One, however, is worthy of insertion in this place on account of the intimate relation of the subject with the spirit and laws of our nation's charter. While at Delhi, a Scotchman called on Mr. Brown to ask his advice with regard to citizenship, asking if he could take the oath to support the Constitution, and help maintain the laws of the country that rob the poor slave of his rights? I never shall forget the sober, thoughtful expression of the good old man's face. God bless him! I know not Mr. Brown's reply — I could not wait for it; but cried out, "No, never!"

The views of Mr. Brown in reference to political action, were briefly these:

Voting — he looked upon as an instrumentality to turn the political machinery of this country to operate in favor of the slave — he thought it calculated to operate on the slaveholder's mind — saying he would count votes! He indulged the idea that mere abstraction in principles or theory would never free the slave. To use his own words, he said that a platform of laws had been framed and laid on the persons of the slaves until they literally crushed them to death, and that on this platform stand the two great political parties and also the American Church — including Methodists, Baptists, Presbyterians, &c. To relieve the slave, each person must jump off, and by so doing counts *one,* and by putting his shoulder under the platform counts *two.* In short, if he jumps off, it is to render some practical aid, and in one way by *voting* he actually is endeavoring to upset this platform now resting upon the heads of the slave.

The writer confesses her inability to do justice to this subject as presented by himself. Suffice it to say that being often used by him as an illustration, it assumed the name of "BROWN'S PLATFORM ARGUMENT" and was considered a very *lucid* argument for the system and the means to be used for its overthrow.

In visiting the southeastern portions of N. Y. State, we were

Advertisement requesting socks and other aid for fugitive slaves (*Albany Patriot,* Jan. 3, 1844).

often compelled to stop at those public places, where the deadly poison of the intoxicating draught spread its pestilential influence to entire villages. Such were the baneful and extended effects of those poisonous streams that no friend of human rights could be heard to effect, if even allowed to speak in behalf of the poor and downtrodden slave. Such was the case in Ulster County, where Mr. Brown had made appointments to lecture. Being thus thwarted in his design, he was led again to examine his duty in relation to the cause of Temperance, and at a point of the enemy where his influence could be most felt and was most needed.

Under these circumstances, he was induced to make an appeal to the public in the form of a circular addressed to the Mayor of Albany, wherein he gave a statement of facts relative to the number of houses used for the sale of spirituous liquors. Such number was no less than *two hundred* through the direct sanction and license of the mayor and authorities of the city. He also depicted the direful effects thereof, and even the *murderous* consequences in some instances, resulting from this legal sanction and approval in combination with the perverted conscience of a professedly Christian people in relation to this subject.

On the publication of this circular, Mr. Brown received many anonymous letters, containing threats of personal violence if he did not quit the city. However, he remained undisturbed, quietly pursuing the duties marked out to him by the leadings of Providence.

LETTER TO THE EDITOR OF *THE AMERICAN FREEMAN*.[21]

Anti-Slavery Rooms,
Albany, 28th *March.* 1844.

Very Dear Sir:— The hearts of the Anti-Slavery friends in this city, have been made glad by the appearance of the *American Freeman.* To one especially, who has for ten years been spending his entire mental and physical energies in advancing a reform, it is truly refreshing to see friends rising up with new energies, and taking the front rank in freedom's holy battles. In the name of the friends of freedom throughout the entire valley of the Hudson, I bid you a hearty "God speed." May the *"American Freeman"* live until the colored men of America shall be as free as the winds that

[21]*This Wisconsin newspaper was based in Prairie Village, the home of Brown's parents. On September 16, 1846, abolitionist singer George W. Clark gave a concert in nearby Southport, Wisconsin, and met with Brown's mother, who tearfully spoke of her son. ("Albany Patriot," Albany Patriot, 2 Feb. 1848: 47.)—Editor.*

sweep over your fertile plains. I almost imagine that your atmosphere has changed. Last August, I was in your town, and saw a man from Md. with his pistols and knives, surrounded by a host of persons who were aiding him in tracking and hunting an innocent girl of sixteen, and I heard that same man-hunter boast to a few of his southern friends, while on our passage to Chicago, that he had all the friends in Milwaukie that he desired, and that he could have taken the girl with perfect ease, had not a few "*nigger thieves*" (as he called them) hid her. But God be praised, Milwaukie is no longer the slave hunter's hunting ground. How does Lawyer Arnold get along? His woman hunting business will I guess be small in future, unless he goes to the land of chains. When I took up your papers, Nos. 1 and 2, I could hardly believe it possible, that such a mighty revolution had been wrought within so short a time. But it is a fashion you western men have of going the "*whole man*" at once. Would to God that Albany Dutchmen could see the truth as soon.

You can appreciate my feelings upon reading your paper, when I indulge myself in telling you a few facts respecting an anti-slavery lecturer, with whom I am well acquainted.[22] He espoused the cause in 1834. Soon after this, he was knocked down in the streets. Then he was whipped with a heavy cowskin more than fifty lashes. Was mobbed times without number almost. On one occasion, he paid for putting in more than seventy lights of glass that had been broken out of his house by a mob. Three times he was cruelly whipped. He was stoned again and again. In the winter of 1837-8, he wore an over coat that was completely besmeared with eggs. He was accustomed to aid slaves from near the Virginia line, a little distance north, and hide them in the woods. His wife would feed these children of sorrow and as her husband was about to leave, would in tears commend him to God, and then rising from prayer, would say, " Go my husband, go, for God will be your shield." At another time, while riding with his wife and child, a gang of ruffians saw him, and one of the number raised his rifle and fired — the ball passed between the horse and the unoffending man. He will carry to his grave the marks of slavery's champions. You will not be surprised that such men rejoice, when accessions are made to the cause of abolition. Every newspaper brings with it a blessed assurance that the cause is onward. It takes off a little of the heavy load that crushed to the earth, the pioneers in this cause.

But Sir, I took my pen only to write a word, and ask you to publish in your paper, a notice of a little work herewith sent, called "*The Legion of*

---

[22]*Brown is here again describing himself in the third person. This use seems more affected than earlier such usage. — Editor.*

Liberty."[23] An excellent friend in our city, who has spent hundreds — yes, thousands of dollars in the cause of the poor, has given me the use of the plates, so that I can publish them quite cheap. Soon as our canal opens, if I can find a traveler who will take them to Buffalo, I shall send five hundred of them to Wisconsin.

Please excuse the liberty I have taken, in so freely writing to a stranger, and yet your paper has been to me a pleasing introduction. Should you visit this city, I shall be very happy to see you.

Truly Yours,
ABEL BROWN, Cor. Sec'y,
Of Eastern N. Y., A. S. Society

THE LEGION OF LIBERTY.

REMONSTRANCE

OF SOME FREE MEN, STATES, AND PRESSES,
TO THE TEXAS REBELLION, AGAINST
THE LAWS OF NATURE AND OF NATIONS.

Ruthless Rapine, Righteous Hope defies.

"Ye serpents ! ye generation of vipers!!
How can ye escape the damnation of hell!!!!"

1843.

Sold at the Patriot Office, No. 9 Exchange st. Albany.
Six cts. single; 50 per dozen; $3 per hundred; $25 per thousand.

Right: **1843 publication by the American Anti-Slavery Society celebrating the writings through the ages in support of freedom.**

---

[23]The Legion of Liberty *was a collection of essays and literary works extolling the virtue of liberty. It was published by the American Anti-Slavery Society.—Editor.*

CHAPTER XVII

LETTERS—ANNIVERSARY OF EASTERN N. Y.
ANTI-SLAVERY SOCIETY—MR. BROWN VISITS
WESTERN N.Y.—LABORS FOR THE CAUSE IN
VARIOUS COUNTIES—RIOTOUS SCENES IN TROY—
MY OWN PERSONAL OBSERVATIONS
OF HIS VIEWS AND CHARACTER

The letter inserted at the end of the last chapter is of interest as pertaining in some degree to the history of Mr. Brown in the allusions incidentally made in reference to himself.

At this season, Mr. Brown was much engaged in preparing the way for the annual convention of the Eastern N.Y. Anti-Slavery Society for which he officiated. His efforts were also enlisted in a series of conventions in behalf of the cause in Dutchess County, where he suffered with other friends much personal violence and abuse. He was even assailed in the night time and forcibly thrust from the side walk. Yet much good was accomplished in arousing the attention of the community to the question of their own responsibilities in reference to this sin of our nation.

On May the 8th, 1844, the anniversary of the Eastern N.Y. Anti-Slavery Society was held at the Apollo Rooms in the city of New York:

The Hall will contain fifteen hundred people. It was crowded to excess, gallery and all, and many left for want of room. The speakers were of the highest order. On the whole our meeting was a great and good, and harmonious one, full of the liveliest and most thrilling interest, even unto the end." Among the results of the society during the year previous, the following are recorded.

First. It has co-operated in the permanent establishment of a weekly Anti-Slavery paper.

Second. More than one hundred thousand Anti-Slavery Tracts have been published and distributed.

Third. From four to nine agents have been constantly engaged.

Fourth. The entire northern half of the field has been made a safe resort for fugitive slaves.

Fifth. The Anti-Slavery vote was increased more than threefold in fifteen counties in Eastern New York over the vote of 1843.

ALBANY PATRIOT.—This is a very large weekly print, published at Albany, N. Y., and edited by W. L. Chaplin, one of the strongest and most able anti-slavery lecturers in the nation. He wields also a strong pen. His style is unpolished and rough but robust and Herculean. We like him because under this rough exterior bears a great, and true, and warm heart. And it is most evident that the severest things our friend Chaplin says, are dictated by the noblest impulses. He hates shams with a perfect hatred. A smooth, oily tongue, canting priest with a hollow heart, is his especial disgust; and wo betide him, if Chaplin should consider him worthy game. So of the cutaneous democracy. Gerrit Smith, Beriah Green, and William Goodell, are constant contributors to the Patriot. It is the most strongly reformatory paper published in the United States. Its mode of attack and its intercourse with its cotemporaries is frequently not to our taste; nevertheless, we say with all our heart God bless the Patriot, and give it a wide circulation. It is the main organ of the progressive potion of the Liberty Party. Will not some of our readers who are able send for it?—*American Freeman.*

This *was* the last anniversary of the Society ever attended by Mr. Brown — to whose efforts it will readily be conceded the Society owed its prosperity and much of its vitality as an organization.[1]

Entry from the *Albany Patriot* reporting the *American Freeman's* comments on its political position (from the *Albany Patriot*, Feb. 2, 1848, p. 47).

Soon after this convention, Mr. Brown visited Western New York for the purpose of seeing his children, and at the same time causing his voice to be heard in behalf of human rights and the holy principles of truth wherever necessity called or opportunity offered.

The following extract, is from a letter to myself in reference to the home[2] of his children under date of May 24, at Fredonia.

... It is very pleasant here. Ma' has a beautiful yard. The flowers are in blossom — Roses, Snowballs, Lillies, &c., &c., and the fine green clover and the noble shade trees. — all encircled by the neat white fence, Robert was preparing when we were here last summer. I wish you were here, and then I should be as happy here as earthly circumstances would permit. My dear boys are here in the room, enjoying a fine spell of playing ball. How truly lovely they are. The cunning of Charles shines finely through his eyes, as with lightning flash, he resents every attempt to pass him by unnoticed.

[1]*So far as is known by this editor, there was only one more annual meeting of the ENYASS in 1845, which was the last known year of its existence.— Editor.*

[2]*This was the home of his first wife's parents; Abel's parents were then living in Wisconsin.— Editor.*

The Apollo Rooms, a major New York City theatre of the antebellum period. The first performance of the New York Philharmonic was held here, as was the 1844 anniversary of the Eastern N.Y. Anti-Slavery Society (New York Philharmonic Archives).

May heaven preserve them uncontaminated and pure, amid the corruptions of this wicked world. I should be very happy to take them home,— but have reluctantly concluded to let them remain. But expect to take Walter with us next Fall, if possible. This is quite a healthy location during the Summer, and I think, it will be as well to let Walter remain; although I am quite sure, that you would be able to teach him many things quite useful, that must be neglected until a future time....

The succeeding article is so characteristic of Mr. Brown's style of speaking on certain occasions that I give it entire:

REV. ABEL BROWN IN BUFFALO.

Dear Sir — Week before last, Wm. J. Graves, the duelist,[3] and Abel Brown, the philanthropist, happened to arrive in our goodly city of the lakes at the same time. On Saturday evening, the 20th instant, Graves was invited by the Whig leaders here to attend amid address a public meeting in their *log* (board and scantling) cabin, called for the purpose of confirming the nominations of Clay and Frelinghuysen. Placards were stuck up in our principal streets, announcing, in staring capitals that the Hon. Wm. J. Graves, from Kentucky, would, by invitation, attend and address the people, and exhorting the lieges to rally to listen to the orator, and respond to the nominations. At an announcement so bold and unexpected, the community were thunderstruck, and for a moment paralyzed — while the Whig leaders seemed equally astonished that the propriety of their course should be questioned; they seemed, indeed, to think it the most unnatural thing in the world, and when expostulated with, resorted to downright denunciation and abuse. But "a change has come over the spirit of their dream" — thanks, mainly to the Rev. Abel Brown, and an awakened public sentiment. The next day, on which day Graves took his departure, all the pulpits in the city were silent about the outrage, save one, and that one was occupied by the Rev. Abel Brown. He preached on Sunday evening, at the Methodist church, Hart's garden, and such a sermon! Buffalo intemperance, theatre and brothel haunting, duelling and pro-slavery, were his themes. Church and clergy were his not forgotten. Mr. Brown thoroughly cleared the skirts of his garments from the blood of the city. Not a stain of it rests upon them. The house was so full that many had to stand. For two hours the audience, made up of all sects and parties, were enchained,

[3]*Kentucky congressman William J. Graves, who in 1838 shot and killed Maine congressman Jonathan Gilley in a duel some say was instigated by Henry Clay. It resulted in the passage of a national law that banned dueling between public officials.— Editor.*

scarcely an individual moving in his place. Many were in tears. Startling truths uttered with the utmost force and directness, were burnt into the conscience. But when the preacher came to speak out the name of Graves, and depicted the crime and outrage of inviting that duelist whose hands, in the language of John Quincy Adams, addressed to one of his seconds, were still "all dripping with a brother's blood," to stand up in this Christian community, and recommend to its suffrages another veteran duelist,[4] a thrill of horror ran through and electrified the assembly. The speaker was more than eloquent. He was sublime. Since that evening no one here has been afraid to call a duelist a murderer and to speak it right out. When cross-grained, knotty sins are to be cut away from a nation's heart, commend me to your strong, truth-edged jackplane. Your fine smoothing plane is not fit for such stuff. The Rev. Abel Brown is both the one and the other, however, as occasion demands. Yours, truly, ANTI-DUELIST.

In reference to Mr. Brown's style or manner of speaking — oftentimes he had told me that he thought he could reach the minds of a certain class better by this method. Though possessed of much ideality and taste for the beautiful in eloquence, whether spoken in the silent voice of nature in meaning accents to the soul, or displayed in the outbursts of a heart glowing with benevolence to his fellow man, it breaks the fetters of sin and oppression by God-like appeals to the slumbering conscience. Yet he sometimes was willing to sacrifice beauty to earnestness and a glowing rhapsody to sober rebuke. Especially was the jackplane necessary where the timber was newly hewn, and was as yet without form or design. A very fine instrument with delicate execution is not adapted to the raw material or "sterner stuff." He therefore, habituated himself to speaking in an abrupt, pointed and severe style for the purpose of riveting truths, or what he termed hammering, so much afraid was he that the nails of his arguments would be loosely set.

This spring we removed to Troy, having secured a very pleasant and eligible situation in a retired part of the city. Here we were cheered and sustained by many kind and Christian friends in the arduous enterprise in which we were engaged. Here we often held meetings in the Reform Churches and at a public hall, wherein to open our mouths for the dumb and plead the cause of the oppressed.

During this season of emigration, we often had the pleasure of affording shelter and relief to many a weary and heart-stricken fugitive.

[4]*A reference to and attack upon Henry Clay, who was running for president.*—*Editor.*

Mr. Brown was often employed to secure the friends of those who had escaped, and an exceedingly interesting case occurred in which a very shrewd and intelligent slave had been directed on his way to the care of Mr. Brown, and in a few weeks his wife was restored to him. She had traveled hundreds of miles with the simple direction of Mr. Brown's address. After spending a week with us, she was conveyed to her husband at a place some distance north of Albany, where a home had been provided by the friends for both William and Mary as a separate and distinct family. Such was their joyful meeting that they remained in silence for some minutes, pacing the room to and fro, and then each burst into a flood of tears. What satisfaction it must have afforded Mr. Brown, to have thus contributed to the security of William and restoration of Mary. One week only elapsed when they were cheered by the addition of a freeborn child, their first and only offspring.

Among our excursions abroad this summer, the following descriptions by Mr. Brown are given.

Keene, Essex Co., N. Y, July 11, 1844.

We took the Steamboat Burlington, commanded by Capt. Sherman,— and, permit me to say, that if you wish to see the most perfect specimen of a steamboat and a steamboat commander, be sure to take passage on time Burlington. I have traveled on (I think) every steamboat route from Maine to Missouri, on lakes, rivers, sounds and seas, and am free to say that Capt. Sherman and the Burlington must bear the palm. I think that even the North River commanders would he improved by a single trip with Capt. S. Parties of pleasure, will find it really a pleasure to give Capt. S. the pleasure of making them as it is their pleasure to be, on any excursion of pleasure through the beautiful and pleasure-loving Champlain. Many a slave has enjoyed the indescribable pleasure of leaping from the liberty-loving "Burlington," to feel the pleasure of being free under the protection of a Queen whose pleasure it is to make the lowest of her subjects happy.

ESSEX COUNTY.

We landed at *Westport* to which place notices had been sent for meetings. At Westport is the residence of Judge Hammond,[5] who by the aid of political abolitionists was elected to the legislature last Fall. Many who gave their votes for him did so under the assurance that he was not a "*Clay man.*" He is a Deacon of the Baptist church. A few years since, when aboli-

[5]*Judge Gideon Hammond was elected president at the organization of the Essex County Anti-Slavery Society in 1837.—Editor.*

tionism was more or less identified with New York Whigism, a number of
the now leading Clay men in that town were very efficient abolitionists.
Knowing that Judge Hammond was an influential man, and professedly a
Christian and a gentleman, and that Westport professed to embrace a large
share of the respectability of Essex Co., I anticipated at least a courteous
reception. In the notice I had sent there I had stated upon what boat I
should leave Whitehall, and requested that *any* who might be interested
to meet me at the landing. On my arrival, I soon learned that instead of
any arrangements for a meeting having been made, a consultation had been
held and an understanding concluded that the object of my visit was to be
defeated. I was informed that the Baptist meeting house would be closed
against me upon the ground that I was in favor of political abolitionism;
although the same house has been opened again and again for Whig and
Locofoco[6] meetings, and for almost every description of meetings. It was
denied me for a lecture without ceremony, and it was said that no house
in the town would be granted me; and every effort that priests and politicians could make was made to prevent it. The Methodist house was however granted. "Then came the tug of war." A consultation was held by
certain men which resulted as follows — notices were sent to the Methodist
and Baptist ministers, of which the following is a copy:

"NOTICE. — Rev. A. Brown, of Albany, will lecture in the Methodist
church, Westport, at half past 7 o'clock, Sunday, P.M., in behalf of
3,000,000 slaves. Mrs. Brown will sing 'The Slave Mother's Lament for
her stolen daughters,' and other appropriate pieces."

The notices were taken by the clergymen with the assurance that they
should be read; but true to the politicians who rule the town, ministers
and all, one minister read a part of the notice, and the other the whole —
and then told their audiences that Mr. Brown, although probably a Minister in respectable standing, had come to that town for the purpose of
getting up a political party, of which they did not approve, and therefore
they (the ministers) could not give it their countenance or support. What
there was in the notice that savored so strong of politics, I am at a loss to
understand. A strong effort was then made in the public audience at the
Methodist church to close the house against me, but the trustees took the
responsibility to open the house. The report was however industriously circulated that there would be no anti-slavery lecture. However, at the time

[6]*Locofoco was a fringe group of the Democratic Party that formed in 1835, advocating for the
rights of the working class. They eventually joined with the Free Soil party during the late 1840s,
advocating for free land. However, their support for abolition went only so far as its benefit to
working-class whites. It derived its unusual name from the brand name of self-igniting matches
that were used at a political rally in New York City around the time of its origin.* — Editor.

appointed, a respectable audience assembled, and (with the exception of a few young loafers kept for the purpose of disturbing anti-slavery meetings) listened with attention. After the lecture, in company with Mrs. Brown, I started for the public house where we had put up. We were however immediately assailed by a body of full grown boys or men, and pelted with eggs until we closed the door of the Hotel against them. They did not even spare Mrs. Brown, but besmeared her with eggs. So much for the respectability of Westport. Their ministers and Politicians shut up their houses of worship and denounce them as unworthy the confidence of the public, and then the unknown rabble pelt them (yes, even the women) with eggs. Would it not be well to send some of the influential men of such a town, men who exert such a mighty influence, to the Legislature or to Congress? Had the ministers and politicians held their peace, no doubt we should have been permitted to lecture in peace and return home in quietness. The next morning we hired the landlord to carry us to Elizabethtown.

ABEL BROWN, Cor. Sec'y.

The following is from a friend in Elizabethtown under date of July 12, 1844.

FOR THE *ALBANY PATRIOT*

Mr. Editor—We have recently been visited by Rev. Abel Brown of your city. Essex county has been quite neglected heretofore as a field for anti-slavery labor. Mr. Glen[7] has been through the county once, and I believe Mr. Brown has visited three towns in the county once before; and although in several towns there have been some two or three out and out abolitionists, yet till recently there has been nothing reliable, in the form of anti-slavery organization. Now, however, in at least five towns out of sixteen in our county, there is an organization on the true plan. We have 150 votes for a Liberty candidate for the Assembly last fall, and this coming fall we mean to give at least 500 for Birney and Morris.[8] I think we have more than doubled our numbers within the last two weeks.

---

[7]*E.M.K. Glen, an antislavery lecturer from Minaville, Montgomery County, N.Y., who was very active in the late 1830s and 1840s.—Editor.*

[8]*James Birney was a Kentucky slaveholder who freed his slaves and devoted the rest of his life to ending slavery. After moving to Ohio, he started a newspaper,* The Philanthropist, *which was attacked by mobs on several occasions. He then moved to New York to become an officer of the American Anti-Slavery Society. When the schism in the society took place over political action in 1840, Birney was named as the presidential candidate of the newly formed Liberty party. He ran for president as its candidate in 1840 and 1844, and in the latter year, he and his running mate, Thomas Morris of Ohio, garnered 62,103 votes.—Editor.*

The tongue of slander had gone with its gall to Moriah, where Mr. Brown next lectured, but during the three meetings he held there, it more than lost its power. The Clayites there are covered with confusion; so at Jay and Keeseville, where every effort of Whig malice was made to embitter the minds of the people against Mr. Brown. The spirit of Liberty at this rate, will soon be completely triumphant in Essex county. No attempt has been made in any instance, however, to discuss principles. At Jay they rallied and with the fragment of the division lately slain at Keeseville, had the folly to attempt a sort of discussion. Mr. Brown being a small man, they thought they could eat him up; but the result was calculated to remind one of the fable of the eagle and the rabbit, which turned out to be no rabbit at all, but a veritable panther, which made a most luscious meal of the eagle. It is very easy to find a reason for the violent opposition made in this county to Mr. Brown. No man that loves the truth, can resist him in his fearless and terrible attack upon the hoary headed cannibal, American Slavery, that has been fed and fattened by this Republican (?) Government, assisted by those who professedly minister at the altar of God, and then receive a large share of its nourishment from the blood of God's own children. Hence the opposition. He is a red hot sword, cutting right through the living flesh of the beast that has its priests in every town. We live here in the midst of a "generation of vipers," and a discourse from Rev. Abel Brown is ever a feast of fat things. I wish you could think best to publish the flaming letter of Burchard; the Whigs hide it here; Burchard has assassinated Clay's Texas letter.

Ever yours,
J. GAY.

[No attribution is given to the following text appended to Gay's letter. — editor]

In the counties of Clinton and Essex, there are a number of intelligent Irishmen and as might be expected they are almost all of them abolitionists. The Catholic minister near Clintonville is in the fullest sense of the term an abolitionist; and uses his voice to influence his people to be found on the side of the oppressed. He secures the papers published in Ireland, and places them in the hands of intelligent men, who are ever ready to prove that the entire Irish nation are calling upon them to take side with the oppressed.

At the mass meeting in Jay, a load of Irishmen and women (many of them Catholics) came six miles to hear Mr. Brown's addresses. Mr. B. says, that he counted twenty-six persons, drawn by that single four-horse team, who spent the entire day at the meeting.

Among the various trials to which Mr. Brown was subject at this period, is found the following account given by himself in reference to a —

RIOT AND MOB IN TROY.[9]

It is once more our painful duty, to chronicle the most heartless and unknown attempt to insult, abuse, assault, trample upon, and kill unoffending citizens, in order to shut out the freedom of discussion and the light of truth from the minds of the respectable, honest and laboring class of the community, that has fallen to our lot for a number of years past. We have recorded accounts of mobs within the few past months, but not where there was such an apparent design to crush discussion at all hazards, as in the present instance. The circumstances are as follows:

The Corresponding Secretary of the E. N. Y. Anti-Slavery Society, Rev. Abel Brown, being under the necessity of spending a few days in Albany and Troy, thought it a favorable opportunity to start a Liberty association in Troy, for the purpose of canvassing the city, and prepare for the Fall campaign.

He accordingly consulted with a number of judicious Anti-Slavery friends, who advised that meetings be held on the Court House steps at 6 1–2 o'clock, P.M. Accordingly handbills were posted about the city, and at the appointed hour Messrs. Brown, Washington, Lane and Shipherd repaired to the Court House. Mr. Lane sang one of Garrison's songs, called *"Independence Day."*

During the singing, Mr. B was informed that a certain lawyer had sent after *"Frank Cleveland"*[10] to attend and make sufficient noise to drown the voice of the speaker and prevent his being heard. An audience gathered round composed chiefly of peaceable and quiet men, who appeared anxious to hear, and Mr. B. commenced by saying, that he had come there to speak in behalf of 3,000,000 of men and women who could not speak for themselves; explained what he meant by slavery, and gave a brief history of the denying of the right of petition; showed that it was denied to slaves; that that class of men were denied even the privilege of telling that the chains of slavery were grievous to be borne. He referred to the treatment received by Hon. J. Q. Adams in the U. S. House of Representatives, when he inquired if a petition from slaves came under a certain rule, and then proceeded to refer to the sentiment of the song that had been sung, and

[9]*Names of some of the more prominent individuals in this account were omitted by Mrs. Brown.—Editor.*
[10]*A local thug.—Editor.*

drew a lively, if not startling description of the difference between the professions, shouts and celebrations of liberty on Independence day, and the real and true state of the case; gave a vivid description of a nation shouting liberty, and at the same moment holding in their iron grasp three millions of men as the most abject slaves, whom they denied even the right of asking for liberty. The speaker then referred to the fact that in this part of the nation we hold such celebrations; even those who uphold and sustain the same laws, shouting liberty to all; he pointed out to them distinctly the hypocrisy of such a course. Ho remarked further, that on last Fourth of July, they celebrated Independence in Troy,—and he understood that even in these times of Temperance (to *their* everlasting shame) they mingled RUM and powder with their Celebration.

The mere reference to the rum Celebration started certain men who had been deeply involved in it, and they demanded that he should "*take it back,*"—*but* Mr. B. said he had made the refereuce to the rum celebration purposely, and could not take it back—for it was a shame to any class of men to get up a rum celebration any where, more especially in *Temperance Troy.* Mr. B. continued; only two or three persons took offence at the remarks respecting rum. All at once a terrible howling was heard at a distance, and soon Frank Cleveland appeared. He ascended the stand and said, the speaker should be heard no more. After a long time spent in trying to persuade him to permit the speakers to he heard, he was called away by a certain lawyer and taken aside, when after a few moments conversation he came directly back: and said, that "*the nigger*" might talk, but Brown should not. The colored man refused to speak, and Mr. Brown said the meeting would adjourn until the next afternoon, when Mr. Washington would speak. The next evening came, and Mr. Washington spoke about one hour, when Mr. Lane attempted to speak and was overpowered by "*Frank.*"

The next afternoon, Mr. Brown spoke again, but was finally interrupted, when it was said that Mr. B. should not talk any more. Mr. B. then adjourned the meeting to a very retired part of the city for the following (Thursday) afternoon. Many threats were made of personal violence but the peace officers seemed not to care; and the more refined portion of partisans laughed at the threats. Thursday P.M. came and Mr. Washington took the stand and spoke until about sundown, when Rev. Merritt Bates,[11] every where known as a mild, kind, Christian minister, yet a firm and decided abolitionist, spoke about ten minutes, and commenced showing the people their political connection with slavery. That was too much for the

---

[11]*Merritt Bates was a Liberty party lecturer, associate of Abel Brown, and in 1844 the founder of the True Wesleyan Methodist Church on Federal Street between River and N. Second streets, which lasted only a few years.—Editor.*

politicians to hear, and immediately, a dreadful howl was heard from about 20 persons who were there for that purpose. It was soon evident, and boldly said, that no man should talk *"political abolition."* There was no effort made by the police officers to quell the rioting, although threats of tar and feathers were made by the mob, and efforts to run over the speakers. The meeting was adjourned until the next afternoon, when another large audience assembled. Mr. Brown was absent during the day, and only arrived in time to request Mr. Washington not to appoint further meetings, as it was necessary that he should accompany Mr. B. to a convention in a distant county. The audience were after many thanks for their respectful attention, dismissed. The mob had been swearing violence during the day, while the more genteel opposers had been saying that Mr. B. ought not to be allowed to speak. The Mayor was seen by the Abolitionists — but he said he had no power to interfere unless violence was used, and the persons of the abolitionists assaulted. The city officers — were many of them among the persons who stood and saw the breaking up of the meetings, and the insulting of the speakers. The mob which by this time, could number some fifty or more, thought that the officers and certain important politicians, had so encouraged them, that they could make a bolder effort; they therefore resolved that they would commence a furious assault upon Mr. Brown, and any others that should be found sustaining him. Mr. B. had only come to the meeting on Friday evening, for a few minutes, had not spoke, and when called for by the audience, declined speaking, was leaving the ground about 8 o'clock, even before it was dark, when from 20 to 50 persons rushed to seize him. The officers found that they were powerless. The lawyer who had been among the most violent denouncers of Mr. B. now made an effort to stop them — yet they pushed Mr. B. down — and jammed him against the iron fence. The friends of Mr. B. appeared determined to protect him, and resisted the mob with so much effort, that Mr. B. passed away. The officers said they would protect him, while the mob followed on all sides, and with horrid oaths and hideous yells made the air resound, until they arrived at the house of the Mayor. The friends asked that Mr. B. might be permitted to enter the house, and find protection from those who had been making every possible effort to injure him. This was, however, peremptorily denied. It was said that Mr. B. had rendered himself obnoxious to the people and he could not be protected there.

The friends then made their way to Rev. Fayette Shipherd's. They were pounded, stoned and beaten the entire distance. The officer left them soon after they started from the house of the Mayor. No arrests were made nor even an attempt to arrest any one, although persons engaged in acts of vio-

lence, must have been seen and known to the high constable. A number
of the abolitionists were severely used in addition to being pelted with
stones — some even were pushed down and trampled upon. A friend who
mingled with the mob as they passed up Albany street, says *their plan* and
design was to *knock Mr. B. down and then trample him to death.* We give
this plain statement of facts from the most authentic sources. What a picture does it present. The freedom of speech trampled in the dust. Innocent and unoffending citizens bruised and stoned, and their lives attempted
in the streets, and the authorities look on and not even make an effort to
arrest the offenders. Yea more, the high constable of the city giving aid and
countenance to the mob by fleeing from those who are being assailed, and
not even attempting to arrest even the most lawless. Why was all this done.
The answer can be given in a few words.

There are many respectable and Christian men in the city who are abolitionists; who feel deeply for the slave, and who, disgusted with the old
pro-slavery parties would, if they understood the designs and plans of the
Liberty party, immediately join it and labor with efficiency to promote its
objects. The only way to keep this class of persons in their ranks, is to keep
the truth from them. To do this it becomes necessary to break up the meetings of the abolitionists; libel and denounce those lecturers who can and
will on any proper occasion, show these inquirers after truth the right way.
Every thing must bow to party interests.

Unfortunately for them, the Whigs are in power-in the city of Troy, and
they are especially interested to keep their predominance — and as a few
votes taken from them would effectually ruin their fair prospects, the offi-
ce-holders and partisans are greatly distressed, lest their gains are taken from
them. We do not suppose that the Whig leaders desired that the abolition
speakers should be mobbed, but they did openly denounce and condemn
them; and countenanced the rioters day after day in preventing their being
heard. That the officers had power to prevent the disturbance is evident,
from the fact that in Whig meetings similar disturbances have been commenced, but always prevented by the police. The Mayor even refused to
take the least action upon the subject, and the high constable looked on
and saw them assaulted and did not arrest the aggressors.

Again, Judge _____, a democrat, called one of the speakers from the
stand and told him he had abused the people, and desired him to break
up the meeting: the same judge threatened to arrest one of the speakers if
he caused disturbance. Now Judge _____ knew that there were only a few
men who did not quietly listen to the speakers, and why should he encourage the disturbers, by attempting to put away the speakers by calling one
a liar &c. &c. Why did he not call off the men who were browbeating the

abolitionists? Really Judge _____ the latter course would have been a little more democratic.

Another, Justice _____, a democrat and a member of the church, stood by and laughed, and thus cheered on the men who were denying to American citizens the freedom of speech. That man had better confess his sins, or leave both the church and the office which he has so disgraced.

To show the spirit which prevailed in the city, in consequence of the Anti-Slavery meetings, as the mob were stoning Mr. B. and his friends in Albany street, between Third and Fifth Streets, certain ladies cried out, 'give it to them, we should like to put the tar on to him ourselves.' If it had been in Kentucky, we should have supposed we were passing the harem of a certain distinguished gentleman. We will not accuse those women of designing to add insult to injury, but we can assure them, that their words caused the stones to be thrown thicker and faster, and it was not their fault, that the abolitionists were not murdered in consequence of it.

The candid reader will ask, Why this outbreak in the law abiding city of Troy. The answer is easy. The two great political parties have both of them nominated men of whom they are ashamed. The Whigs would be ashamed to see Henry Clay marching through the streets with his sixty slaves. The Democrats know that their candidate's views of Texas and slavery only need be known to be hated — yet both parties have so far advocated the claims of their candidates as to destroy what little of moral principle remained, after the campaign of 1840. Their papers cast off all pretence of recognizing God's commands in their political affairs, and even the mass of clergymen are such perfect dupes of the politicians, that they durst not preach the duty of electing "righteous rulers." Their hearers are so absorbed in electing men whom they know fear not God, or regard (colored) men, that they would not suffer any minister to preach such doctrines and enjoy their support.

The people are, therefore, in a most horrible condition — being left without the fear of rebuke, the baser sort have committed the horrible deeds recorded above. "When the wicked bear rule the people mourn." This is emphatically true in the present case — and may a righteous God open the eyes of the community to see their wretched condition, before all moral principle is swept from their remembrance. But, inquires another, why should they be so enraged about abolitionists holding meetings and exposing the wickedness of slaveholding, the miseries of the slave, and the propriety of emancipation? Certainly, the talk of abolitionists cannot be worse than slavery and slaveholders who are tolerated; yea, made welcome in Troy. No one even thought of mobbing them. Why not hear Mr. Brown? Certainly the numerous lawyers and politicians can answer him, if he is half as incorrect as they pretend! Be patient, readers, and you shall know why the party in power are so enraged at Messrs. Brown, Bates and every other man who will faithfully show them their duty.

The two great political parties are both of them slaveholding parties: and they have for years, secured the aid of your votes to help them carry on their infamous wickedness, and knowing that you are honest men and hate oppression, they dare not suffer you to be shown your true position, lest you forsake their party.

In connection with the preceding statements, Mr. Brown gives an exposition of the various topics on which he intended to have lectured, and in conclusion adds:

> Thus we have briefly stated a few points of difference between the parties, which it was Mr. Brown's intention to have stated in his public lectures, and for attempting to state which, he has been so cruelly mobbed — and for which certain persons say he shall not stay in Troy. Time must determine. A.

The abolitionists of Troy were not to be defeated. An adjourned meeting was commenced the following week in a retired part of the city near the house of Rev. Mr. Shipherd. The rioters were punctual to the hour of appointment; Mr. Bates, a Wesleyan preacher both dauntless and firm, commenced speaking upon one of those little summits for which Troy is remarkable, *an offset*.[12] The mobocrats proceeded to the spot, and in a moving column endeavored to crowd the speaker from his position, and thus precipitate him headlong to the ground. He, however, evaded the result by retiring with the rest of the assembly within the walls of Rev. Mr. Shipherd's church (near at hand) as was their intention to do on the approach of night. The house was filled with those who came to listen to the truths promulgated. Several speakers were in attendance. Mrs. Brown, being invited to ascend the platform, sung to them the affecting song of the Slave Mother's lament.

> Hark! from the South, a voice of woe —
> The wild Atlantic in its flow,
> Bears on its breast the murmur low —
> My child is gone.

[12]*A stone ledge projecting from a wall, which was used by those speaking to an assembled audience. — Editor.*

Like savage tigers o'er their prey,
They tore him from my heart away —
And now I cry by night, by day —
My child is gone.

The hideous yells without were occasionally mingled with this song, although some of the mobocrats within the house listened with fixed attention and acknowledged its pathos.

Mr. Brown arrived about nine o'clock (with valise in hand), having just returned from a convention in some of the northern counties. He soon ascended the platform and commenced speaking. The disturbance increased, accompanied by sounds in harmony with their discordant spirits, when a number of the rioters entered and stood in front of the pulpit ready to seize him in case he faltered, or should descend to escape. However, he remained firm and unmoved at his post, continuing to address the audience. The mobocrats finally retreated (with the exception of a few under the guise of friends) and joined in the disturbance without the house — when a volley of stones were thrown at the windows, scattering fragments of glass in every direction. The audience rose simultaneously upon their feet; Mr. Brown continued to speak in a tone both fearless and strong for the purpose of inducing them to remain and not expose themselves to the fury of the elements without. All that I noticed of his saying at this critical moment was — "I know not, but I am as well prepared to die now, as I should be forty years hence." The mobocrats finding their efforts unavailing to secure Mr. Brown by frightening the audience from the house, set fire to certain combustible materials near the windows.

Previous to these scenes, between two and three hundred citizens of all parties had petitioned the Mayor to send officers to protect the people and arrest the rioters, but he did not arrive until sent for and told that the mob had broken in the windows. He advised the abolitionists, "to go home and go to bed and go to sleep." During the presence of the Mayor and police officers, Mr. Brown and myself left the house through the back door. The rioters numbering one hundred or more soon dispersed, and we returned to our homes by different and circuitous routes — myself in company with friends, while Mr. Brown in disguise went into the open streets to watch the movement of his enemies, who had so signally essayed to destroy his life.

This was the last scene of warfare in which he personally suffered (with which I am acquainted). Mr. Brown was never well afterward. The exhaustion and fatigue, consequent to this continued struggle with the violence inflicted upon his person altogether, contributed to weaken and *destroy* that life so generously sacrificed in the cause of the oppressed. The following Sabbath (Aug. 11th), Mr. Brown preached in reference to the riotous proceedings and the duty of abolitionists in conflict with the enemies of God.

He loved his enemies and could pray in the spirit of Him who cried — "Father forgive them, for they know not what they do." He ever felt that the injuries done his person, or even character, were not so much in hostility to himself as to the cause he espoused; in short to the truth itself— so far as he was able to present its claims to the hearts and consciences of men.

Those poor, ignorant and deluded men, who inflicted violence upon his person, he blamed less than their instigators and supporters. He looked upon Frank Cleveland, the reputed leader of the mob in Troy as being at the time under the influence of intoxicating spirit, and also hired to do the devil's work. One day, while walking in the streets with Mr. Brown, we met Frank. Mr. Brown immediately bade me go forward while he stopped and expostulated with him in reference to his conduct. Mr. Brown remarked on his return home that Frank seemed heartily ashamed of what he had done. This, Mr. Brown performed as a Christian duty and not from any desire to extort a confession from him for his evil doing, or from any personal consideration.

Mr. Brown was previously known and hated in Troy by a certain class of persons — ere he took up his abode in the city on account of his engagedness in the reforms of the day, and his enemies, during the excitement referred to, did not hesitate to allude to many circumstances connected with his ministry of blessing and benefiting his fellow-beings. In one instance, sometime previous, Mr. Brown received the entreaties of a Christian mother to search for a lost daughter, once his Sabbath School Scholar, and whom she suspected had found her way to some house of infamy in the city of Troy. Mr. Brown succeeded in finding her, and also assisted her in her determination to leave the place. On conveying her trunk to the hotel, certain persons interested in her detention discovered the design and prevented her escape. Mr. Brown consequently received much abuse and his watch was stolen from him, on which account a trial was held at Court in reference to the whole affair. It resulted in breaking up some two or three houses of this description. This case misconstrued, formed a subject of vilification and abuse among other assertions equally ridiculous and absurd, such as that I was not his lawful wife, &c. Some of the reports of our enemies, (aside from their calumny) were really amusing, and calculated rather to produce a smile than a tear.

Mr. Brown continued to labor in the cause of the slave with the same zeal and determination that had hitherto characterized his career.

Among the variety of conventions attended by Mr. Brown at this closing period of his life were the counties of Clinton, Saratoga, Montgomery and Schenectady.

One account given by himself exhibits a pleasing contrast to those miserable, fiendish scenes described.

SARATOGA COUNTY AWAKE AT LAST.

Edinburgh, Sept. 10, 1844.

We are at this hour (10 o'clock at night, Sept. 10) just closing up a great Liberty Convention in Edinburgh. The large church in which we have met has been well filled during the day, notwithstanding the loco-focos have held a mass meeting within a mile of us. The excellent Edinburgh Band has been in attendance during the day and evening, and have given us fine music, and made us a donation in cash into the bargain. The pro-slavery parties are making their last dying efforts, but I am very happy to see that they all feel the force of our Liberty addresses, and must soon submit to our principles. The Band here refused to play for the Polk convention, choosing rather to join with and cheer on Liberty's host by their soul-stirring music.

Indeed this is a grand Convention — a new era in Saratoga Abolitionism. The house is still full, and the audience have just voted unanimously to stay another hour, and hear another Liberty speaker. The friends have concluded to raise $100 to employ an anti-slavery agent to go through the county to circulate tracts, papers, petitions, &c. and to lecture and wake up the people to the interests of Liberty. We have called another Convention, to meet in Corinth, week after next. Liberty is progressing. Adieu.

A. BROWN.

The last convention I ever attended abroad with my husband was at Corinth. The occasion was one never to be forgotten. At the time I was visiting Saratoga — enjoying its waters and scenes — when Mr. Brown, agreeable to appointment, arrived. On approaching my boarding place, the first I noticed was his limping movement in walking, assisted by his cane. He had unfortunately sprained his foot very badly in descending the platform at a convention in Utica the week previous. He was also apparently much worn with exertion and fatigue, and his brother at home endeavored to dissuade him from attending the convention, but Mr. Brown true to his appointment was not to be detained. He therefore came with the ease and rapidity of the cars to Saratoga. A gentleman was already in waiting for him to convey him to Corinth that night. He was very anxious to proceed, but with a severe thunder shower approaching, I persuaded him to remain on condition that I would start with him at 3 o'clock in the morning. We accordingly started, having some sixteen miles or more to ride in an open carriage. It was very dark and cold. We arrived in season to attend the convention at the usual hour of meeting on Sabbath day. After enjoying the morning's repast and a comfortable fire, we were invited to ride four miles farther to the place of the convention, where we found an extensive collection of people within and around a large barn fitted up for the occasion. We did not find the Saviour literally "in the manger," but excluded from the sanctuary, which was dedicated to "purposes, more sacred" than that of discussing the rights of the poor slave. We found his words of denunciation, pity and rebuke as uttered to the Scribes and Pharisees of old equally applicable to the present time.

The barn was in a very dilapidated condition, and being obliged to occupy the north side opposite the entrance, there seemed no security from the cold except what was found in a Buffalo skin suspended back of the platform, as good as a damask curtain behind a pro-slavery pulpit and better (under the circumstances). Mr. Brown stood leaning upon his cane, at the same time forwarding me his cloak for protection from the cold, so careful was he always for my health and comfort.

The season was, notwithstanding, one of great interest to our cause, and we were very happy in finding warm hearts and listening ears to the story of the slave's wrongs, friends who in imitation of our Saviour were determined to "remember those in bonds as bound with them."[13]

---

[13]*One of the most common abolitionist aphorisms. — Editor.*

PERSONAL OBSERVATIONS

Many little incidents occurred while traveling with Mr. Brown indicative of his disposition to oblige and render himself serviceable to others by acts of kindness apparently trivial and insignificant in themselves, yet bearing their due proportion of weight in the estimation of his character. At one time on board a canal boat, a lady with an infant loudly crying in her arms was pacing the cabin, much agitated, and evidently mortified at the supposed annoyance to the passengers when Mr. Brown mildly accosted her and said, let me take the little darling. He gently hushed it, reclining on his bosom while he softly paced to and fro the same floor, producing a smile in the surrounding passengers at the sudden transition of the child to perfect composure on being transferred from its mother's arms to a stranger's embrace.

His politeness at home was common, and seemed as natural as the most scrupulous observance of the same among strangers. It was not mere formal etiquette, but a kind and constant regard for the welfare of those around him, manifested in those minute attentions which help to fill up life's brief measure and contribute to its highest enjoyment.

Tranquil was his mind under all circumstances — serene in the high hopes and trust his soul enjoyed in the love of his Saviour.

IN HIS DEVOTEDNESS — he was truly "a man of one idea" — but that a world-embracing idea in his desire to bless and benefit mankind. And there was no moral subject of the age in which he did not feel a deep interest. He also considered the progress of science and the arts as contributing to the supply and convenience of our temporal wants, and ultimately to the advancement of moral truth.

THE LAWS OF HEALTH — Indeed, all those subjects connected with our physical being he regarded in the light of moral obligation in obedience to the laws of God. He knew no difference, made no distinction between the violation of a physical law and that of a moral *law*. He viewed them both as equally destructive to the wellbeing of individuals and nations. He did not in the language of mere moralists and sentimentalists speak of the laws of nature in contradistinction to the laws of God, but viewed each as belonging to one grand system in the infinite order and harmony of the Divine will.

"Of the spirit, there are divers operations" according to the different gifts, natural temperament, disposition, &c. induced by circumstances or otherwise. I do not say that Mr. Brown was a perfect man, or that he always acted with discretion and wisdom; this cannot, perhaps, be awarded to the best of men, but taking into consideration his ardent temperament, his mental activity, and the peculiar circumstances in which he was placed, he acted more bravely and more conscientiously than most men, thrown into the same vortex of malice, rage and hatred toward the principles of his advocacy.

In writing his Biography, I know that he would not wish me to pass a mere eulogy upon his virtues, but to give a true picture of his life and hold up his defects as a warning to others. This trait of his was peculiar to himself being rarely seen among men, a willingness to be told of his errors or faults that he might correct them. He used often to say that in preaching against the sins of his fellow men, there was this advantage, that "they would turn right about and tell him of some fault," whose correction he never despised but would bethink himself whether indeed he deserved the censure. If in the wrong, he did not hasten to justify himself, for he counted not that he was already perfect but as "being in the flesh and liable to err." He strove to bring every power and faculty of both body and mind into subjection to the will of Christ, I am assured. His secret devotions, his sense of unworthiness and humility in view of his imperfections, his faith in Christ as the author of his salvation, his unwavering trust in God, his firm resolution in the discharge of duty, opposed to every obstacle of Satan's device — and above all, his willingness to sacrifice every personal consideration for the promotion of Christ's kingdom and the advancement of his cause — all show him to have been actuated by any motive rather than selfishness, a foolish ambition, or vain glory.

No greater test of the sincerity of an individual in any great and good cause can be given than that he has shown himself willing to suffer. Indeed, he has been made a willing sacrifice in the labors, toil and privations he has endured to accomplish the design of his mission. Such was Abel Brown — eccentric, as his course often appeared even to his best friends, they can conscientiously award this meed of praise due to his services as a disinterested and devoted Christian, seeking to promote the interests of humanity and to aid in restoring the God-given rights of the slave to liberty and the blessings of freedom. He considered the Christian's duty not confined to the attention of himself, but extending to all his fellow-beings in common with his race. The Christian warfare he considered must be aggressive in order that sin be rebuked. He seemed to think one ought to be thankful to be told of his faults. He looked upon sin as a disease — and that it be the greatest kindness to convince a person of his true state, and point him the remedy in Christ. Public sins, he thought, should be rebuked in a public manner, that the evil might thereby be effectually eradicated. Finally, he deemed it as the only true method of combating such sins as slavery and kindred evils.

Although his denunciations were severe, and he "cried aloud and spared not" when necessity required, and his opponents were never flattered into accordance with him, yet when converted they were radically so, and permanently abided in the good work.

He abhorred sectarianism in the latter part of his life. As proof of this, a clergymen in New England asked Mr. Brown in reference to a Thanksgiving Discourser for what particular blessings should we be thankful, to which he replied, for the increase of liberality among Christians. I cannot vouch for his views in this particular at an earlier period unless the sentiment uttered in a preceding letter to his sister be an indication to this effect in which he says, "if the Baptists would only lay aside their party feelings, &c." Still, he ever held the doctrine of Immersion as of binding obligation on every believer of Christ (as I have heard him express in private conversation), on the ground of obedience to a plain command as given by Jesus Christ himself, who also left his example with his own words to St. John the Baptist, saying, "for thus it becometh us to fulfill all righteousness." Mr. Brown held what he termed a rebuking connection with the pro-slavery portion of the Baptist Church, who would have been very glad to have excised him from their denomination, could they have found sufficient excuse as in vain they sought.

He saw clearly the iniquity of partisans and professed Christian apologists for slaveholding — those who cried "peace, peace, when there is no peace," — and he, a warrior in the Anti-Slavery field, should he not do battle for the slave, or should he turn coward and prove recreant to the high trust commissioned to him as an Ambassador of the Saviour of men, who came on Earth to proclaim liberty to the captive.

During the last days of Mr. Brown, he seemed deeply impressed with the shortness of time and the injunction to "work while the day lasts, lest the night approach wherein no man can work." It seemed by him literally fulfilled in his constant aim to finish the work appointed for him to do. And several times, he publicly remarked that he no longer anticipated *rest* this side of the grave. He seemed also to experience deep searchings of heart, and he particularly requested the prayers of Mr. Shipherd's church in Troy after preaching to them. And in allusion to his trials and sufferings from his enemies, he asked them to pray that he might have more Christian dignity — more of meekness united with true courage in defense of the right. I never shall forget the expression of his countenance as with childlike simplicity he made this request. We had previously talked over the matter in relation to the subject of exciting and arousing the morbid passions of men by his plain, pointed rebukes. He was anxious to know if there was anything in his manner that might be obviated. Not that he had rebuked too sharply, but whether he might not administer his reproofs with more coolness and gentleness, or as he expressed, with greater Christian dignity.

CHAPTER XVIII

The Family Circle—The visit
of Alvan Stewart—His Letter—
Our Parting—His last Journey for
the Slave—His Visit at Rochester—Free
Mission Meeting—The last Letters—His
Sickness and Death—Correspondence
of the Mosher Family—Effusions
of Grief—Funeral Services—An Obituary
Notice—Resolutions—Monumental
Inscriptions—Conclusion

Our family, the few last months of his life, consisted of a brother from Wisconsin and a colored girl for whom he was guardian in connection with myself and Mr. Brown—and a happy family we were. Our morning and evening devotions will ever be remembered with heartfelt gratitude. It is not for me to extol our own mode of worship, especially within our family circle, but in order more fully to portray the life of him of whom I am writing, I allude more especially to those seasons as conducted by him. No stiff formality characterized those hours. The same easy, affable manner displayed in his usual address also found its way to the family altar. Instead of occupying the time wholly himself, we would first read in rotation, then sing together, and then my husband would lead in our petitions, or as often ask some other member of the family to engage in this exercise. How much consolation those hours *now* afford my soul, and I rarely think of him except upon the bended knee alone or at the family altar. I can even now seem to hear that voice of supplication to the Father of mercies, and hear that song so dear to him—

201

as with great earnestness, he would sing — "What mean ye, that ye bruise and bind my people, saith the Lord."[1]

The pressing cares of Mr. Brown in the cause of the slave had prevented his being at home but little of the time during the summer and autumn. In the month of October he was called to attend a court in Poughkeepsie in relation to an occurrence which happened in April, and already noted in a previous chapter.

The following letter from Mr. Stewart, for the Albany Patriot, presents a further account of the case and of the continued trials to which Mr. Brown was subject.

Albany, Oct. 14, 1844.

EDITOR OF THE PATRIOT:

Sir — I cannot refuse to record the gratification I feel to Him, who rules the hearts of men, for the two delightful Anti-Slavery meetings I have held in the last three days. One at Poughkeepsie, on Friday the 11th inst., and the other at Troy last evening the 13th

The Rev. Abel Brown held an Anti-Slavery meeting in a country town of Dutchess county some months since, and was attacked by a most ferocious mob in the course of the evening. The Rev. Mr. Van Loon, the distinguished Anti-Slavery orator, was speaking when a set of *vile beings* came in with large quantities of liver, lights and putrid meat, and threw these missiles at the head and person of Mr. Brown and others, and hallooed with the shouts of fiends let loose. Mr. Brown defended himself with a board* without using violence to any man, and his friends went before the grand jury of Dutchess and got the mobocrats indicted — when one of the mob crew perjured himself, by swearing before a grand jury, that Mr. Brown committed an assault and battery, to try which indictment against Brown at the present Oyer and Terminer,[2] before Judge Ruggles and his associates. — Mr. Brown had written to me a pressing letter to come down and aid as counsel on the trial. But the court refused to try it, and it will

---

*Mr. Van Loon has since told me that Abel used the board to protect himself while speaking — by holding it before his face. The mob surrounding the house, as also the rioters within, prevented the escape of the speakers, and they were consequently compelled to receive such abuse as savage men saw fit to inflict without being shown even the protection of a board to ward off the offensive missiles hurled at them. — C.S. Brown.

[1]From an 1839 poem by Eliza Lee Follen that became a popular hymn. The text is likely Isaiah 3:15: "What mean ye that ye beat my people to pieces, and grind the faces of the poor?" saith the Lord God of hosts. — Editor.

[2]Legal term meaning trial or hearing. — Editor.

go over to the June sessions, when I hope we shall try the mobocrats as well as the abused and worthy friend of men.

The last meeting for the slave we held in Troy was on the occasion of Mr. Stewart's visit in company with Mr. Brown on his return home from Poughkeepsie.

Mr. Brown had previously made arrangements to visit western New York for the purpose of holding a series of conventions in behalf of his agency, and to obtain subscriptions and funds for the Albany Patriot — as one of its Proprietors — and to sustain *which he* had spent much time and effort during the last four or five months of his life.

As Mr. Brown anticipated spending some weeks in his contemplated tour, I embraced the opportunity of visiting my friends in Massachusetts during the same time, where also my husband intended on his return to meet me in company with his son Walter on the anniversary of Thanksgiving.

On the morning of his departure from home, he prayed with unusual fervor and earnestness that he might go out with a single eye to the glory of God.

The idea of parting, each for opposite routes carrying us some four hundred miles from each other, was indeed painful, and my own heart began to relent. But Mr. Brown endeavored to console me and brushed away my tears (as he was wont to do) and said, you are going to see your friends (whom I had not seen for nearly ten months). He first went over to Albany on some preliminary business in the morning with the intention of taking the evening train, and being obliged to start from Albany myself the coming morning, I went over once more to see him. And there we severed — never more in earthly forms to meet. How little of fate we know. We blindly wander forth, and when we give the parting hand, it may be the last affection's grasp can yield, and when the eye turns silently away in the fond adieu, it may be forever to close on us.

Wearied with exertion and worn in countenance, yet uncomplaining, he pursued his way the same evening, Oct. 14, 1844.[3] He reached

---

[3]*Brown was accompanied by a runaway slave lecturer, James Baker, who apparently remained with him until he called on the Moshers and his illness turned for the worse. Baker then left and went to Fredonia, where he met Eber Pettit, who took Baker under his wing and helped him with the purchase of his wife from slavery. Pettit tells Baker's story in his 1879 book about the Underground Railroad, but refers to Baker as Jo Norton.* (Albany Patriot, 12 February 1845: 54; Harrold: 98–99; Eber M. Pettit, Sketches in the History of the Underground Railroad, *Fredonia, N.Y.: W. McKinstry & Son, 1879: 34–54.)—Editor.*

Rochester in time to attend a meeting for Free Missions of the Baptist denomination held on the 15th inst. He spoke with great solemnity and earnestness — and it was observed on the occasion that he told them it was probably the last time he should ever address them. Held up to view the position of the Baptist denomination in reference to Missions, he said, as one clergyman present remarked, "what no other man dared say."

A severe change taking place in the weather, in consequence of a tremendous gale extending from the Lakes to this place, Mr. Brown suffered much from cold in connection with overexertion and fatigue. On his way from Rochester to Canandaigua, he left the cars at Victor about midnight. Not being able to find lodging at the hotel, and neither being able to find his friend, Mr. Clark[4] (who had so often cheered our conventions with his music), he was obliged to call at the private house of a stranger. Knocking at the door, he related to the man of the house his predicament and unfortunate position, and asked the favor of being permitted to stop a few hours. Then early in the morning, he wished to be conveyed to Canandaigua to meet an appointment as an Abolition lecturer. Upon this announcement, the man bid him be-gone, telling him, "he would shoot him, unless he cleared out instantly." Mr. Brown with valise in hand was then obliged to walk three miles in a stormy night before he could find a resting place.

This memorable night, in the fate of his death, is ever portrayed to my mind in the words of "the poor wayfaring man of grief." A song of solemn import ever to Mr. Brown when singing. Dark and dreary was that hour when at midnight 'mid raging winds and tempest driven, he a shelter sought wherein to lay his shrinking shivering frame — O, sadly mournful, though methinks, his Saviour was with him still. He prayed, yes, I know he prayed; he thought of her, who in her native nest far away was borne, and he thanked the Lord that she was sweetly slumbering; nor did he forget that poor man, who had thus turned him from his door, but more in pity than in hate, cried, Father forgive him this murderous will, the deed he would fulfill. Dear Saviour, how has he treated thee? For "inasmuch," as me he sheltered not, even this to thee was done.

Mr. Brown reached Canandaigua the following morning at the appointed Convention Oct. 21st, yet was unable to say but little in con-

[4]George W. Clark, noted Liberty singer from Canandaigua, was an ardent abolitionist and leading Liberty party spokesman. He sang at many conventions, and collected the Liberty songs from his repertoire in a book called The Liberty Minstrel. — Editor.

sequence of cold, exhaustion and fatigue produced by his walk and exposure the previous night.

Having promised to write Mr. Brown at his request immediately on my arrival home, I did so, and will insert one single clause of this last communication to him from myself under date of Oct. 16.

How much I thought of you all the way from Albany; yes, my dear husband — and I prayed that our hearts might still be united, though so far absent from each other; and immediately, I seemed spiritually to perceive the person of our Saviour, with each and both of our hearts in his possession. Blessed thought! May it indeed be so.

You need much strength to go through your arduous duties, and I pray that God may give it thee.

Receiving no intelligence from Mr. Brown for some two or three weeks, I was filled with anxiety and fearful apprehension for his safety when I received a letter from him, written at Honeoye, Ontario Co., bearing date of Oct. 30th, in which he wrote:

I am under the necessity, of informing you, that I have been sick in this place about ten days. I have had a violent attack of fever. Have been among the most kind friends, who have watched over me and taken the very best of care. I was so broken of my rest at Rochester and elsewhere, that I was obliged to give up and be sick. Another man went on and filled a part of my appointments.

There has been a terrible snow storm here. The snow is some eight inches deep and still coming. It looks queer. All around me dressed in winter. I am entirely rid of the fever, and recovering as fast as can be expected, but it will probably be some four or five days before I shall be able to be about as usual.

I trust you will he patient, and hope and wait until I return. Above all things, I charge you not to come to me.

Trust in God and do good,— and God will take care of thy husband.

If I am *dangerously* ill, I will inform you.

My love to all,
ABEL.

He also writes on the following day, Nov. 1st, of his intention to start on the morrow for Canandaigua on his way to Buffalo and home to see his children.

From the letters, written during this period of the sickness and death of Mr. Brown, the following particulars are given [no attribution is given for the following passage — Editor].

Mr. Brown went to Canandaigua on Saturday, Nov. 1, as he anticipated; and called at the house of our friend Mosher — as a sick man. Greeted Mrs. Mosher cordially on his arrival. Spoke of pursuing his journey on Monday. He seemed to have no correct idea of his situation — appeared worn and exhausted, and perfectly restless. In the afternoon, he tried to get some sleep, for he said, he had not rested one night well since he left Albany; but his efforts were in vain. On Sabbath morning, he rose and dressed himself and came down from his room alone, and while partaking of his food, was asked by Mrs. Mosher, if he did not wish them to write me to come. No, he replied, "I told her she must not come." Immediately after, he became speechless — and remained so for two hours. On applying cold water to his head he recovered; when he remarked, "I thought, I should never speak again — that my labors on earth were ended, and that I should soon commence them in Heaven." Mrs. Mosher told him that she also thought they were soon to close. He did not make her much reply, as he became delirious. At his particular request, he was placed under the care of a Homeopathic Physician.[5]

Mrs. Mosher writes:

Sabbath evening he rested pretty well, and I retired, — and left Mr. Mosher sitting up with him. About ten o'clock, he commenced praying and talking very loud — I thought him dying — and I believe he thought so too. "O, I want to see my blessed Saviour, to go home and be forever at rest — Yes," he repeated, "rest from all the labors of earth." We asked him if he would like to see you. "O yes," he exclaimed, "I guess I should. She is a good woman, she took care of my soul." On being asked if we should send for you, he replied, "you must send for her, you will won't you."

On Monday he had a very sick day, mind wandering most of the time. Tuesday morning he appeared very sensible — wished to get up and sit by the fire. Said, he felt better, and thought he should get well. Mr. Stringham came in and he conversed with him fluently, and seemed in his right mind. He remarked to him, that he was among his friends now, but thought it would be better if he was with some of his relatives. Said the room in

---

[5]*Homeopathy, an alternative approach to medical care that during this time used dilute solutions of substances that caused symptoms of disease in healthy persons, was in vogue among many abolitionists, including William Lloyd Garrison. — Editor.*

which he was sick, was a pleasant one (it was a large bed-room off the sitting-room). After conversing some time with him, Mr. S. mentioned something about election;[6] he groaned very deeply; his attention was immediately diverted, but he did not again appear so sensible that day. Mr. Adsit came in at one time, and he called him Brother Adsit, and wished him to sit nearer the bed that he might see him better.

His appetite seemed good most of the time, and I never gave him any food or drink, or administered to his wants in any way, without thinking of you — he appeared so thankful, and would sometimes remark, "I think I must make you some trouble."

He spoke at one time of his little boys, and said he was intending to take the oldest one home with him. Whenever we spoke of you, he would say that he wished much to see you, but you must not come as it would be a short time before he should go home. He seemed to anticipate much pleasure at being at your father's on Thanksgiving and mentioned it two or three times. When one person called, he would say, he was getting well, was in no pain, was not sick. The next moment he would say he was suffering exceedingly, was very sick.

I do not think of any thing that would give him comfort that he did not have. All our services were cheerfully performed. Mr. Brown prayed to be made one of Christ's "little ones," and after that, this passage of Scripture was constantly in my mind, "Inasmuch as ye have done it unto one of these," &c. Dr. Matthews of our village attended Mr. Brown for three days; we then had a Council of Physicians. The disease was in his head and beyond the reach of Medical skill; they called it the fever on the brain or dropsy in the brain.[7]

On Wednesday we could see that he failed rapidly. Wednesday night he was taken with raving spasms which lasted about five minutes each, at intervals of two or three hours during which he seemed impressed with the idea that he was surrounded with a mob in pursuit of his life. "Must I be sacrificed, he would exclaim,— Let me alone every one of you." He did not use the least violence to any one but was trying to get out of the way. On Thursday we perceived that he could not live. He did not make

[6]*Henry Clay was defeated by James Polk in the 1844 Presidential election, to which Mr. Stringham was referring. This was because he lost the state of New York. Carrying New York, Polk's margin of victory was 170–105 electoral votes. However, if Clay had carried New York, he would have won 141–134. The vote in New York was very close and turned on the votes taken away from Clay by the Liberty party. Consequently the efforts of Liberty spokesmen like Abel Brown proved instrumental to Clay's defeat.—Editor.*

[7]*Brown apparently was suffering from encephalitis or meningitis, which is a viral infection of the brain. Untreated, the mortality rate is more than 50 percent, and even today nearly 100 percent of those who survive suffer some permanent motor impairment.—Editor.*

much enquiry about any one. His mind was so disordered, that he could not think of what he seemed inclined to tell us. Friday, about ten o'clock, he had a very violent spasm, after which he settled down quietly, did not move, but continued to sink away until 5 o'clock, when he breathed his last without a struggle.

Not receiving the first intelligence of his relapse and sickness until the day of his death, I was unable to be present through this scene of trial and suffering, and could not reach Canandaigua to attend the last mournful rites of my dear departed husband! Having started to see him on receipt of the news of his dangerous illness, I intercepted a letter on my way containing information of his death and supposed burial. I immediately proceeded to my home in Troy and being under peculiar circumstances, I had no heart to go farther or to visit the grave that contained the lifeless remains of him I so much loved and of whom I had been so suddenly bereaved.

The kindness of those friends with whom it was my husband's privilege to spend his last expiring days can never be forgotten, and will be remembered in that better world when we tune our harps anew to Christian love and holy gratitude.

The following letter from a sister of Mr. Mosher and then member of his family and written on the event of Mr. Brown's death is truly worthy of insertion, and on memory's page will ever be sacredly cherished.

After alluding to his frenzied imagination caused by the cruel attacks of mob violence, she proceeds:

> But he has gone where earthly fears will never more distress. The blessed Saviour has called him home. We will hereafter contemplate him as an inhabitant of that blessed abode. A shining spirit in the courts of our God. His labors for suffering humanity are ended and he has gone to reap the reward of his faithfulness.
>
> Many are those who in obedience to that blessed command of our Saviour, "will mourn with those who mourn, and weep with those who weep." Tears pleasant in memory of his many virtues, and bitter when we reflect on how much we have lost, now are flowing from many eyes. But your grief my dear sister, must far exceed ours. You have lost your dearest earthly friend, your all — "cut down and withered in an hour." Those affectionate and endearing relations which in *life* afforded a pleasing satisfaction, are become the channel of a deeper and more poignant grief in his death. And this grief is rendered still more aggravating by the thought, that you were

not near to smooth his dying pillow But be comforted, dear friend, there was a "friend that sticketh closer than a brother," that received his departing spirit. You will not weep as those who cannot realize, the love which our blessed Saviour bears his children when he afflicts them.

"Behind a frowning Providence, he hides a smiling face." You may not realize this at first, but you will see that it is all love — unbounded love.

The Roman matron, when asked for her jewels, presented her children saying, — "These are my jewels." So to the Christian of nobler views, *his friends* are his greatest earthly treasures, and when God has taken them to himself, he feels that his treasure is laid up in Heaven, and shall not his heart be there also? But why need I offer words of human consolation, there is a void in the bereaved heart that nothing earthly can fill. There is a purer source of comfort, the voice of an indulgent heavenly Father speaks to him in every sorrow, "be not dismayed, I will not leave you comfortless." To that exhaustless fountain you will go and find relief.

Mr. Brown's death was peaceful. Not a struggle was perceived. It was the remark of all present that they never witnessed a more quiet death. It is to us a consoling thought, for we feared it would be otherwise.

May the Lord sanctify this heavy affliction according to his merciful design. Your sincere friend,

LAURA MOSHER

It was indeed a consolation that Mr. Brown thus quietly sank to rest.

Calm as the breath of even[ing] — was his last expiring hour, as through the valley of death he passed from the dreamy shadows of earth to the realities of the spirit world! Not the sun declining,[8] in all its soft radiance beaming such visions as that hour revealed, and I have often thought of the transport of this scene on finding himself safely lodged in his Saviour's arms instead of a merciless mob expiring alike with his fevered brain.

On the morning after the news of my husband's death, when alone and overpowered with grief too deep for utterance even in prayer, his happy spirit seemed to say, "sing Catharine, sing," and immediately my soul gave vent to the following effusion in strains of melody before unknown.

> Abel, dearest Abel — sing, sing with me;
> How pure thy strain — for thou hast gone,

[8]*He died with the setting sun at 5:00 on November 8, the day before his 34th birthday.* — Editor.

Illustration from original publication of *Memoir of Rev. Abel Brown.*

Forever to be blest!
Be thou my guardian Angel,
For thou art kind and gentle, Abel.
How expressive thy hand,
When raised in defence of truth;
How expansive thy mind — When plans thou devised;
To execute with zeal — what thy heart did feel.
I feel thy presence near,
To love, direct and cheer;
Thou art my love, my Abel — Still, though in Heaven, thou art;
Earth thou hast not left,
Except its pains, its sorrows;
And all that annoyed thy soul,
E'er thou left this earthly goal!
Sing Spirit, sing — thou lovedst to hear me,
Now join with me, Or, rather; let me join with *thee!*

The music of another land hath spoken,
No after sound is sweet! this weary thirst!
And I have heard celestial fountains burst!
What love shall quench it?
But Oh, sweet friend! we dream not of love's might,
Till death has robed with soft and solemn light
The image we enshrined! Before that hour
We had but glimpses of time o'ermastering power
Within us laid!—then doth the spirit flame,
With sword-like lightning rend its mortal frame.

The wings of that which pants to follow fast,
Shake their clay-bars, as with a prisoned blast
The sea is in our souls!

He died, *he* died

On whom my lone devotedness was cast!
I might not keep one vigil by his side,
I whose wrung heart watched with him to the last;
I might not once, his fainting head sustain,
Nor bathe his parched lips in the hour of pain,
Nor say to him farewell!

An account of the funeral obsequies as given by Mr. Mosher in a letter to myself is as follows:

The Funeral services of Mr. Brown were held at the Baptist Church in Canandaigua on the Sabbath following his death. The Discourse on the occasion was given by the Rev. Mr. Adsit, and was based on the Declaration of St. Paul—"I have fought the good fight," 2 Timothy 4:7.[9] After narrating Paul's arduous and numerous struggles in the Christian warfare, so fully recorded in the Acts of the Apostles, he drew a parallel between the conflicts of the Apostle and those of our beloved brother Brown, showing in a very lucid manner that the great object each had in view was similar in its nature, and the means used to accomplish this object were the same; that the weapons of their warfare were not carnal, but spiritual, mighty through God to the pulling down of strong holds; that each ended their warfare in the midst of their conflict, and entered into their eternal rest.

---

[9]*"I have fought the good fight." Paul wrote this to his protégé Timothy before his death. He had accomplished what God had set out for him, and was ready to go on to his reward.—Editor.*

Mr. Adsit alluded in a very striking manner to the treatment Mr. Brown had received in Canandaigua; but he rejoiced that there was sufficient humanity left in the hearts of men to treat the lifeless remains with respect, that they could be received into the sanctuary from which Mr. Brown was excluded when alive.

The relics of Mr. Brown were deposited in a part of the village burial ground, appropriated by the authorities for the use of the Baptist Church in Canandaigua.

Death of Abel Brown.

At a meeting of the colored citizens of Canandaigua, held at the colored schoolhouse, on Monday evening, Nov. 11th, 1844, for the purpose of expressing their sorrow at the decease of the late Rev. ABEL BROWN, and also to sympathise with the friends of impartial Liberty on account of the loss of so able and efficient an advocate of the cause of the down-trodden and oppressed colored man, on motion, G. W. Tucker of Detroit, Michigan, was called to the Chair, and H. W. Johnson appointed Secretary—Prayer by B. H. Sims. On motion of Austin Seward, a committee of three were appointed to draught resolutions expressive of of the feelings of the meeting. On motion, A Seward, R. Valentine, and D. H. Ray, were appointed to act as such committee. The committee then retired, and returned in a few minutes and reported through their chairman, the following preamble and resolutions which were accepted and laid upon the table for further consideration.

We, the colored citizens of Canandaigua here assembled, feeling profound respect and love for the late Rev. Abel Brown, and deep and pungent grief for the loss we, the slaves and the friends of humanity have sustained, by the death of this, our distinguished and devoted friend. By his zeal and indefatigable perseverance, and the energy of his labors in the cause of human liberty, and by his exposures and fatigue while travelling to promote the cause he loved, he has been early called from this, into a world of spirits, and we trust, is now reaping the reward of his labors, and has entered into that rest prepared for all those who love the Lord Jesus Christ, and their fellow men, of whatever color or clime.

Report of Abel Brown's funeral in *The Albany Patriot*, Nov. 27, 1844.

Through the kindness of friends, a meeting was also held in Troy in relation to the event of Mr. Brown's death — and the remarks given and sympathy manifested, afforded much consolation to my bereaved heart.

Rev. Mr. Garnet gave the Discourse from the following words, "Wist ye not that I must be about my Father's business," Luke 2:49.[10] He then vividly portrayed the character of Mr. Brown, as manifested in his devotion and service to the will of his Divine Master, and that death found him still engaged about his Father's business, which work formed the only absorbing idea of his soul in mortal life, and the prelude to scenes of activity still more glorious and extensive beyond the

[10]*Modern translation: "Didn't you know I had to be in my Father's house?" Jesus was 12 and went to Jerusalem with his parents for Passover. When his family was traveling back home, they were a day's journey away when they realized he was not among their group. Jesus had stayed in Jerusalem and was in the temple courts listening to the teachers of the law and asking questions that belied his age, and everyone was amazed at his understanding and wisdom. His parents were upset and asked why he would treat them as he had. His response was that they should have known he would be in his Father's house. The Rev. Garnet is probably saying by way of this example that Abel's life was about God's business first and foremost. — Editor.*

grave. He also alluded to the riotous proceedings in Troy in opposition to the efforts of Mr. Brown and the circumstance of his being haunted by those who had pursued his life in his hours of delirium when sick, as an evidence of the sufferings he had previously endured.

Extracts from an obituary notice of Mr. Brown from the *American Freeman*, published in Wisconsin:

It has pleased the great Head of the Church to summon to a sphere of duty nearer his throne, the spirit of our brother, Abel Brown. "Blessed are the dead which die in the Lord from henceforth: Yea, saith the Spirit, that they may rest from their labors; and their works do follow them."

Our friends in the west have no doubt marked the prominent part, which the Providence and Spirit of God called him to perform in the anti-slavery warfare; and would naturally feel desirous to learn something more of his history.

His love to Christ and the souls of men, were evinced by his indefatigable labors in the Temperance, Sabbath School and Moral Reform enterprises. The Spirit of Christ is a Missionary Spirit, and this he possessed in no common degree; and but for the influences now operating in the church, and in the civil government, to reduce to and retain in heathenism, millions of our brethren and sisters at home, he would have delighted to exhibit to the benighted of other lands the glory of the Cross. But he felt that the reproach of our own hand must be wiped away — duty — the souls of our brethren and sisters in bonds — the honor of Christ — the purity and reputation of the Church, and the permanent existence and successful result of the *Missionary cause* itself— each and all required the removal of slavery from our land. Commencing, therefore, with the foundation, and throwing his whole soul into the glorious cause, alike regardless of the attacks of bitter foes and false brethren, leaving a time-serving policy to those who had less confidence in Christ, he hastened on to meet the consequences of obedience to God. And though sometimes surrounded by men of blood, the invisible hand of the Saviour shielded him, the Spirit whispered peace to his soul; he felt "safe under the shadow of the Almighty — the munition of rocks was his defence.'

He sustained for the last four years past, the relation of Agent to the Eastern N. Y. Anti-Slavery Society. In every department of the Anti-Slavery enterprise, he exhibited a spirit that could not rest while so much was at stake and so much required to be done. In circulating anti-slavery publications, in urging religious denominations to practice the principles they avowed, and [to assist] by their presses, ministers, influence, and benevolent societies, our colored brother, who was bleeding in the porch of the sanctuary — in bringing the political parties at the north, from under the thraldom in which they were kept by the slave-power — in assisting, as a member of the vigilance committee, trembling Americans, to the number of *not less than* one *thousand*, to the shelter afforded by a monarchial government, from the inhuman monsters walking at large and claiming property in human flesh. He was a pattern to believers — a living argument against unbelief.

As a lecturer, he produced an impression deep and lasting; and if some of his arrows were not finely polished, they were less easily removed from the mind in which they had been fastened.

His visit to this place will be held in long remembrance. We little expected, however, that it was the last interview till the sea shall give up her dead....

That same Jesus, whose little ones had so often been assisted by his servant, fulfilled the promise made to those who consider the cause of the poor, and made all his bed in his sickness. True, he was absent from his beloved companion, and his little ones, but he received from the friends with whom he stayed, all that attention and aid, that the most affectionate of earth could impart.

"Thou art gone to the grave!" Yes — and art useful there. "Being dead he yet speaks," calling on those who sympathize with Christ's suffering little ones to press forward; and, methinks, when the pearly gates were opened to receive his disembodied spirit, the glorified tuned their harps to a new and more melodious note as he mingled with them; and he, and the hosts above, and the Lamb in the midst of the throne, mark with interest the most intense, the progress of humanity, liberty and love. May we follow his faith, possessing which, we shall be instant in season and out of season, till the message is heard.

"Child, thy Father calls, come home."

The following Resolutions were passed by the colored citizens of Canandaigua, Nov. 11, 1844, ... for the purpose of expressing their sorrow at the decease of the late Rev. Abel Brown, and also to sympathize with the friends of impartial liberty, on account of the loss, of so able and efficient an advocate of the cause of the down-trodden and oppressed...."

We, the colored citizens of Canandaigua here assembled, feeling profound respect and love for the late Rev. Abel Brown, and deep and pungent grief for the loss we, the slaves and the friends of humanity have sustained, by the death of this, our distinguished and devoted friend. By his zeal and indefatigable perseverance, and the energy of his labors in the cause of human liberty, and by his exposures and fatigue while traveling to promote the cause he loved, he has been early called from this, into a world of spirits, and we trust, is now reaping the reward of his labors, and has entered into that rest prepared for all those who love the Lord Jesus Christ, and their fellow men, of whatever color or clime. Therefore,

Resolved, That the Christian church has been deprived of one of her brightest ornaments by the death of the Rev. Abel Brown.

Resolved, That while we acquiesce with the will of Heaven, we cannot do otherwise than lament over the loss of so valuable a friend of humanity, and so uncompromising an advocate of the cause of the crushed and bleeding slave.

Resolved, That in this sudden dispensation of Providence, we feel that we are bereft of one of the most efficient advocates of the cause of our countrymen, and the eloquent narrator of the story of our wrongs — and while memory performs its sacred office, his name shall live to the grateful recollections of colored Americans.

Resolved, That we, as colored citizens partially free, feel his loss to be a heavy calamity to us, and not only to us, but every lover of his country.

Resolved, That we deeply sympathise with the afflicted companion and children, and commend them to the God of the widow, and the father of the fatherless, as one who is ever ready and willing to succor the needy and shield the innocent and unprotected, and with their tears of sorrow and affliction, shall be mingled our tears of heart-felt sorrow.

After a few eloquent and impressive remarks by A. Seward, D. H. Ray, G. W. Tucker and others, the resolutions were unanimously adopted. On motion, it was resolved that the proceedings of this meeting be signed by the Chairman and Secretary, and be published in the Ontario Repository, the Ontario Messenger, the Liberty Press and Albany Patriot, the meeting then adjourned.

G.W. TUCKER, Chairman.

H.W. JOHNSON, Secretary.

A Monument has been erected to the memory of my departed husband, bearing the following inscription.

ABEL BROWN,

A faithful minister of Him who
proclaimed Liberty to the captive.

A Hero, in the fearless advocacy of truth,
and in vindication of the oppressed.
A Martyr, in his devotion and self-sacrifice to
the calls of bleeding humanity.
His memory lies embalmed in the heart of many a fugitive,
and on the leaves of Immortality his deeds are inscribed.
Rev. Abel Brown was born at Springfield, Mass., Nov. 9, 1810.
Died Nov. 8, 1844, at Canandaigua, N. Y.
The Free Church of Canandaigua, and other friends
of the slave, erect this monument, as a record
of his resting-place, and a tribute to his worth.

CONCLUSION.

In preparing these Memoirs, I would say that *one* consideration, not the least important that I have had in view, has been to preserve a transcript of the life and character of my departed husband for the special benefit of his orphan children — two of whom being deprived of both parents in early life, and one of my own bearing both the name and impress of his father yet to him unseen with mortal eyes, and whatever he may learn of him may herein be gathered, as with care I have penned each leaf bearing the mementos of precious deeds performed and lofty principles maintained 'mid the stormy rage of persecution and strife of foes.

But the love and affection of that heart I cannot portray, as the spirit alone can give life and expression even to the brightest page that memory's hand with skill can trace; yet however faint the portraiture may be, I hope that my efforts have not altogether been in vain to add a new testimony to the efficacy of Christian principle, as exemplified in the disinterested motives and services of the subject of this Volume.

Appendix I

Excerpt from "Impressions and Incidents Connected with the Life of Rev. Charles B. Ray"

by Mrs. C. S. Brown Spear[1]

This letter of Catharine Brown was written sometime after 1883 for inclusion in the biographical sketch of Charles Ray prepared by his family and published in 1887 (Florence T. Ray, *Sketch of the Life of Rev. Charles B. Ray*, New York: Press of J. J. Little & Co., 1887: 64–67).

When I first knew [Mr. Ray], in the city of New York in the spring of '43, he was Corresponding Secretary of a Committee of Vigilance in the escape and protection of fugitive slaves. When Abel and myself were about to be united in the holy bonds of matrimony, he said, "Whom shall we have to perform the ceremony?" He made mention of a number of clergymen of this city, and the question was asked by myself with regard to each one, "Is he an Abolitionist?" And he as often said, "No!" At last he said, "Why not have Mr. Ray?" I readily assented, and so I felt approved and blessed in thus being united by this godly man, having been co-workers in the glorious cause of emancipation and in aiding fugitives to a land of freedom! I met him in convention on the fiftieth anniversary of our cause in this city. It was a glorious occasion!

During our sojourn in New York State after our marriage, Abel was connected with the Vigilance Committee of New York, being the "forwarding merchant" for this species of property in Albany where his office was located, and in constant communication with Mr. Ray and others. One day on his return from a meeting

[1] *Mrs. Brown had since remarried. — Editor.*

217

The Rev. Charles Ray, New York City minister and secretary of the New York Committee of Vigilance, one of the nation's foremost Underground Railroad organizations (from Florence T. Ray, *Sketch of the Life of Charles Ray.* New York: Press of J.J. Little & Co., 1887).

of the committee in this city, he said, "Oh, Catharine, we have had one of the finest specimens I have ever seen. The man is a musician; he plays the violin nearly as well as your brother James, and you will think so when you hear him."

Soon after, Abel took him with us to a convention at Canandaigua. He played at my solicitation in the cars, while stopping at Utica, and he was indeed truly artistic. He had played at a theater in one of the cities at the South and was also a leader of a band of musicians. One being a white man, he took him for his master and thus escaped. He improvised accompaniments to my anti-slavery songs. He had thrown away his horn from fear of detection. He was nearly a white man

and this helped him in his pursuit of freedom! Many interesting facts of a novel character, but nevertheless true, might be given of escaped fugitives, inasmuch as "Truth is stranger than fiction."

An extremely interesting case occurred, concerning a fugitive forwarded by Mr. Ray to Albany, care of Mr. Abel Brown. William arrived one morning during the absence of Abel, and was sheltered and cared for by his companion in labors three days, constantly in dread of being taken by his pursuers! The account of himself as a slave and of his journey on his way to a land of freedom was so peculiar that I wished to retain him. Abel, in the meantime, had found a place near Lake Champlain for this class of human beings, to which the fugitive was immediately conveyed. He was very intelligent, could read and write, and by the aid of his own pass had effected his escape. Although often accosted as a runaway, he deliberately showed them his "Ticket of Leave," that proved sufficient. He had been three months on his way from Virginia, always traveled in the daytime, and slept in grave-yards at night. "The best place in the world, because there they would not look for me," he said. Abel wrote for William's wife. She came all the way with a little scrap of paper with the words, "Abel Brown, Albany." (She was a free woman.) After keeping her a week, she was sent for by the friends of her "dear William," and conveyed to his place of safety. On her arrival both were so much affected that neither could speak for some time, when she gave burst to a flood of tears, and the fountain of her lips was unsealed. They were provided by friends with a home of their own whence they repaired, and lived happily together in the full tide of domestic happiness, never before experienced while in a land of slavery.

Appendix II

Excerpt from Reply
of C.S.B. Spear of Passaic,
N.J., to Wilbur Siebert

Catharine Brown (by then Catharine Spear) wrote this letter sometime during the 1890s in response to the inquiry Siebert sent to likely participants or friends and relatives of likely participants in the Underground Railroad. They formed the basis for much of the information he collected for his classic work, *The Underground Railroad: From Slavery to Freedom*, published in 1898. ("Reply of C.S.B. Spear of Passaic, N.J.," Ohio Historical Society, Columbus, Oh., Wilbur Henry Siebert Collection, Series IV, New York.)

This road [the Underground Railroad] was established for that species of property who were Fugitive Slaves. My companion [Abel Brown] and myself were agents in behalf of this flying property, connected with "Committees of Vigilance" in various towns and cities enroute to the land of freedom. Mr. Brown was also corresponding secretary of fifteen counties — bordering on the Hudson River....

The first information I received concerning Rev. Abel Brown was on the occasion of his visit to my native town in Mass. He came in company with a fugitive slave, Lewis Washington. A minister called on myself to announce his coming and said, I regard Mr. Brown as a second Moses, having aided "a thousand slaves" in their escape to a land of freedom. I had previously received an invitation from Rev. Charles T. Torrey to engage in the same business with himself at Albany. Afterward, having an appointment with Mr. Brown, I joined a company of anti-slavery friends to attend an anniversary Convention in New York. Meeting Mr. Brown, we soon became united and engaged in behalf of fugitive slaves in the city of New York. Horace Dresser, our anti-slavery lawyer, was ever ready to aid and defend any case requiring adjudi-

cation. The writ of 'habeas corpus"
was always on our side for we were
only assisting our fellow beings in
maintaining their natural and God
given rights. An Association was
formed. Mr. Doubleday was Secretary.
....

A very interesting case occurred
while in New York of an escaped slave,
a musician. He had taken a white man
with him as his master. He, the fugitive, was almost as white himself being
a Quadroon. He had played at Richmond Theatre. He took with him his
violin and horn, but was obliged to
throw the latter away from fear of detection. On one journey through the
state of New York, he accompanied
myself in singing Anti-slavery songs.
We left him at Buffalo, and it was well
we did for in our excursion around the
Lakes a Slave hunter came on board
and searched our cabin. At our office
in Albany we had frequent calls and
provided for them food and clothing.
One morning a Refugee called
coming from North Carolina. He had

been three months traveling on foot
during the daytime and at night
sought shelter in the grave yards. Best
places in the world, he said, because
free from invasion. He had written his
own pass and was often examined and
as often had shown his pass. He called
for a Bible to show me how well he
could read. He was constantly in fear
of apprehension. Some one knocked
at my office door. I locked him in my
sleeping rooms. When safe he came
out covered with feathers. He had
hidden under the bed. Mr. Brown returned and during his absence had secured for him a place in the country;
so it was fortunate that I had not sent
him away for he might have missed
the good home. His wife soon came
having only for direction Abel Brown,
Albany, and little, scraps of paper ...
word was sent to the man in care of
her husband, and a carriage with driv-
ers to convey her to the place. When
they met, neither one could speak a
word....

C. Swan Brown Spear

Index

223

Johnson, H.W. 215
Johnson, William 121
Johnson, William P. 119, 119n.12
Johnston, William 119n.12
Jones, Dr. C. 65; letter to 67
Jordan, NY 119n.11
Judson, Adoniram 37n.1, 69n.5

Keeseville, NY 186
Kingsley, Mr. 173

Lake Champlain 170, 218
Lake George 167
Lane, James D. 148, 149n.7
Lane, Lunsford 143, 143n.9
Lane Seminary 71n.7
Lanesboro, MA 100n.12
Lattimore, George 143, 143n.10
Leavitt, Joshua 75n.5; letter to 75
Lee, Rev. Luther 161n.9
Lee, Stephen 167
Leggett, Joseph W. 168, 168n.16, 169
Legion of Liberty 177n.23
The Liberator: letter to 95n.8
Liberia 120n.13
Liberty Minstrel 204n.4
Liberty Party 47n.1, 154n.1, 159, 163,
  166n.14, 168n.16, 171n.18, 185, 187, 188,
  190, 204n.4; role in defeat of Henry Clay's
  bid for president in 1844 election 207n.6
Liberty Press 157n.4, 215
Liberty Street Church, Troy, NY 120n.13
Lincoln, Abraham 120n.13
Little York, PA 80
Lockport, NY 21
Loco-focos 184, 184n.6, 195
Loguen, Jermaine 126n.4
London, England 140n.4
Lord Nelson 53
Louisville, KY 80
Lovejoy, Elijah 76n.6, 163n.12
Lovejoy, Owen 163, 163n.12
Loveridge 122
Lowell, MA 172
Lyman, Timothy 11

Madison County 12
Maine 183
Marshall, Henry 126n.3
Marshall, MI 159
Maryland 142
Massachusetts Abolition Society 85, 91
Matthew, Theobald 108
Matthews, Dr. 207
McDonald, Mrs. 112
McDonough (steamboat) 34
Mercer, Reuben: letter to 87
Michigan: state of abolitionist movement
  156, 159
Michigan Freeman 159n.6

Middlebury, VT 161n.9
Milwaukee, WI 160, 163
Minaville, NY (Montgomery County) 185n.7
Miner, Rev. [Ovid] 161n.9
Mink, Charles W. 121, 122
Mississippi River 43, 157
Missouri 44, 163, 183
Missouri River 44n.4, 56n.7
Mix, Willian 133
Moore, Noadiah 171, 171n.18
Moresville, NY 171
Moriah, NY 186
Morris, Thomas 185n.8
Morrisville, NY 22, 29
Mosher, John 153, 203 n.3, 206, 211
Mosher, Laura: letter to C.S. Brown 208–209
Mosher, Mrs. 206
Mumford, Rev. 173
Munroe, Thomas 57
Murphy, Hon. R.W. 133
Murray, Brother 103
Myers, Stephen 133n.7

National Negro Convention 120n.13
Nebraska 56n.7
Nelson, Father 89
Nelson, Lord 54n.4
Nelson, NY 46
New Orleans 116, 117
New Windsor, NY 173
New York Baptist Register 76, 84, 98
New York City 55n.5, 101, 111, 116, 117,
  120n.13, 178, 220
New York Committee of Vigilance 47n.1, 119,
  120n.13, 148n.5
New York State 55n.5
New York State Antislavery Society 47n.1,
  129n.1, 173n.20
New York State Baptist Antislavery Conven-
  tion 139–140
Newburgh, NY 173
Niagara Falls, NY 155
Norfleet, Brother 55, 55n.6
Norfolk, VA 143n.10, 149n.7
North Carolina 152, 153
Northampton MA 11, 85, 87, 92, 95n.8

Oberlin, OH 161n.9
Oberlin College 71n.7
Oberlin tent 164
Oberlin-Wellington Rescue 108n.2
O'Connell, Daniel 108, 108n.4
Ohio Western Reserve 140
Omaha, NE 44n.4
Ontario Repository 215
Ontario Messenger 215
Orange County, NY 172
Organization of Radical Abolitionists 47n.1
Oswego, NY 55, 108n.2, 119n.11
Ottoe Indians 44